Christmas

RDA ENTHUSIAST BRANDS, LLC
MILWAUKEE, WI

Contents

Taste of Home

© 2019 RDA Enthusiast Brands, LLC.
1610 N. 2nd St., Suite 102, Milwaukee WI
53212-3906

International Standard Book Number:
D 978-1-61765-901-0
U 978-1-61765-902-7
International Standard Serial Number:
1948-8386
Component Number:
D 119600044H
U 119600046H

Deputy Editor: Mark Hagen
Senior Art Director: Raeann Thompson
Editor: Hazel Wheaton
Art Director: Maggie Conners
Designer: Arielle Jardine
Senior Copy Editor: Dulcie Shoener

Cover:
Photographer: Mark Derse
Food Stylist: Shannon Norris
Set Stylist: Melissa Franco

Pictured on front cover:
Chocolate Amaretti, p. 203; Finnish
Pinwheels, p. 201; Linzer Cookies,
p. 196; Norwegian Cookies, p. 201;
Pfeffernuesse, p. 203; Pizzelle, p. 194;
Swedish Spritz, p. 204

Pictured on back cover:
Apple & Herb Roasted Turkey, p. 45;
Christmas Elf Cake Pops, p. 159

Holly Illustration:
Shutterstock/Leigh Prather

Printed in U.S.A.
1 3 5 7 9 10 8 6 4 2

1

2

14

13

*Welcome your loved ones home
with Taste of Home Christmas*

1. MAKE-AHEAD APPETIZERS
Whether you're hosting a family dinner or a party with friends, these make-in-advance bites let you spend less time in the kitchen and more time with your loved ones.

2. EASY OPEN HOUSE
Open-house parties sound intimidating, with long run times and guests who come and go, but they're easy to pull together! These 20 recipes make it simple for you to make your home a welcoming place.

3. HOLIDAY FEASTS
Choose one of three extravagant feasts built around a stunning turkey, lamb or meatless entree—or choose from the delicious a la carte options to create your own menu.

4. FESTIVE BREADS
The holidays are the time to pull out the stops and indulge in homemade breads and baked goods—as the finishing touch to a feast or as the star of a holiday brunch.

5. FLAVORS OF THE SEASON
Peppermint, ginger, orange and cranberry... these tastes and aromas are forever linked with memories of the Christmas season. We offer up recipes that feature each of these timeless flavors.

6. CHRISTMAS FAST & SLOW
These 16 delicious savory recipes can be made in either a slow cooker or the Instant Pot®— so you can adjust your kitchen time to your holiday schedule.

12

11

7. JOY TO THE SWIRLED
Cinnamon rolls, jelly-roll cakes, roulade, pinwheels and palmiers...every one of the 17 recipes in this chapter celebrates the swirl. Bring a touch of magic to your holiday table with spirals, twists and twirls!

8. SEASONAL GET-TOGETHERS
Gather the kids for a holiday sleepover, celebrate with a country-style Christmas dinner, or kick back with your friends after the rush is over. We've got just the menu for whatever party you have planned.

9. ELF ON THE SHELF
At the beginning of the season, we welcome the arrival of the elf on the shelf. At the end, we say goodbye. This new holiday tradition is the perfect theme for a kids party.

10. OFFICE PARTY
The challenge of the office potluck is to bring something that travels well, reheats easily and pleases a crowd. These 17 recipes give you plenty of options that raise the bar for the office Christmas party.

11. PERFECT PIES
At the end of the holiday meal, what's more welcome than a pie? Here are 17 pies and tarts to choose from, plus four distinctly different desserts inspired by classic Christmas pies.

12. OLD-WORLD COOKIES
Celebrate the holidays with cookies made from traditional European and Scandinavian recipes. These delicious morsels have been passed down through the generations—with some new-world tweaks along the way!

13. CHRISTMAS CANDIES
Fudge, caramels, hard candy, toffee and more—handmade Christmas candy makes the season bright and is the perfect gift for teachers, co-workers and neighbors.

14. SHOWSTOPPING DESSERTS
When you want to end the evening with a bang, try one of these truly spectacular sweets. These 19 unabashedly decadent desserts will have everyone at the table ready to give you a standing ovation!

MAKE-AHEAD APPETIZERS

For the perfect holiday party, have a spread of dips, appetizers and all kinds of finger food just waiting for your guests to arrive. Then you can mingle, instead of toiling in the kitchen!

KALAMATA CHEESECAKE APPETIZER

PICTURED ON P. 6

It's believed the Greeks served cheesecake at the first Olympics, so this appetizer has history on its side as a celebration offering. Ingredients in this version tame the kalamata olives, so even if you shy away from dishes with them, you'll be glad you tried this one. For even milder flavor, use black or green olives.
—Theresa Kreyche, Tustin, CA

PREP: 30 MIN. • **BAKE:** 25 MIN. + CHILLING
MAKES: 24 SERVINGS

- 1¼ cups seasoned bread crumbs
- ½ cup finely chopped pecans
- ⅓ cup butter, melted

FILLING
- 11 oz. cream cheese, softened
- 1 cup sour cream
- 1 Tbsp. all-purpose flour
- ¼ tsp. salt
- ¼ tsp. pepper
- 1 large egg, room temperature
- 1 large egg yolk, room temperature
- ½ cup pitted kalamata olives, chopped
- 2 tsp. minced fresh rosemary
  Optional: Halved pitted kalamata olives and fresh rosemary sprigs

1. Preheat oven to 350°. In a small bowl, combine bread crumbs and pecans; stir in butter. Press onto the bottom of a greased 9-in. springform pan. Place pan on a baking sheet. Bake for 12 minutes. Cool on a wire rack.
2. In a large bowl, beat the cream cheese, sour cream, flour, salt and pepper until smooth. Add egg and egg yolk; beat on low just until combined. Fold in chopped olives and minced rosemary. Pour over the crust. Return pan to baking sheet.
3. Bake until the center is almost set, for 25-30 minutes. Cool on a wire rack for 10 minutes. Loosen edges of cheesecake from the pan with a knife. Cool 1 hour longer. Refrigerate overnight.
4. Remove the rim from the pan. Top with halved olives and rosemary sprigs if desired.
1 SLICE: *142 cal., 12g fat (6g sat. fat), 45mg chol., 223mg sod., 6g carb. (1g sugars, 0 fiber), 3g pro.*

MAKE A CHEESE BOARD: SIMPLE & GORGEOUS

A cheese board can be as simple or complex as you like. You can do a lot of the prep work in advance, including cutting the cheeses into cubes or wedges. Slice hard cheeses into small, thin pieces; semi-soft cheeses into long wedges; and soft cheeses into short, thick wedges. Store the cheese in airtight containers in the refrigerator until an hour before you arrange the board; cheese tastes best at room temperature.

Choose 4-5 different kinds of cheese. Mix up the variety with soft (goat cheese), semisoft (mozzarella or burrata), firm (Asiago or manchego), blue (Stilton or Gorgonzola) and aged (sharp cheddar) cheeses. Then start adding! Good add-ins are condiments like mustard, chutney or honey, cured meats, nuts, and fresh or dried fruits. For fresh fruit, think apple slices, orange segments, fresh figs, grapes or cherries on the stem. Some kind of bread—crusty baguette slices, melba toast or crackers—is always welcome, as it makes a great palate-cleanser between different types of cheese. Crackers should be plain, rather than heavily herbed or spiced; you always want the flavor of the cheese to dominate. Likewise, place condiments off to the side, rather than on top of the cheese.

When arranging the plate, place the cheese first, then arrange the rest according to size (largest to smallest). Don't forget cheese spreaders, one for each type of cheese. If you have neat handwriting, display tags for the different cheeses is an elegant touch!

CHEESE/GRAPE APPETIZERS

These small bites are well-worth the time they take. Serve them as part of an antipasto or cheese platter alongside your favorite wine.
—*Eleanor Grofvert, Kalamazoo, MI*

PREP: 35 MIN. • **BAKE:** 10 MIN. + COOLING
MAKES: ABOUT 5 DOZEN

- 4 oz. sliced almonds (about 1 cup)
- 1 pkg. (8 oz.) cream cheese, softened
- 2 oz. crumbled blue cheese, room temperature
- 2 Tbsp. minced fresh parsley
- 2 Tbsp. heavy whipping cream, room temperature
- 1 to 1¼ lbs. seedless red or green grapes, rinsed and patted dry
  Appetizer skewers or toothpicks

1. Preheat oven to 275°. Pulse almonds in a food processor until finely chopped (do not overprocess). Spread in a 15x10x1-in. pan; bake until golden brown, 6-9 minutes, stirring occasionally. Transfer to a shallow bowl; cool slightly.
2. In another bowl, mix cream cheese, blue cheese, parsley and cream until blended. Insert a skewer into each grape. Roll grapes in the cheese mixture, then in the almonds; place on waxed paper-lined baking sheets. Refrigerate, covered, until serving.
5 APPETIZERS: *146 cal., 11g fat (6g sat. fat), 28mg chol., 124mg sod., 8g carb. (7g sugars, 1g fiber), 4g pro.*

CRANBERRY CREAM CHEESE SPREAD

This festive dip is a snap to make, taking only 10 minutes from start to finish. Thanks to its hint of sweetness, both adults and kids will gobble it up.
—*Frankie Robinson, Lockhart, TX*

TAKES: 10 MIN. • **MAKES:** 1½ CUPS

- 1 pkg. (8 oz.) reduced-fat cream cheese
- ½ cup dried cranberries, chopped
- ½ cup chopped dried apricots
- 1 tsp. grated orange zest
  Assorted crackers

In a large bowl, beat the cream cheese, cranberries, apricots and orange zest until blended. Chill until serving. Serve cheese spread with crackers.
2 TBSP. SPREAD: *76 cal., 4g fat (3g sat. fat), 13mg chol., 84mg sod., 9g carb. (6g sugars, 1g fiber), 2g pro.*
DIABETIC EXCHANGES: *1 fat, ½ starch.*

LAYERED MEDITERRANEAN DIP WITH PITA CHIPS

Not your ordinary layered dip, this bold combination of hummus and Greek yogurt will be a new most-requested recipe at your next gathering.
—Elizabeth Dumont, Madison, MS

PREP: 15 MIN. + CHILLING • **BAKE:** 10 MIN.
MAKES: 5 CUPS (120 CHIPS)

- 1 cup (8 oz.) plain Greek yogurt
- 1 medium seedless cucumber, chopped
- 1 tsp. white wine vinegar
- 2 tsp. minced fresh mint or 1 tsp. dried mint
- 1 carton (10 oz.) hummus
- 1 medium red onion, chopped
- 1 cup chopped roasted sweet red peppers, drained
- 2 pkg. (4 oz. each) crumbled feta cheese
- ½ cup pitted Greek olives, sliced
- 2 plum tomatoes, chopped
  Optional: Minced fresh parsley and additional minced fresh mint

PITA CHIPS
- 20 pita pocket halves
- ¼ cup olive oil
- ½ tsp. salt
- ¼ tsp. pepper

1. Line a strainer with a coffee filter or 4 layers of cheesecloth; place over a bowl. Place yogurt in prepared strainer and cover (with edges of cheesecloth if using). Refrigerate 8 hours or overnight. In a small bowl, combine the strained yogurt, cucumber, vinegar and mint.
2. Spread hummus in a 9-in. deep dish pie plate. Layer with onion, peppers, feta cheese, olives, tomatoes and yogurt mixture. Top with parsley and additional mint if desired. Chill until serving.
3. Preheat oven to 400°. Cut each pita half into 3 wedges, then separate each wedge into 2 pieces. Place in a single layer on ungreased baking sheets. Brush both sides with olive oil; sprinkle with salt and pepper. Bake until crisp, about 8-10 minutes, turning once. Serve with dip.
¼ CUP DIP WITH 6 CHIPS: 178 cal., 8g fat (2g sat. fat), 8mg chol., 478mg sod., 20g carb. (2g sugars, 2g fiber), 6g pro.

HERBED CHEESE WAFERS

These bite-sized snacks are rich, buttery and full of flavor. You can either serve them alone or for dipping.
—Mildred Sherrer, Fort Worth, TX

PREP: 10 MIN. + CHILLING
BAKE: 10 MIN./BATCH
MAKES: ABOUT 4½ DOZEN

- ¾ cup butter, softened
- ½ cup shredded cheddar cheese
- ⅓ cup crumbled blue cheese
- 1 Tbsp. minced fresh tarragon or 1 tsp. dried tarragon
- ½ tsp. dried oregano
- 1 small garlic clove, minced
- 2 cups all-purpose flour

1. In a large bowl, beat butter, cheeses, tarragon, oregano and garlic until well mixed. Beat in flour (the dough will be crumbly). Shape into a 14-in. roll. Wrap tightly with plastic. Refrigerate rolls for 4 hours or overnight.
2. Cut into ¼-in. slices; place on ungreased baking sheets. Bake at 375° until golden brown and crisp, 10-12 minutes. Cool on wire racks.
3 WAFERS: 138 cal., 9g fat (6g sat. fat), 26mg chol., 131mg sod., 11g carb. (0 sugars, 0 fiber), 3g pro.

HERBED LEEK TART

This savory tart is a favorite among family and friends! It's delicious and different— and surprisingly easy to make.
—Jean Ecos, Hartland, WI

PREP: 25 MIN. • **BAKE:** 20 MIN. + COOLING
MAKES: 2 TARTS (8 SERVINGS EACH)

- 3 cups thinly sliced leeks (about 4 medium)
- ½ cup chopped sweet red pepper
- 4 garlic cloves, minced
- 2 Tbsp. olive oil
- 1½ cups shredded Swiss cheese
- 2 Tbsp. Dijon mustard
- 1 tsp. herbes de Provence
- 1 pkg. (15 oz.) refrigerated pie crust
- 1 tsp. whole milk
- 2 Tbsp. chopped almonds or walnuts, optional

1. Preheat oven to 375°. In a large skillet, saute the leeks, red pepper and garlic in oil until tender. Remove from the heat; cool 5 minutes. Stir in cheese, mustard and herbs; set aside.
2. On a lightly floured surface, roll each sheet of crust into a 12-in. circle. Transfer to parchment-lined baking sheets. Spoon leek mixture over crust to within 2 in. of edges. Fold the edges of the crust over the filling, leaving the center uncovered. Brush folded crust with milk; sprinkle with nuts if desired.
3. Bake until the crust is golden and the filling is bubbly, 20-25 minutes. Using parchment, slide tarts onto wire racks. Let cool for 10 minutes before cutting. Serve warm. Refrigerate leftovers.
1 PIECE: *194 cal., 12g fat (5g sat. fat), 14mg chol., 177mg sod., 17g carb. (2g sugars, 1g fiber), 5g pro.*

CHICKEN SALAD CAPRESE

This distinctive, flavorful salad and bread combination will get rave reviews— guaranteed! It also makes a tasty side dish.
—Frances Pietsch, Flower Mound, TX

PREP: 40 MIN. • **BAKE:** 5 MIN.
MAKES: 8 CUPS SALAD
(6½ DOZEN CROSTINI)

- 2 cups shredded rotisserie chicken
- 1 lb. fresh mozzarella cheese, cubed
- 2 cups grape tomatoes, halved
- 1 can (14 oz.) water-packed artichoke hearts, rinsed, drained and coarsely chopped
- ½ cup pitted Greek olives, thinly sliced
- ¼ cup minced fresh basil
- ¼ cup olive oil
- 2 garlic cloves, minced
- ½ tsp. salt
- ½ tsp. coarsely ground pepper

CROSTINI
- 2 French bread baguettes (10½ oz. each)
- 4 garlic cloves
- ¼ cup olive oil
- 1 tsp. salt

1. In a large bowl, combine the first 6 ingredients. In a small bowl, whisk the oil, garlic, salt and pepper; drizzle over the chicken mixture and toss to coat. Refrigerate until serving.
2. Cut baguettes into ½-in. slices. Place on ungreased baking sheets. Bake at 425° until lightly browned, 2-4 minutes. Cut garlic in half lengthwise; rub over bread. Brush with oil and sprinkle with salt. Bake until crisp, 2-3 minutes longer. Serve crostini topped with salad.
1 CROSTINI: *179 cal., 10g fat (3g sat. fat), 19mg chol., 316mg sod., 16g carb. (1g sugars, 1g fiber), 7g pro.*

HERB DIP WITH BABY VEGETABLES

When you're having a large party and focusing on the entrees, it's smart to have snacks and nibbles ready ahead of time. There's nothing simpler than making dip a day or two ahead and putting it out for guests. I'm a huge fan of ranch, so this is my pick.
—Michelle Clair, Seattle, WA

PREP: 10 MIN. + CHILLING • **MAKES:** 2 CUPS

2	cups sour cream
¼	cup ranch salad dressing mix
2	Tbsp. onion soup mix
¼	cup minced fresh parsley
2	Tbsp. chopped fresh rosemary
	Fresh rainbow baby carrots and watermelon (or plain) radishes

Stir together the first 5 ingredients; refrigerate, covered, overnight. Sprinkle with additional parsley and rosemary before serving with rainbow carrots and assorted radishes.

2 TBSP. DIP: 76 cal., 6g fat (4g sat. fat), 7mg chol., 559mg sod., 5g carb. (1g sugars, trace fiber), 1g pro.

SPANISH MARINATED MUSHROOMS

I had some amazing marinated mushrooms in a little tapas bar in Seville when I was stationed in Spain with the U.S. Navy. A couple of months ago, I decided to see if I could make something close, and here's what I came up with. The longer you keep them refrigerated, the stronger the vinegar taste will be.
—Patricia Mitchell, Ingleside, TX

PREP: 15 MIN. + MARINATING • **MAKES:** 32 SERVINGS

2	cups water
1	cup red wine vinegar
3	Tbsp. olive oil
1	Tbsp. sugar
1	Tbsp. dried basil
2	garlic cloves, minced
1½	tsp. salt
1	tsp. dried oregano
½	tsp. crushed red pepper flakes
2	lbs. small fresh mushrooms

In a large shallow dish, combine the first 9 ingredients. Add the mushrooms; turn to coat. Cover; refrigerate for at least 8 hours or overnight. Drain and discard the marinade before serving.

¼ CUP: 10 cal., 0 fat (0 sat. fat), 0 chol., 21mg sod., 1g carb. (0 sugars, 0 fiber), 1g pro.

FESTIVE GUACAMOLE APPETIZERS

For ages, my brother's family and I have gotten together on Christmas Eve, and we always eat snacks while we open our presents. This pretty Tex-Mex spin on the classic appetizer pizza is one we have again and again.
—*Laurie Pester, Colstrip, MT*

PREP: 1 HOUR • **BAKE:** 10 MIN. + COOLING
MAKES: 40 APPETIZERS

- 2 tubes (8 oz. each) refrigerated seamless crescent dough sheet
- 1½ tsp. taco seasoning, divided
- 20 pretzel sticks, broken in half
- 4 oz. cream cheese, softened
- 1 cup guacamole
- 2 medium sweet yellow peppers
- 1 medium sweet red pepper
- 1 medium green pepper
  Chopped fresh cilantro, optional

1. Preheat oven to 375°. On an ungreased baking sheet, unroll one tube of crescent dough and press into a 13x8-in. rectangle. Prick with a fork; sprinkle with ¾ tsp. taco seasoning. Repeat with the remaining dough and seasoning.
2. Bake until golden brown, 10-12 minutes. Transfer to wire racks to cool completely.
3. Cut each rectangle crosswise to make 4 strips (about 8x4-in.). Cut each strip into 5 triangles, reserving the scraps at each end for another use. To add a "trunk" to each "tree," insert a pretzel piece into the base of each triangle.
4. Beat cream cheese and guacamole until smooth; spread over the trees. Halve and seed peppers. Cut 40 stars from yellow peppers using a ¾-in. star-shaped cookie cutter. Dice and julienne the remaining peppers to use as tree decorations. Decorate the trees with pepper pieces and, if desired, cilantro. Refrigerate until ready to serve.
1 APPETIZER: *57 cal., 3g fat (1g sat. fat), 3mg chol., 133mg sod., 6g carb. (1g sugars, 1g fiber), 1g pro.*

CRANBERRY-GLAZED LAMB SKEWERS

Lamb marinated with savory cranberry sauce—I love making this for Christmas parties! Guests will appreciate that it's not your average appetizer.
—*Kim Yuille, Brooklyn, NY*

PREP: 25 MIN. + MARINATING
BROIL: 5 MIN. • **MAKES:** 16 APPETIZERS

- 2 cans (14 oz. each) whole-berry cranberry sauce
- 2 Tbsp. brown sugar
- 2 Tbsp. chili powder
- 1 Tbsp. garlic powder
- 1 tsp. paprika
- ½ tsp. salt
- 2 lbs. boneless leg of lamb, cut into ¼-in.-thick strips

1. In a small bowl, combine the first 6 ingredients, stirring to dissolve sugar; transfer 1½ cups of the mixture to a large shallow dish. Add the lamb; turn to coat. Cover and refrigerate for several hours or overnight. Cover the remaining cranberry mixture; refrigerate.
2. Remove lamb from marinade; discard marinade. Thread the lamb strips, weaving back and forth, onto 16 metal or soaked wooden skewers. Arrange in greased foil-lined 15x10x1-in. baking pans. Broil 4 in. from the heat until the lamb reaches the desired doneness, about 2-3 minutes on each side.
3. Meanwhile, in a small saucepan, bring the reserved cranberry mixture just to a boil over medium heat, stirring frequently. Serve alongside the lamb.
1 SKEWER: *141 cal., 3g fat (1g sat. fat), 34mg chol., 135mg sod., 17g carb. (11g sugars, 1g fiber), 11g pro.*

MINI MUFFULETTA

Mediterranean meets comfort food when French rolls are slathered with olive spread and stuffed with layers of salami and cheese. You can make these the night before and cut them into appetizer-sized slices just before serving.
—Gareth Craner, Minden, NV

PREP: 25 MIN. + CHILLING
MAKES: 3 DOZEN

- 1 cup pimiento-stuffed olives, drained and chopped
- 1 can (4¼ oz.) chopped ripe olives
- 1 Tbsp. balsamic vinegar
- 1½ tsp. red wine vinegar
- 1½ tsp. olive oil
- 1 garlic clove, minced
- ½ tsp. dried basil
- ½ tsp. dried oregano
- 6 French rolls, split
- ½ lb. thinly sliced hard salami
- ¼ lb. sliced provolone cheese
- ½ lb. thinly sliced cotto salami
- ¼ lb. sliced part-skim mozzarella cheese

1. In a large bowl, combine the first 8 ingredients; set aside. Hollow out the tops and bottoms of rolls, leaving ¾-in. shells (discard the removed bread or save for another use).

2. Spread olive mixture over tops and bottoms of rolls. On roll bottoms, layer the hard salami, provolone cheese, cotto salami and mozzarella cheese. Replace the tops.

3. Wrap rolls tightly in plastic. Refrigerate overnight. Cut each into 6 wedges; secure with toothpicks.

1 APPETIZER: *108 cal., 7g fat (2g sat. fat), 16mg chol., 454mg sod., 6g carb. (0 sugars, 0 fiber), 6g pro.*

HOT CRAB PINWHEELS

A friend gave me the recipe for these crabmeat bites. What amazed me most is that my husband, who hates seafood, just couldn't stop eating them!
—Kitti Boesel, Woodbridge, VA

PREP: 15 MIN. + CHILLING • **BAKE:** 10 MIN. • **MAKES:** 3 DOZEN

- 1 pkg. (8 oz.) reduced-fat cream cheese
- 1 can (6 oz.) crabmeat, drained, flaked and cartilage removed
- ¾ cup diced sweet red pepper
- ½ cup shredded reduced-fat cheddar cheese
- 2 green onions, thinly sliced
- 3 Tbsp. minced fresh parsley
- ¼ to ½ tsp. cayenne pepper
- 6 flour tortillas (6 in.)

1. Beat cream cheese until smooth; stir in crabmeat, red pepper, cheese, green onions, parsley and cayenne. Spread ⅓ cup of the filling over each tortilla; roll up tightly. Wrap each roll in plastic, twisting the ends to seal; refrigerate at least 2 hours.
2. Preheat oven to 350°. Unwrap rolls; trim the ends and cut each roll into six slices. Place rolls on baking sheets coated with cooking spray. Bake until bubbly, about 10 minutes. Serve warm.
1 PINWHEEL: *44 cal., 2g fat (1g sat. fat), 10mg chol., 98mg sod., 3g carb. (0 sugars, 0 fiber), 2g pro.*

EASY SMOKED SALMON

I found this in a magazine years ago, and it became my favorite way to prepare salmon. It's such an elegant appetizer!
—Norma Fell, Boyne City, MI

PREP: 10 MIN. + MARINATING • **BAKE:** 35 MIN. + CHILLING
MAKES: 16 SERVINGS

- 1 salmon fillet (about 2 lbs.)
- 2 Tbsp. brown sugar
- 2 tsp. salt
- ½ tsp. pepper
- 1 to 2 Tbsp. liquid smoke

1. Place salmon, skin side down, in an 11x7-in. baking pan coated with cooking spray. Sprinkle with brown sugar, salt and pepper. Drizzle with liquid smoke. Cover and refrigerate 4-8 hours.
2. Drain; discard liquid. Bake, uncovered, at 350° until fish flakes easily with a fork, 35-45 minutes. Let cool to room temperature. Cover and refrigerate for 8 hours or overnight.
2 OZ. SALMON: *110 cal., 6g fat (1g sat. fat), 33mg chol., 327mg sod., 2g carb. (0 sugars, 1g fiber), 11g pro.*
DIABETIC EXCHANGES: *2 lean meat.*

SMOKED SALMON & DILL DEVILED EGGS

Take this perennial party food and give it an upscale twist with smoked salmon. Your guests will be delighted with the results.
—Jan Valdez, Chicago, IL

TAKES: 25 MIN. • **MAKES:** 16 APPETIZERS

8	hard-boiled large eggs
1	pkg. (3 oz.) smoked salmon or lox, finely chopped
6	Tbsp. sour cream
1	Tbsp. chopped fresh dill or 1 tsp. dill weed
1	tsp. cider vinegar
1	tsp. Dijon mustard
¼	tsp. cayenne pepper

Cut eggs lengthwise in half. Remove yolks; set whites aside. In a small bowl, mash yolks. Add the remaining ingredients; mix well. Spoon into egg whites. Refrigerate until serving.

1 STUFFED EGG HALF: *57 cal., 4g fat (2g sat. fat), 111mg chol., 147mg sod., 1g carb. (0 sugars, 0 fiber), 4g pro.*

PEAR WALDORF PITAS

Here's a guaranteed table-brightener for a brunch, luncheon or party. Just stand back and watch them disappear! I tuck each one into a colorful paper napkin for an eye-catching presentation.
—Roxann Parker, Dover, DE

PREP: 20 MIN. + CHILLING • **MAKES:** 20 MINI PITAS

2	medium ripe pears, diced
½	cup thinly sliced celery
½	cup halved seedless red grapes
2	Tbsp. finely chopped walnuts
2	Tbsp. lemon yogurt
2	Tbsp. mayonnaise
⅛	tsp. poppy seeds
20	miniature pita pocket halves
	Lettuce leaves

1. In a large bowl, combine the pears, celery, grapes and walnuts. In another bowl, whisk the yogurt, mayonnaise and poppy seeds. Add to pear mixture; toss to coat. Refrigerate for 1 hour or overnight.

2. Line the pita halves with lettuce; fill each with 2 Tbsp. of the pear mixture.

1 PITA HALF: *67 cal., 2g fat (0 sat. fat), 0 chol., 86mg sod., 12g carb. (3g sugars, 1g fiber), 2g pro.*
DIABETIC EXCHANGES: *1 starch.*

PUTTANESCA MEATBALL SLIDERS

With the just-spicy-enough flavors of a classic and hearty Italian dish, these tender meatballs stand apart from the rest. Top with zesty sauce and serve on soft dinner rolls: They'll quickly win over a crowd.
—Amy Coeler, Lemoore, CA

PREP: 50 MIN. • **COOK:** 25 MIN.
MAKES: 15 SLIDERS

- 1 can (28 oz.) whole tomatoes, undrained
- 1 medium onion, finely chopped
- 3 Tbsp. olive oil
- 2 garlic cloves, minced
- 1 tsp. crushed red pepper flakes
- ½ tsp. fennel seed, crushed
- 1 Tbsp. chopped capers
- ⅛ tsp. salt
- ¼ tsp. pepper

MEATBALLS
- 1 cup shredded Parmesan cheese, divided
- ½ cup panko (Japanese) bread crumbs
- ¼ cup 2% milk
- 1 large egg, beaten
- 2 Tbsp. minced fresh parsley
- 1 garlic clove, minced
- ½ tsp. pepper
- ¼ tsp. salt
- ½ lb. lean ground beef (90% lean)
- ½ lb. ground pork
- 1 Tbsp. canola oil
- 15 dinner rolls

1. Place tomatoes in a food processor; cover and process until pureed. Set aside. In a large skillet, saute onion in oil until tender. Add the garlic, pepper flakes and fennel; cook 2 minutes longer. Stir in the tomatoes, capers, salt and pepper. Bring to a boil. Reduce the heat; simmer until thickened, about 15-20 minutes, stirring occasionally.

2. Meanwhile, in a large bowl, combine ½ cup of cheese, the bread crumbs, milk, egg, parsley, garlic, pepper and salt.

Crumble the meat over the bread crumb mixture and mix well. Shape into fifteen 1½-in. balls.

3. In a large skillet, brown the meatballs in oil; drain. Transfer meatballs to sauce; simmer, uncovered, until a thermometer reads 160°, about 15-20 minutes.

4. Place a meatball on each roll. Top with sauce and remaining cheese.

FREEZE OPTION: Freeze rolls in resealable freezer bags. Freeze meatball mixture in freezer containers. To use, partially thaw in refrigerator overnight. Microwave, covered, on high in a microwave-safe dish until heated through, gently stirring and adding a little water if necessary. Place a meatball on each roll and top as directed.

1 SERVING: *248 cal., 11g fat (3g sat. fat), 55mg chol., 482mg sod., 23g carb. (4g sugars, 2g fiber), 13g pro.*

EASY OPEN HOUSE

How to create an inviting buffet for an open house party?
Prepare in advance, restock cool items from the fridge,
and keep hot dishes warm in a chafing dish or
slow cooker—always ready for new arrivals!

SHREDDED LAMB SLIDERS

Lamb, a wonderful special-occasion meat, is a big crowd-pleaser in these delicious sliders. I served up about 1,500 in two days when I made them for the Great American Beer Fest, using every little bit to satisfy the very last customer.
—Craig Kuczek, Aurora, CO

PREP: 45 MIN. • **COOK:** 6 HOURS
MAKES: 2 DOZEN

- 1 boneless lamb shoulder roast (3½ to 4¼ lbs.)
- 1½ tsp. salt
- ½ tsp. pepper
- 1 Tbsp. olive oil
- 2 medium carrots, chopped
- 4 shallots, chopped
- 6 garlic cloves
- 2 cups beef stock

PESTO

- ¾ cup fresh mint leaves
- ¾ cup loosely packed basil leaves
- ⅓ cup pine nuts
- ¼ tsp. salt
- ¾ cup olive oil
- ¾ cup shredded Parmesan cheese
- ⅓ cup shredded Asiago cheese
- 24 slider buns
- 1 pkg. (4 oz.) crumbled feta cheese

1. Sprinkle roast with salt and pepper. In a large skillet, heat oil over medium-high heat; brown meat. Transfer to a 6- or 7-qt. slow cooker. In the same skillet, cook and stir the carrots, shallots and garlic until crisp-tender, about 4 minutes. Add stock, stirring to loosen browned bits from pan. Pour over the lamb. Cook, covered, on low until the lamb is tender, 6-8 hours.

2. Meanwhile, for the pesto, place the mint, basil, pine nuts and salt in a food processor; pulse until chopped. Continue processing while gradually adding oil in a steady stream. Add cheeses; pulse just until blended.

3. When lamb is cool enough to handle, remove meat from bones; discard bones. Shred meat with 2 forks. Strain cooking juices, adding vegetables to the shredded meat; skim fat. Return the cooking juices and meat to slow cooker. Heat through. Serve on buns with pesto and feta.

1 SLIDER: *339 cal., 22g fat (7g sat. fat), 56mg chol., 459mg sod., 16g carb. (2g sugars, 1g fiber), 18g pro.*

CURRIED VEGETABLE SOUP

I created this recipe uniting my favorite spices with frozen vegetables to save time. It's easy to scale up to feed a crowd. I usually prepare enough to make sure there are leftovers. For a buffet, keep this soup warm in a slow cooker, and set yogurt out in a separate dish to let guests serve themselves.
—Heather Demeritte, Scottsdale, AZ

PREP: 10 MIN • **COOK:** 25 MIN. • **MAKES:** 6 SERVINGS (2 QT.)

- 1 Tbsp. canola oil
- 2 garlic cloves, minced
- 1 pkg. (16 oz.) frozen broccoli florets
- 1 pkg. (16 oz.) frozen cauliflower
- 5 cups vegetable broth
- 2 tsp. curry powder
- ½ tsp. salt
- ½ tsp. pepper
- ⅛ tsp. ground nutmeg
  Plain Greek yogurt, optional

1. In a 6-qt. stockpot, heat oil over medium heat. Add garlic; cook and stir until fragrant, 1 minute. Add the remaining ingredients; bring to a boil. Reduce heat; simmer, covered, until vegetables are tender, 8-10 minutes.
2. Remove soup from heat; cool slightly. Process in batches in a blender until smooth; return to pot and heat through. If desired, top with yogurt to serve.
1⅓ CUPS: *84 cal., 3g fat (0 sat. fat), 0 chol., 793mg sod., 10g carb. (4g sugars, 4g fiber), 4g pro.*

CUTLERY AT THE READY

When hosting an open house, you don't want your guests searching for the silverware, and you don't want your setup to look clumsy or awkward. Here are some ideas for making the most utilitarian objects part of your pretty display.

MAKE INDIVIDUAL BUNDLES

1. Place cutlery diagonally on the napkin; leave about a third of the napkin showing at the bottom. Fold the bottom corner over the cutlery.
2. Fold over the left side of the napkin.
3. Fold over the right side of napkin and tuck underneath the bundle.
4. Tie the bundle with foil garland, raffia or ribbon.

GO VERTICAL

Set out standing containers—one each for forks, knives and spoons. You can use any pretty container, such as a vase, large-mouth Mason jars... even flower pots!

GO HORIZONTAL

Lay out utensils in a rectangular basket or decorative tray.

DRESS UP HOUSEHOLD WARES

Lay a pretty piece of cloth or a holiday-themed towel over a standard utensil drawer organizer and fold the edges underneath. The cutlery can nestle into the recesses, just as it would in the drawer.

APPLE BACON PORK ROLL-UPS

I am so proud of this delicious creation— it's easy to make, but impressive enough to use for parties.
—*Cyndy Gerken, Naples, FL*

PREP: 25 MIN. • **BAKE:** 20 MIN.
MAKES: 8 SERVINGS

- ½ lb. bacon strips, chopped
- 2 Tbsp. olive oil, divided
- 2 Tbsp. butter, divided
- ½ cup chopped red onion
- 5 medium apples, peeled and finely chopped
- ½ cup packed brown sugar
- 2 Tbsp. minced fresh parsley
- 8 thin-cut boneless pork loin chops (about 3 oz. each)
- 8 slices Swiss cheese
- ½ tsp. salt
- ¼ tsp. pepper

1. Preheat oven to 400°. In a large skillet, cook bacon over medium heat until crisp, stirring occasionally. Remove with a slotted spoon; drain on paper towels. Remove drippings, reserving 1 Tbsp. for cooking pork chops.
2. In the same skillet, heat 1 Tbsp. each oil and butter over medium heat. Add onion; cook and stir until tender, for 3-4 minutes. Add apples and brown sugar; cook and stir until the apples are tender, 4-5 minutes. Stir in parsley and bacon; remove from pan. Cool slightly. Remove 1 cup mixture for the filling.
3. Pound each pork chop with a meat mallet to ¼-in. thickness. Layer each with 1 slice cheese and 2 Tbsp. filling to within 1 in. of edges. Roll up chops from a short side; secure with toothpicks. Sprinkle salt and pepper over roll-ups.
4. In the same skillet, heat the reserved drippings and the remaining oil and butter over medium-high. Starting with the seam side, brown roll-ups on both sides. Transfer to a 13x9-in. baking pan. Bake until golden brown and the pork is tender, 15-20 minutes. Discard toothpicks; serve with remaining apple mixture.
1 PORK ROLL-UP WITH ⅓ CUP APPLE MIXTURE: *370 cal., 20g fat (8g sat. fat), 70mg chol., 404mg sod., 25g carb. (22g sugars, 2g fiber), 23g pro.*

FINNISH MULLED WINE

I found this recipe stuck in the pages of my Finnish grandmother's Bible. It takes 24 hours to make—but can be stored tightly bottled in the fridge for up to two weeks.
—*Judy Batson, Tampa, FL*

PREP: 15 MIN. + CHILLING • **COOK:** 30 MIN.
MAKES: 6 SERVINGS

- ⅔ cup vodka
- ⅔ cup port wine
- 15 whole cloves
- 3 cinnamon sticks (3 in.)
- 2 orange zest strips (1 to 3 in.)
- 1 orange slice
- 1 lemon zest strip (1 to 3 in.)
- 1 lemon slice
- 1 piece fresh gingerroot (about 2 in.), peeled and thinly sliced
- 1 tsp. cardamom pods
- 3 cups dry red wine
- 1 cup packed brown sugar
  Optional: Raisins and blanched almonds

1. In a large bowl, combine the first 10 ingredients. Refrigerate the mixture, covered, overnight.
2. Transfer to a large saucepan; stir in red wine and brown sugar. Bring just to a simmer (do not boil). Reduce heat; simmer gently, uncovered, until the flavors are blended, about 30 minutes, stirring to dissolve sugar. Strain.
3. Serve warm over raisins and blanched almonds, if desired.
⅔ CUP: *339 cal., 0 fat (0 sat. fat), 0 chol., 18mg sod., 43g carb. (38g sugars, 0 fiber), 0 pro.*

CRAB CAKE STUFFED MUSHROOMS

These tender mushrooms with their crispy golden topping are always popular at parties! The crab filling is a delicious special occasion treat. Serve them while they're warm.
—Nancy Aiello, Bloomery, WV

PREP: 15 MIN. • **BAKE:** 20 MIN. • **MAKES:** 1½ DOZEN

- 18   medium fresh mushrooms
- 1   can (6 oz.) crabmeat, drained, flaked and cartilage removed
- ⅓   cup mayonnaise
- 3   Tbsp. seasoned bread crumbs
- 2   Tbsp. grated Parmesan cheese
- 1   garlic clove, minced
      Minced fresh parsley, optional

1. Preheat oven to 400°. Remove stems from the mushrooms (discard stems or save for another use); set the caps aside.
2. In a small bowl, combine the crab, mayonnaise, bread crumbs, cheese and garlic. Stuff crab mixture into the mushroom caps. Place on a greased baking sheet.
3. Bake until mushrooms are tender, 20-25 minutes. If desired, sprinkle with parsley before serving.

1 STUFFED MUSHROOM: *51 cal., 4g fat (1g sat. fat), 10mg chol., 81mg sod., 2g carb. (0 sugars, 0 fiber), 3g pro.*

WILD RICE & LENTIL SALAD

This healthy, protein-packed salad is a perfect main dish for the vegetarians who grace your holiday table—or as a side in smaller portions. My family loves it for the flavors, and my friends love it because I offer them a healthy alternative to meat.
—Mary Leverette, Columbia, SC

PREP: 15 MIN. • **COOK:** 20 MIN. • **MAKES:** 8 SERVINGS

- 1   pkg. (2¾ oz.) quick-cooking wild rice
- 1   cup dried lentils, rinsed
- 2   cups water
- ¼   cup olive oil
- 2   Tbsp. lemon juice
- 2   Tbsp. red wine vinegar
- 1   garlic clove, minced
- ½   tsp. salt
- 2   medium tomatoes, chopped
- 6   green onions, chopped
- 2   cups fresh arugula or baby spinach
- ¼   cup crumbled feta cheese

1. Prepare wild rice according to package directions. Drain; rinse with cold water. Place the lentils in a small saucepan. Add water; bring to a boil. Reduce the heat; simmer, covered, until tender, 20-25 minutes. Drain; rinse with cold water.
2. Whisk oil, lemon juice, vinegar, garlic and salt until blended. In a large bowl, combine rice, lentils, tomatoes and green onions; drizzle with the dressing. Just before serving, stir in the arugula and cheese.

¾ CUP: *461 cal., 19g fat (5g sat. fat), 15mg chol., 283mg sod., 51g carb. (4g sugars, 18g fiber), 21g pro.*

SMOKED SALMON PASTA

This pasta originally came to be from the miscellaneous ingredients in my fridge, and depending on who I make it for, it changes a little each time I make it. The recipe makes enough for a party or for leftovers, which is a bonus because it's excellent the next day, whether you serve it cold or reheated.

—Jackie Hennon, Boise, ID

TAKES: 25 MIN. • **MAKES:** 8 SERVINGS

- 1   lb. uncooked spiral or penne pasta
- 2   Tbsp. olive oil
- 2   large tomatoes, diced
- 2   cups water-packed artichoke hearts, drained and chopped
- 1½ cups kalamata olives, pitted and halved
- 1   cup chopped oil-packed sun-dried tomatoes
- ¾   cup chopped onion
- 8   oz. smoked salmon fillets
- 2   Tbsp. sun-dried tomato pesto
- 2   tsp. dried basil
- ¾   tsp. crushed red pepper flakes
- ¼   cup grated Parmesan cheese
- ¼   cup crumbled feta cheese

1. In a large saucepan, cook the pasta according to the package directions for al dente. Meanwhile, in a Dutch oven, heat olive oil over medium-low heat. Add the next 5 ingredients. Break the salmon into bite-sized pieces; add to tomato mixture. Stir in pesto, basil and red pepper flakes. Cook, stirring occasionally, until the vegetables are crisp-tender, 8-10 minutes.
2. Drain pasta. Add to the salmon mixture; stir to combine. Top with cheeses.
¾ CUP: *433 cal., 16g fat (3g sat. fat), 11mg chol., 924mg sod., 55g carb. (4g sugars, 4g fiber), 17g pro.*

Holiday Helper
The main ingredient amounts in this recipe are meant to be made to taste; if you want more salmon in your pasta, feel free to use more!

SPICY BEEF BRISKET

My family fell in love with this brisket the first time I tried the recipe. The no-fuss preparation and long cooking time make it perfect to have simmering away while you take care of party preparations and other courses.

—Mary Neihouse, Fort Smith, AR

PREP: 5 MIN. • **BAKE:** 3 HOURS
MAKES: 10 SERVINGS

- 1   fresh beef brisket (3 to 4 lbs.)
- 1   can (15 oz.) tomato sauce
- 1   can (10 oz.) diced tomatoes and green chilies, undrained
- 1   envelope onion soup mix
- ¼   tsp. garlic powder

Preheat oven to 325°. Place the brisket on a rack in a shallow greased roasting pan. In a small bowl, combine remaining ingredients; pour over the brisket. Cover and bake until the meat is tender, about 3 hours. To serve, thinly slice the brisket across the grain.
NOTE: This is a fresh beef brisket, not corned beef.
4 OZ. COOKED BEEF: *195 cal., 6g fat (2g sat. fat), 58mg chol., 601mg sod., 5g carb. (1g sugars, 1g fiber), 29g pro.*
DIABETIC EXCHANGES: *4 lean meat.*

STOLLEN BUTTER ROLLS

Our family enjoys my stollen so much that I can't serve it just as a holiday sweet bread. I created this dinner roll—buttery, less-sweet—so we can satisfy our stollen cravings anytime.
—Mindy White, Nashville, TN

PREP: 45 MIN. + RISING • **BAKE:** 15 MIN.
MAKES: 2 DOZEN

- 1 pkg. (¼ oz.) active dry yeast
- ¼ cup warm water (110° to 115°)
- 1 cup 2% milk
- 2 large eggs, room temperature
- ½ cup butter, softened
- 1 Tbsp. sugar
- 1 tsp. salt
- 4¼ to 4¾ cups all-purpose flour
- ¾ cup chopped mixed candied fruit
- ¾ cup dried currants
- ½ cup cold butter, cut into 24 pieces (1 tsp. each)

1. In a small bowl, dissolve yeast in warm water. In a large bowl, combine milk, eggs, butter, sugar, salt, the yeast mixture and 3 cups of flour; beat on medium speed until smooth. Stir in enough of the remaining flour to form a soft dough (dough will be sticky).
2. Turn dough onto a floured surface; knead until smooth and elastic, about 6-8 minutes. Place in a greased bowl, turning once to grease the top. Cover and let rise in a warm place until doubled, about 1 hour.
3. Punch dough down; turn onto a floured surface. Knead candied fruit and currants into the dough (knead in more flour if necessary). Divide and shape into 24 balls; flatten slightly. Place 1 tsp. cold butter in the center of each circle. Fold circles in half over butter; press the edges to seal. Place in a greased 15x10x1-in. baking pan. Cover; let rolls rise in a warm place until doubled, about 45 minutes.
4. Preheat oven to 375°. Bake until golden brown, 15-20 minutes. Cool rolls in the pan 5 minutes; serve warm.
FREEZE OPTION: Freeze cool rolls in airtight containers. To use, microwave each roll on high until warmed, 30-45 seconds.
1 ROLL: *198 cal., 9g fat (5g sat. fat), 37mg chol., 178mg sod., 28g carb. (9g sugars, 1g fiber), 4g pro.*

RUTABAGA CARROT CASSEROLE

This scoop-able side with its sweet, crunchy topping makes a delightful alternative to the traditional sweet potato casserole.
—Joan Hallford, North Richland Hills, TX

PREP: 30 MIN. • **BAKE:** 30 MIN.
MAKES: 8 SERVINGS

- 1 large rutabaga, peeled and cubed
- 3 large carrots, shredded
- 1 large egg
- 2 Tbsp. brown sugar
- 1 Tbsp. butter
- ½ tsp. salt
- ¼ tsp. ground nutmeg
  Dash pepper
- 1 cup cooked brown rice
- 1 cup fat-free evaporated milk
TOPPING
- ¼ cup all-purpose flour
- ¼ cup packed brown sugar
- 2 Tbsp. cold butter
- ½ cup chopped pecans

1. Place rutabaga in a Dutch oven, cover with water and bring to a boil. Cook, uncovered, until tender, 15-20 minutes, adding carrots during the last 5 minutes of cooking; drain.
2. Preheat oven to 350°. In a large bowl, mash the rutabaga mixture with egg, brown sugar, butter, salt, nutmeg and pepper. Stir in rice and milk. Transfer to an 11x7-in. baking dish coated with cooking spray.
3. For the topping, combine the flour and brown sugar; cut in butter until crumbly. Stir in the pecans. Sprinkle over top of casserole. Bake, uncovered, until bubbly, 30-35 minutes.
½ **CUP:** *249 cal., 11g fat (3g sat. fat), 39mg chol., 267mg sod., 34g carb. (21g sugars, 4g fiber), 6g pro.*
DIABETIC EXCHANGES: *2 starch, 2 fat.*

CARAMEL CHEX MIX

This wonderfully crunchy snack is loaded with cereal, pretzels and nuts—and coated with a not-too-sweet brown sugar mixture. Package this up as gifts, or set out a bowl at your party and watch it disappear by the handful.
—Samantha Moyer, Oskaloosa, IA

PREP: 10 MIN. • **BAKE:** 15 MIN. + COOLING • **MAKES:** 3 QT.

- 2 cups each Rice Chex, Corn Chex and Wheat Chex
- 2 cups miniature pretzels
- 2 cups pecan halves
- 2 cups salted cashews
- ¾ cup butter, cubed
- ¾ cup packed brown sugar

1. Preheat oven to 350°. In a large bowl, combine the cereal, pretzels and nuts. In a small saucepan, combine butter and brown sugar. Bring to a boil; cook and stir until thickened, for 2 minutes. Pour over the cereal mixture; toss to coat.

2. Spread into two greased 15x10x1-in. baking pans. Bake for 8 minutes. Stir; bake 6 minutes longer. Transfer to waxed paper-lined baking sheets. Cool completely. Store the mix in airtight containers.

¾ CUP: 383 cal., 27g fat (8g sat. fat), 23mg chol., 333mg sod., 34g carb. (14g sugars, 3g fiber), 6g pro.

SHRIMP & CUCUMBER CANAPES

These cute stacks really stand out in a holiday appetizer buffet. Tasty, cool and crunchy, they come together in a snap.
—Ashley Nochlin, Port St. Lucie, FL

TAKES: 25 MIN. • **MAKES:** 2 DOZEN

- ½ cup ketchup
- 4 tsp. Creole seasoning, divided
- 1 Tbsp. finely chopped onion
- 1 Tbsp. finely chopped green pepper
- 1 Tbsp. finely chopped celery
- ¼ tsp. hot pepper sauce
- 1 pkg. (8 oz.) cream cheese, softened
- 24 English cucumber slices
- 24 peeled and deveined cooked medium shrimp
- 2 Tbsp. minced fresh parsley

1. For the sauce, combine ketchup, 2 tsp. of Creole seasoning, the onion, green pepper, celery and pepper sauce. In another bowl, combine cream cheese and remaining Creole seasoning.

2. Spread or pipe the cream cheese mixture onto cucumber slices. Top each with a shrimp and a dab of the cocktail sauce. Sprinkle with parsley.

NOTE: The following mix of spices may be substituted for 1 tsp. Creole seasoning: ¼ tsp. each salt, garlic powder and paprika plus a pinch each of dried thyme, ground cumin and cayenne pepper.

1 CANAPE: 50 cal., 3g fat (2g sat. fat), 26mg chol., 218mg sod., 2g carb. (1g sugars, 0 fiber), 3g pro.

MUSHROOM OLIVE BRUSCHETTA

After experimenting with ingredients and flavor combinations, I came up with this variation on traditional tomato-based bruschetta. I've also used this recipe as a stuffing for chicken breast, and sometimes will add a little feta cheese. You can make it ahead of time and keep it in the refrigerator, but be sure to bring it to room temperature before serving—that's how it tastes best!
—Colleen Blasetti, Palm Coast, FL

PREP: 40 MIN. • **BAKE:** 10 MIN.
MAKES: 2 DOZEN

- 1¾ cups sliced baby portobello mushrooms
- ¼ cup chopped onion
- 1 anchovy fillet
- 1 Tbsp. olive oil
- ½ tsp. minced garlic
- ½ cup finely chopped tomatoes
- ¼ cup chopped pitted green olives
- ¼ cup chopped ripe olives
- 1 Tbsp. capers, drained
- ¼ tsp. dried thyme
- ¼ tsp. dried basil
- ¼ tsp. dried oregano
- ⅛ tsp. pepper
- 24 slices French baguette (½ in. thick)
- 2 Tbsp. butter, melted
- ¼ cup grated Parmesan cheese

1. Preheat oven to 375°. In a large skillet, saute mushrooms, onion and anchovy in oil until vegetables are tender. Add garlic; cook 1 minute longer. Remove from heat. Stir in the tomatoes, olives, capers, thyme, basil, oregano and pepper.
2. Place baguette slices on an ungreased baking sheet. Brush with butter; sprinkle with Parmesan cheese. Bake until lightly browned, 8-9 minutes. With a slotted spoon, top each slice with about 1 Tbsp. mushroom mixture.

1 APPETIZER: *44 cal., 2g fat (1g sat. fat), 3mg chol., 127mg sod., 5g carb. (0 sugars, 0 fiber), 2g pro.*

BUTTERNUT & CHARD PASTA BAKE

This recipe is made for butternut squash lovers, with pureed squash in the sauce and squash pieces in the casserole alongside an ideal companion, Swiss chard. This is a veggie hybrid of ever-popular holiday sides.
—Arlene Erlbach, Morton Grove, IL

PREP: 25 MIN. • **BAKE:** 30 MIN.
MAKES: 9 SERVINGS

- 3 cups uncooked bow tie pasta
- 2 cups fat-free ricotta cheese
- 4 large eggs
- 3 cups frozen cubed butternut squash, thawed and divided
- 1 tsp. dried thyme
- ½ tsp. salt, divided
- ¼ tsp. ground nutmeg
- 1 cup coarsely chopped shallots
- 1½ cups chopped Swiss chard, stems removed
- 2 Tbsp. olive oil
- 1½ cups panko (Japanese) bread crumbs
- ⅓ cup coarsely chopped fresh parsley
- ¼ tsp. garlic powder

1. Preheat oven to 375°. Cook the pasta according to the package directions for al dente; drain. Place ricotta, eggs, 1½ cups squash, the thyme, ¼ tsp. salt and the nutmeg in a food processor; process until smooth. Pour into a large bowl. Stir in pasta, Swiss chard, shallots and the remaining squash. Transfer to a greased 13x9-in. baking dish.
2. In a large skillet, heat oil over medium-high heat. Add bread crumbs; cook and stir until golden brown, about 2-3 minutes. Stir in the parsley, garlic powder and the remaining salt. Sprinkle crumbs over the pasta mixture.
3. Bake, uncovered, until set and topping is golden brown, about 30-35 minutes.

1 CUP: *223 cal., 6g fat (1g sat. fat), 83mg chol., 209mg sod., 33g carb. (4g sugars, 2g fiber), 9g pro.*

8-in. square baking dish. Bake, uncovered, until a knife inserted in the center comes out clean, 40-45 minutes.

2. In a small saucepan over medium heat, melt butter; stir in the brown sugar and apple juice. Cook and stir until the sugar is dissolved. Remove from the heat; stir in extracts. Serve warm with bread pudding. Refrigerate leftovers.

1 PIECE WITH 2 TBSP. SAUCE: *413 cal., 19g fat (11g sat. fat), 87mg chol., 349mg sod., 57g carb. (44g sugars, 1g fiber), 6g pro.*

JALAPENO GREEN BEANS

This simple green bean dish gets a bit of a kick from a jalapeno pepper. If you don't like it spicy, reduce the amount of jalapeno by half—or eliminate it completely.
—Deirdre Cox, Kansas City, MO

TAKES: 25 MIN. • **MAKES:** 4 SERVINGS

- 2 Tbsp. olive oil
- 1 jalapeno pepper, thinly sliced
- 1 shallot, thinly sliced
- 1 lb. fresh green beans, cut into 2-in. pieces
- ½ tsp. salt
- 2 Tbsp. lemon juice

In a large skillet, heat oil over medium-high heat. Add jalapeno and shallot; cook and stir 2-3 minutes or until tender. Add beans and salt; cook and stir 8-10 minutes longer or until beans are tender, reducing heat if necessary. Drizzle with lemon juice. Serve immediately.

NOTE: Wear disposable gloves when cutting hot peppers; the oils can burn skin. Avoid touching your face.

½ CUP: *106 cal., 7g fat (1g sat. fat), 0 chol., 303mg sod., 11g carb. (4g sugars, 4g fiber), 2g pro.*
DIABETIC EXCHANGES: *1½ fat, 1 vegetable.*

BREAD PUDDING WITH SAUCE

This warm pudding is a traditional winter favorite, and for a good reason. The rich, cinnamony flavor is perfect for the holidays, and the decadent, buttery sauce is such an amazing complement. You can use actual rum instead of extract, just for grown-ups.
—Peggy Goodrich, Enid, OK

PREP: 15 MIN. • **BAKE:** 45 MIN.
MAKES: 9 SERVINGS

- 2 large eggs
- 2 cups milk
- ½ cup sugar
- ¼ cup butter, melted
- 1 tsp. ground cinnamon
- ¼ tsp. salt
- 6 cups cubed day-old bread
- ½ cup golden raisins, optional

BROWN SUGAR BUTTER SAUCE
- ½ cup butter
- 1 cup packed brown sugar
- 3 Tbsp. unsweetened apple juice
- 2 tsp. rum extract
- 1 drop orange extract

1. Preheat oven to 350°. In a large bowl, whisk eggs, milk, sugar, butter, cinnamon and salt. Gently fold in bread cubes and raisins if desired. Transfer to a greased

FLUFFY CRANBERRY DELIGHT

This was originally my daughter's recipe, and either she or I will make it for our holiday get-togethers. It can be served as a fruit salad along with the meal or later as a light dessert. It's particularly pretty in a cut-glass bowl on a buffet.
—Ruth Bolduc, Conway, NH

PREP: 20 MIN. + CHILLING • **MAKES:** 10 SERVINGS

4	cups cranberries
1½	cups sugar
¾	cup water
1	envelope unflavored gelatin
¼	cup lemon juice
2	Tbsp. orange juice
1½	cups heavy whipping cream
3	Tbsp. confectioners' sugar
1	tsp. vanilla extract

1. In a saucepan, bring the cranberries, sugar and water to a boil. Reduce heat and cook until the berries burst. Strain through a food mill or sieve into a large bowl.
2. Stir in gelatin, lemon juice and orange juice. Cool until the mixture coats the back of a spoon.
3. In a small bowl, whip the cream until soft peaks form. Add confectioners' sugar and vanilla; beat until stiff peaks form. Fold into the cranberry mixture. Chill until set.
1 SERVING: *273 cal., 13g fat (8g sat. fat), 49mg chol., 16mg sod., 39g carb. (36g sugars, 2g fiber), 2g pro.*

BOURBON BAKED HAM

Because of its simple ingredient list, easy preparation and unbeatable flavor, this baked ham recipe is one you'll come to rely on often. The honey-bourbon glaze looks lovely and helps seal in the meat's juices.
—Jean Adams, Waycross, GA

PREP: 15 MIN. • **BAKE:** 2 HOURS 20 MIN. • **MAKES:** 15 SERVINGS

1	bone-in fully cooked spiral-sliced ham (7 to 9 lbs.)
1	cup honey
½	cup bourbon
½	cup molasses
¼	cup orange juice
2	Tbsp. Dijon mustard

1. Preheat oven to 325°. Place the ham on a rack in a shallow roasting pan. Score the surface of the ham, making diamond shapes ½ in. deep. Bake for 2 hours.
2. Meanwhile, in a small saucepan over medium-low heat, combine the remaining ingredients; cook and stir until smooth.
3. Brush ham with some of the glaze. Bake until a thermometer reads 140°, 20-25 minutes longer, brushing occasionally with the remaining glaze.
6 OZ. COOKED HAM: *379 cal., 5g fat (1g sat. fat), 47mg chol., 1958mg sod., 43g carb. (25g sugars, 0 fiber), 38g pro.*

PUMPKIN SAGE BEURRE NOISETTE COOKIES

In a world of pumpkin spice flavor, these fluffy cookies are my top choice. The infusion of fresh sage gives a surprising savory note. You can use mashed sweet potatoes or yams instead of the pumpkin if you prefer.
—*Jill LeMasters, Ravenna, OH*

PREP: 25 MIN. + STANDING
BAKE: 10 MIN/BATCH • **MAKES:** 26 COOKIES

- ½ cup butter, cubed
- ½ cup fresh sage, thinly sliced
- ¼ cup sugar
- ¼ cup packed brown sugar
- 1 large egg, room temperature
- ½ cup canned pumpkin
- 1 cup all-purpose flour
- ½ tsp. baking soda
- ½ tsp. ground cinnamon
- ¼ tsp. salt
- ¼ tsp. ground ginger
- ¼ tsp. ground cloves
  Dash ground nutmeg
  Confectioners' sugar

1. In a small heavy saucepan, melt butter over medium heat. Add sage; heat until golden brown, stirring constantly, about 5-7 minutes. Remove from heat; discard the sage. Let stand until firm.
2. Preheat oven to 375°. In a large bowl, cream the sage butter and sugars until light and fluffy. Beat in egg and pumpkin. In another bowl, whisk flour, baking soda, cinnamon, salt, ginger, cloves and nutmeg; gradually beat into the creamed mixture.
3. Drop dough by rounded tablespoonfuls 1 in. apart onto parchment-lined baking sheets. Bake cookies until lightly browned, 10-12 minutes. Remove to wire racks to cool. Dust tops with confectioners' sugar. Store in an airtight container.
1 COOKIE: *69 cal., 4g fat (2g sat. fat), 17mg chol., 79mg sod., 8g carb. (4g sugars, 0 fiber), 1g pro.*

Holiday Helper
To make a vegan version, use a vegan buttery spread in place of the butter, and instead of an egg, soak 1 Tbsp. flax seed meal in 3 Tbsp. water for 5 minutes.

APRICOT-APPLE CIDER

Dried apricots give this comforting cider a delicious twist. Add cranberries and winter spices and you have a perfect drink to warm your guests' hearts.
—*Ginnie Busam, Pewee Valley, KY*

PREP: 20 MIN. • **COOK:** 3 HOURS
MAKES: 13 SERVINGS (2½ QT.)

- 8 cups unsweetened apple juice
- 1 can (12 oz.) ginger ale
- ½ cup dried apricots, halved
- ½ cup dried cranberries
- 2 cinnamon sticks (3 in.)
- 1 Tbsp. whole allspice
- 1 Tbsp. whole cloves
  Additional cinnamon sticks, fresh cranberries, optional

In a 5-qt. slow cooker, combine apple juice and ginger ale. Place the apricots, cranberries, cinnamon sticks, allspice and cloves on a double thickness of cheesecloth; bring up the corners of the cloth and tie with string to form a bag. Place in slow cooker; cover. Cook on high for 3-4 hours. Discard spice bag. Garnish individual servings with cinnamon sticks and cranberries, if desired.
¾ CUP: *79 cal., 0 fat (0 sat. fat), 0 chol., 8mg sod., 20g carb. (17g sugars, 0 fiber), 0 pro.*

HOLIDAY
FEASTS

*Three specially designed full-course menus provide
perfect plans for celebrations to remember—
plus a bonus selection of a la carte dishes
gives you even more tempting options.*

Lamb Feast

Smoky & Spicy
Vegetable Bisque, p. 39

Roquefort Pear Salad, p. 41

Plum-Glazed Lamb, p. 39

Rustic Squash Tarts, p. 40

Wild Rice Mushroom Bake, p. 42

Minty Peas & Onions, p. 42

Poached Pears with
Vanilla Sauce, p. 43

PLUM-GLAZED LAMB

Fruity and flavorful, this wonderful glaze is simple to prepare. The recipe makes enough glaze to baste the lamb during roasting and still leaves plenty to pass when serving.
—Ann Eastman, Santa Monica, CA

PREP: 5 MIN. • **BAKE:** 1¾ HOURS
MAKES: 6 SERVINGS

- 1 bone-in leg of lamb (4 to 5 lbs.)
  Salt and pepper to taste
- 2 cans (15 oz. each) plums, pitted
- 2 garlic cloves
- ¼ cup lemon juice
- 2 Tbsp. reduced-sodium soy sauce
- 2 tsp. Worcestershire sauce
- 1 tsp. dried basil

1. Preheat oven to 325°. Place lamb on a rack in a shallow baking pan, fat side up. Season with salt and pepper. Bake lamb, uncovered, 1¾-2¼ hours or until meat reaches desired doneness (for medium-rare, a thermometer should read 135°; medium, 140°; medium-well, 145°).
2. Meanwhile, drain plums, reserving ½ cup of the syrup. Place the plums, reserved syrup, garlic, lemon juice, soy sauce, Worcestershire sauce and basil in food processor; cover and process until smooth. Set aside half of the plum sauce.
3. Baste lamb every 15 minutes during the last hour of roasting. In a small saucepan, simmer reserved sauce 5 minutes; serve with meat.
5 OZ. COOKED LAMB: *338 cal., 10g fat (4g sat. fat), 137mg chol., 283mg sod., 23g carb. (18g sugars, 2g fiber), 39g pro.*

SMOKY & SPICY VEGETABLE BISQUE

On an ordinary night, I make my bisque a complete meal by serving it with a side of bruschetta or a Caprese salad. For a special-occasion feast, it makes a great first course, setting off the richer dishes beautifully with a bit of heat and smoke.
—Juliana Inhofer, Rocklin, CA

PREP: 1 HOUR • **COOK:** 30 MIN.
MAKES: 6 SERVINGS

- 2 large onions, cut into 8 wedges
- 4 large tomatoes, cut into 8 wedges

- 1 large sweet red pepper, cut into 8 wedges
- 4 garlic cloves, halved
- ¼ cup olive oil
- 2 cans (14½ oz. each) reduced-sodium chicken broth
- ½ cup fat-free half-and-half
- ½ cup coarsely chopped fresh basil
- 1 small chipotle pepper in adobo sauce, seeded
- ½ tsp. pepper
- ¼ tsp. salt
  Fresh basil leaves, optional

1. Preheat oven to 425°. Line a 15x10x1-in. baking pan with foil and coat the foil with cooking spray. Place the onions, tomatoes, red pepper and garlic in pan. Drizzle with oil and toss to coat.
2. Bake, uncovered, until vegetables are tender and browned, 40-45 minutes, stirring occasionally.

3. In a large saucepan, combine the broth, half-and-half, chopped basil, chipotle pepper, pepper, salt and the roasted vegetables. Bring to a boil. Reduce heat; simmer, uncovered, for 20-25 minutes. Cool slightly.
4. In a blender, process the soup in batches until smooth. Return all to the pan; heat through. Garnish with basil leaves if desired.
NOTE: Wear disposable gloves when cutting hot peppers; the oils can burn skin. Avoid touching your face.
1 CUP: *157 cal., 9g fat (1g sat. fat), 0 chol., 528mg sod., 15g carb. (9g sugars, 3g fiber), 5g pro.*

RUSTIC SQUASH TARTS

Of all the delicious side dishes you'll have at your holiday meal, this one will surprise guests the most. Flaky, rustic-looking pastry shells hold a sweet and spicy pecan layer under the perfectly roasted squash slices.
—Ann Marie Moch, Kintyre, ND

PREP: 30 MIN. • **BAKE:** 35 MIN.
MAKES: 2 TARTS (8 SERVINGS EACH)

- 1 medium butternut squash, peeled, seeded and cut into ⅛-in. slices
- 1 medium acorn squash, peeled, seeded and cut into ⅛-in. slices
- 2 Tbsp. water
- ¼ cup olive oil
- 1 Tbsp. minced fresh thyme
- 1 Tbsp. minced fresh parsley
- ½ tsp. salt
- ¼ tsp. pepper
- ½ cup all-purpose flour
- ½ cup ground pecans
- 6 Tbsp. sugar
- ½ tsp. ground nutmeg
- ½ tsp. ground cinnamon
- 1 pkg. (17.3 oz.) frozen puff pastry, thawed
- 1 large egg, lightly beaten
- 2 Tbsp. butter

1. In a large microwave-safe bowl, combine butternut and acorn squash and water. Cover and cook on high for 5 minutes or until crisp-tender. Drain; return to bowl. In a small bowl, combine oil, thyme, parsley, salt and pepper; drizzle onto squash and toss to coat. In another bowl, combine the flour, pecans, sugar, nutmeg and cinnamon; set aside.

2. Unfold the pastry sheets on a lightly floured surface. Roll each pastry to ⅛-in. thickness; transfer each to an ungreased baking sheet. Sprinkle with the pecan mixture. Arrange the squash slices to within 1½ in. of edges, alternating slices of butternut and acorn squash.

3. Fold up edges of the pastry over the filling, leaving centers uncovered. Brush the pastry with egg. Dot the squash with butter. Bake tarts at 375° until golden brown, for 35-40 minutes.

1 SLICE: *279 cal., 15g fat (4g sat. fat), 17mg chol., 196mg sod., 34g carb. (7g sugars, 5g fiber), 4g pro.*

ROQUEFORT PEAR SALAD

Guests brought this salad to a party we hosted last summer. Now it's a mainstay at most of our get-togethers. It's great all year, but the elegant combination of pears and rich cheese really is perfect for the holidays.
—Sherry Duval, Baltimore, MD

TAKES: 20 MIN. • **MAKES:** 10 SERVINGS

- 10 cups torn salad greens
- 3 large ripe pears, sliced
- ½ cup thinly sliced green onions
- 4 oz. crumbled blue cheese
- ¼ cup slivered almonds, toasted

MUSTARD VINAIGRETTE
- ⅓ cup olive oil
- 3 Tbsp. cider vinegar
- 1½ tsp. sugar
- 1½ tsp. Dijon mustard
- 1 garlic clove, minced
- ½ tsp. salt
- Pepper to taste

In a large bowl, combine the salad greens, pears, onions, cheese and almonds. In a jar with a tight-fitting lid, combine vinaigrette ingredients; shake well. Pour over salad; toss to coat.

1¼ CUPS: *171 cal., 12g fat (3g sat. fat), 9mg chol., 303mg sod., 14g carb. (8g sugars, 4g fiber), 4g pro.*
DIABETIC EXCHANGES: *2½ fat, 1 vegetable, ½ fruit.*

SET THE TABLE— COMPANY'S COMING!

A formal feast can leave you wondering about the correct placement of flatware, plates, napkins and glassware. Don't add stress to your dinner plans, and keep the focus on the food, your family and friends, with this simple guide.

The dinner plate is always the center of the place setting; everything else is placed around it. Arrange the flatware in the order in which it will be used.

Forks go to the left of the plate. If you're serving a salad, place a small salad fork to the left of the dinner fork. Dessert forks can either be placed to the right of the dinner fork or brought to the table when dessert is served. Place the napkin under the forks or on the plate.

The knife and spoons go to the right of the plate. (Soup or dessert spoons can also be brought to the table as those courses are served.) Place the knife with its sharp edge toward the plate. If soup is to be served, set the bowl on the plate.

Smaller plates for salad or bread go above and to the left of the forks. Position the butter knife across the butter plate.

The cup and saucer go above the spoons with the handle to the right.

Water glasses and wine glasses (both red and white, if necessary) go to the left of the coffee cup, with the water glass on the right.

MINTY PEAS & ONIONS

Mother always relied on peas and onions when she needed a side dish that she knew everyone would love. Besides being easy to prepare, this dish was a favorite with everyone in our family. It was handed down to my mother by my grandmother.
—Santa D'Addario, Jacksonville, FL

TAKES: 20 MIN. • **MAKES:** 8 SERVINGS

- 2 large onions, cut into ½-in. wedges
- ½ cup chopped sweet red pepper
- 2 Tbsp. vegetable oil
- 2 pkg. (16 oz. each) frozen peas
- 2 Tbsp. minced fresh mint or 2 tsp. dried mint

In a large skillet, saute the onions and red pepper in oil until the onions just begin to soften. Add peas; cook, uncovered, stirring occasionally, for 10 minutes or until heated through. Stir in mint and cook for 1 minute.

1 SERVING: *134 cal., 4g fat (1g sat. fat), 0 chol., 128mg sod., 19g carb. (9g sugars, 6g fiber), 6g pro.*
DIABETIC EXCHANGES: *1 starch, 1 fat.*

WILD RICE MUSHROOM BAKE

Wild rice adds rich and wonderful flavor to this casserole. I like to serve it on special occasions—it's a surprising and appealing alternative to potatoes or a traditional pilaf.
—Jann Marie Foster, Minneapolis, MN

PREP: 15 MIN. + SOAKING • **BAKE:** 1 ½ HOURS
MAKES: 10 SERVINGS

- 1 cup uncooked wild rice
- 2 cups boiling water
- 1 lb. sliced fresh mushrooms
- 1 medium onion, chopped
- 2 Tbsp. butter
- ¾ cup uncooked long grain rice
- ½ cup sliced almonds
- 3 cups chicken broth
- 1½ cups heavy whipping cream
- 1 tsp. salt
- ⅛ tsp. pepper
- 3 Tbsp. grated Parmesan cheese

1. Place the wild rice in a large bowl and cover with boiling water; soak for 1 hour. Drain and set aside.
2. In a large skillet, saute mushrooms and onion in butter until tender. In a large bowl, combine the mushroom mixture, wild rice, long grain rice, almonds, broth, cream, salt and pepper.
3. Transfer to a greased 2½-qt. baking dish. Cover and bake at 350° for 75 minutes. Uncover; sprinkle with the Parmesan cheese. Bake until the rice is tender, 10 minutes longer.
¾ CUP: *318 cal., 19g fat (10g sat. fat), 56mg chol., 583mg sod., 31g carb. (3g sugars, 2g fiber), 8g pro.*

POACHED PEARS WITH VANILLA SAUCE

This dessert makes a great ending to an indulgent feast—elegant and delicious but not too heavy. Whole pears are lightly spiced and chilled, then served with a heavenly custard sauce.
—Al Latimer, Bentonville, AZ

PREP: 25 MIN. • **COOK:** 25 MIN. + CHILLING
MAKES: 6 SERVINGS

- 2⅓ cups sugar, divided
- 2 tsp. cornstarch
- 1 cup milk
- ½ cup heavy whipping cream
- 4 large egg yolks, lightly beaten
- 1 tsp. vanilla extract
- 10 cups water, divided
- 2 Tbsp. lemon juice, divided
- 6 medium firm pears, stems attached
- 1 tsp. grated lemon zest
- 1 cinnamon stick (3 in.)
- 3 whole cloves

1. In a heavy 2-qt. saucepan, combine ⅓ cup sugar and the cornstarch; gradually stir in milk and cream until smooth. Bring to a boil over medium heat; cook and stir for 2 minutes. Remove from the heat.
2. Gradually add a small amount of the hot mixture to egg yolks; return all to the pan, stirring constantly. Cook and stir over medium-low heat until mixture thickens slightly, 15 minutes (do not boil). Stir in vanilla. Pour into a bowl; place a piece of waxed paper or plastic wrap on top of the sauce. Cover and refrigerate.
3. In a large bowl, combine 6 cups water and 1 Tbsp. lemon juice. Peel the pears, leaving stems attached. Immediately plunge pears into lemon water. In a large saucepan, combine lemon zest and the remaining sugar, water and lemon juice. Bring to a boil. Add cinnamon stick, cloves and pears. Reduce heat; cover and simmer until pears are tender, 20-25 minutes.
4. Carefully remove pears to a plate. Discard cinnamon stick and cloves. Drizzle syrup over pears. Loosely cover and refrigerate for 2-3 hours. To serve, place pears on dessert plates; drizzle with the chilled vanilla sauce.
1 SERVING: 539 cal., 13g fat (7g sat. fat), 174mg chol., 33mg sod., 107g carb. (96g sugars, 4g fiber), 4g pro.

APPLE & HERB ROASTED TURKEY

My daughter loves to help me make this moist roasted turkey with herbs. Her job is to hand Mommy the ingredients—if she doesn't eat the apples first!
—*Kimberly Jackson, Gay, GA*

PREP: 20 MIN.
BAKE: 3 HOURS + STANDING
MAKES: 14 SERVINGS

- ¼ cup minced fresh sage
- ¼ cup minced fresh rosemary
- 1 turkey (14 lbs.)
- 1 medium apple, quartered
- 1 medium onion, halved
- 1 celery rib, halved
- ½ cup butter, melted
- ½ cup apple jelly, warmed

1. Preheat oven to 325°. Combine sage and rosemary. With your fingers, carefully loosen skin from the turkey breast; rub herbs under the skin. Secure the skin to the underside of breast with toothpicks.
2. Place turkey breast side up on a rack in a roasting pan. Stuff with apple, onion and celery. Brush with butter.
3. Bake, uncovered, until a thermometer reads 180°, basting occasionally with pan drippings, 3-3½ hours. (Cover loosely with foil if the turkey browns too quickly.) Brush with apple jelly. Cover and let stand 15 minutes before removing toothpicks and carving.
8 OZ. COOKED TURKEY: *626 cal., 31g fat (11g sat. fat), 262mg chol., 222mg sod., 10g carb. (9g sugars, 0 fiber), 72g pro.*

POTATO PUMPKIN MASH

I swirl fresh pumpkin into potatoes for a little extra holiday color. No more plain white potatoes for us! If you'd like, you can use butternut squash instead. Either way it's super pretty.
—*Michelle Medley, Dallas, TX*

PREP: 20 MIN. • **COOK:** 25 MIN.
MAKES: 8 SERVINGS

- 8 cups cubed peeled pie pumpkin (about 2 lbs.)
- 8 medium Yukon Gold potatoes, peeled and cubed (about 2 lbs.)

- ½ to ¾ cup 2% milk, divided
- 8 Tbsp. butter, softened, divided
- 1 tsp. salt, divided
- 1 Tbsp. olive oil
- ¼ tsp. coarsely ground pepper

1. Place the pumpkin in a large saucepan; add water to cover. Bring to a boil. Reduce heat; cook, uncovered, for 20-25 minutes or until tender.
2. Meanwhile, place potatoes in another saucepan; add water to cover. Bring to a boil. Reduce heat; cook, uncovered, for 10-15 minutes or until tender.

3. Drain potatoes; return to pan. Mash the potatoes, adding ¼ cup milk, 4 Tbsp. butter and ½ tsp. salt. Add additional milk if needed to reach desired consistency. Transfer to a serving bowl; keep warm.
4. Drain pumpkin; return to pan. Mash the pumpkin, gradually adding the remaining butter and salt and enough remaining milk to reach the desired consistency; spoon pumpkin mixture evenly over potatoes. Cut through with a spoon or knife to swirl. Drizzle with olive oil; sprinkle with pepper. Serve immediately.
¾ CUP: *214 cal., 13 g fat (8 g sat. fat), 31 mg chol., 384 mg sod., 23 g carb., 2 g fiber, 3 g pro.*

SOUTHERN CORNBREAD DRESSING

This big-batch recipe is one of my favorite holiday side dishes, and it's economical, too! No matter where you are in the country, your guests will appreciate a taste of the South.
—Margaret Kendall, McConnelsville, OH

PREP: 20 MIN. • **BAKE:** 40 MIN.
MAKES: 10 SERVINGS

  8   cups coarsely crumbled cornbread
  4   hard-boiled large eggs, chopped
  1   medium green pepper,
       finely chopped
  1   medium onion, finely chopped
  2   celery ribs, finely chopped
  ½   cup turkey giblets, finely chopped
  2   garlic cloves, minced
1½   tsp. poultry seasoning
  ½   tsp. salt
  ½   tsp. pepper
  3   large eggs, lightly beaten
  3   cups chicken broth

1. Preheat oven to 350°. In a large bowl, combine the first 10 ingredients. In another bowl, whisk eggs and broth. Add to the bread mixture; stir until moistened.
2. Transfer to a greased 13x9-in. baking dish. Bake, uncovered, 40-45 minutes or until lightly browned and a thermometer inserted in the center reads 160°.
¾ CUP: *264 cal., 6g fat (1g sat. fat), 182mg chol., 987mg sod., 39g carb. (4g sugars, 3g fiber), 12g pro*

 Holiday Helper
Very fresh eggs can be hard to peel, but if you store them in the refrigerator for 7-10 days before cooking them, the shells will come off more easily. Gently tap or roll eggs on the counter to crack the shell before peeling—the smaller pieces will usually come off more easily and without tearing the whites.

POMEGRANATE SPLASH SALAD

The sparkling pomegranate gems make this salad irresistibly beautiful. My family loves it at holiday gatherings when pomegranates are in season. Even the children can't get enough of this antioxidant-rich delight.
—Emily Jamison, Champaign, IL

TAKES: 15 MIN. • **MAKES:** 8 SERVINGS

- 4 cups fresh baby spinach
- 4 cups spring mix salad greens
- ¾ cup crumbled feta cheese
- ¾ cup pomegranate seeds
- ¾ cup fresh or frozen raspberries
- ⅓ cup pine nuts, toasted

CRANBERRY VINAIGRETTE
- ½ cup thawed cranberry juice concentrate
- 3 Tbsp. olive oil
- 2 Tbsp. rice vinegar
  Dash salt

In a large bowl, combine the first 6 ingredients. In a small bowl, whisk the vinaigrette ingredients. Serve with salad.

1 CUP WITH ABOUT 4½ TSP. VINAIGRETTE: *164 cal., 10g fat (2g sat. fat), 6mg chol., 140mg sod., 16g carb. (11g sugars, 2g fiber), 4g pro.*
DIABETIC EXCHANGES: *2 fat, 1 starch.*

FOOLPROOF GRAVY

A turkey dinner isn't complete without gravy—this can't-miss recipe is just the thing. Use the drippings from your roasted turkey, and the gravy is done in just 20 minutes.
—Edie DeSpain, Logan, UT

TAKES: 20 MIN. • **MAKES:** 2⅓ CUPS

  Drippings from 1 roasted turkey
- ½ to 1 cup turkey or chicken broth
- ¼ cup plus 1 Tbsp. all-purpose flour
- ½ cup fat-free milk
- 1 tsp. chicken bouillon granules
- ¼ tsp. poultry seasoning
- ⅛ tsp. white pepper

1. Pour turkey drippings into a 2-cup measuring cup. Skim and discard the fat. Add enough broth to the drippings to measure 2 cups; transfer to a small saucepan and bring to a boil.
2. In a small bowl, whisk flour and milk until smooth; gradually stir into the drippings mixture. Stir in bouillon granules, poultry seasoning and white pepper. Return to a boil, stirring constantly; cook and stir for 2 minutes or until thickened.

2 TBSP.: *165 cal., 17g fat (7g sat. fat), 17mg chol., 103mg sod., 2g carb. (0 sugars, 0 fiber), 0 pro.*

THYME GREEN BEANS WITH ALMONDS

Thyme is a lovely addition to this classic vegetable side dish. It's a snap to make for family, yet special enough to serve guests.
—Kenna Baber, Rochester, MN

TAKES: 25 MIN. • **MAKES:** 8 SERVINGS

- 2 lbs. fresh green beans, trimmed
- 2 Tbsp. butter
- 1 Tbsp. minced fresh thyme or
     1 tsp. dried thyme
- ½ tsp. salt
- ½ tsp. pepper
- ⅓ cup slivered almonds, toasted

1. Place beans in a steamer basket. Place basket in a large saucepan over 1 in. of water; bring to a boil. Cover and steam until crisp-tender, 10-12 minutes.
2. In a large skillet, melt butter; add the beans, thyme, salt and pepper. Cook and stir until heated through, 5 minutes. Sprinkle with almonds.

1 CUP: *83 cal., 5g fat (2g sat. fat), 8mg chol., 183mg sod., 8g carb. (3g sugars, 4g fiber), 3g pro.*

CRANBERRY-APPLE LATTICE PIE

Two popular fall fruits bring out the best in each other, while rum works its own magic. Few people pass up a piece of this pie.
—Sonja Blow, Sherman Oaks, CA

PREP: 40 MIN. + CHILLING
BAKE: 65 MIN.
MAKES: 8 SERVINGS

- 2½ cups all-purpose flour
- 1   Tbsp. sugar
- ¾   tsp. salt
- ½   cup cold unsalted butter, cubed
- ⅓   cup cold shortening
- 5   to 7 Tbsp. ice water

FILLING
- ½   cup dried currants or raisins
- 2   Tbsp. dark rum or water
- 1   cup fresh or frozen cranberries, divided

- ¾   cup sugar, divided
- 6   medium baking apples, such as Fuji or Braeburn (about 2 lbs.), peeled and cut into ¼-in. slices
- 2   Tbsp. quick-cooking tapioca
- 1   Tbsp. lemon juice
- 2   tsp. grated lemon zest
- ½   tsp. ground cinnamon

EGG WASH
- 2   tsp. sugar
     Dash ground cinnamon
- 1   large egg
- 1   Tbsp. 2% milk or heavy whipping cream

1. In a small bowl, mix flour, sugar and salt; cut in butter and shortening until crumbly. Gradually add water, tossing with a fork until dough holds together when pressed. Divide the dough in half. Shape each half into a disk; wrap each disk and refrigerate for 30 minutes or overnight.
2. In a small bowl, combine currants and rum; let stand for 20 minutes.
3. Place ¾ cup cranberries and ¼ cup sugar in a food processor; pulse until the cranberries are coarsely chopped. Transfer to a large bowl. Add the apples, tapioca, lemon juice, lemon zest, cinnamon, the remaining sugar and the currant mixture; toss to combine. Let stand for 15 minutes.
4. On a lightly floured surface, roll one half of dough to a ⅛-in.-thick circle; transfer to a 9-in. deep-dish pie plate. Trim pastry to ½ in. beyond rim of plate. Add filling.
5. Roll remaining dough to a ⅛-in.-thick circle; cut into ½-in.-wide strips. Arrange strips over filling in a lattice pattern. Trim and seal strips to edge of bottom pastry. Place remaining cranberries in the spaces between lattice strips.
6. For egg wash, in a small bowl, mix the sugar and cinnamon; set aside. In another bowl, whisk egg and milk; brush over the lattice. Sprinkle with sugar mixture.
7. Bake on a lower oven rack at 400° for 25 minutes. Reduce oven temperature to 325°; bake until crust is golden brown and filling is bubbly, 40-45 minutes longer.
8. Cool on a wire rack for 30 minutes; serve warm.

1 PIECE: *508 cal., 21g fat (9g sat. fat), 54mg chol., 235mg sod., 75g carb. (38g sugars, 4g fiber), 6g pro.*

VEGGIE LASAGNA

This delectable, vegetable-rich lasagna, with its fresh, full-bodied flavor, is a true special-occasion indulgence. To save time, prepare the carrot and spinach layers in advance.
—Mary Jane Jones, Williamstown, WV

PREP: 70 MIN.
BAKE: 1¼ HOURS + STANDING
MAKES: 12 SERVINGS

- 1 pkg. (16 oz.) frozen sliced carrots
- ¼ cup finely chopped onion
- 2 Tbsp. butter
- 1 cup ricotta cheese
- ¼ tsp. each salt and pepper

SPINACH LAYER
- 2 shallots, chopped
- 1 Tbsp. olive oil
- 2 pkg. (10 oz. each) frozen chopped spinach, thawed and squeezed dry
- 1 cup ricotta cheese
- 1 large egg
- ¼ tsp. each salt and pepper

EGGPLANT LAYER
- 1 medium eggplant, peeled and cut into ¼-in. slices
- 3 garlic cloves, minced
- 6 Tbsp. olive oil
- ½ tsp. salt
- 2½ cups marinara sauce
- 12 lasagna noodles, cooked and drained
- ¼ cup minced fresh basil
- 4 cups (16 oz.) part-skim shredded mozzarella cheese
- 3 cups grated Parmesan cheese

1. Cook carrots according to package directions; drain and cool. In a small skillet, saute onion in butter until tender. In a food processor, puree the carrots, onion, ricotta, salt and pepper. In the same skillet, saute shallots in oil until tender. Puree the shallots, spinach, ricotta, egg, salt and pepper.
2. In a large skillet, cook eggplant and garlic in oil over medium heat in batches until tender, about 7-10 minutes; drain. Sprinkle with salt.
3. Spread ½ cup marinara sauce in a greased 13x9-in. baking dish. Layer with 4 noodles, carrot mixture, ½ cup sauce, 1 Tbsp. basil, 1 cup mozzarella and ¾ cup Parmesan. Top with 4 noodles, eggplant,

½ cup sauce, 1 Tbsp. basil, 1 cup of mozzarella and ¾ cup Parmesan.
4. Layer with the remaining noodles, the spinach mixture, ½ cup sauce, 1 Tbsp. basil, 1 cup mozzarella and ¾ cup of Parmesan. Top with the remaining sauce, basil, mozzarella and Parmesan (dish will be full).
5. Cover and bake at 350° for 1 hour. Uncover; bake 15 minutes longer or until bubbly. Let stand 15 minutes.
1 PIECE: *496 cal., 27g fat (13g sat. fat), 77mg chol., 954mg sod., 37g carb. (12g sugars, 5g fiber), 29g pro.*

WHIPPED SQUASH

This is an excellent way to serve butternut squash. Its rich flavor and golden harvest color really come through in this smooth vegetable side dish.
—Dorothy Pritchett, Wills Point, TX

TAKES: 30 MIN. • **MAKES:** 6 SERVINGS

- 1 butternut squash (about 2½ lbs.), peeled, seeded and cubed
- 3 cups water
- ¾ tsp. salt, optional, divided
- 2 Tbsp. butter
- 1 Tbsp. brown sugar
- ⅛ to ¼ tsp. ground nutmeg

1. In a saucepan over medium heat, bring the squash, water and ½ tsp. of salt (if desired) to a boil. Reduce heat; cover and simmer for 20 minutes or until the squash is tender.
2. Drain; transfer to a bowl. Add butter, brown sugar, nutmeg and the remaining salt (if desired); beat until smooth.
¾ CUP: *86 cal., 4g fat (0 sat. fat), 0 chol., 37mg sod., 14g carb. (0 sugars, 0 fiber), 1g pro.*
DIABETIC EXCHANGES: *1 starch, ½ fat.*

2. In a large skillet, saute onion in oil until tender. Add garlic and pepper flakes; cook 1 minute longer. Stir in kale and cook until wilted, for 3-4 minutes.

3. Stir in pine nuts and currants; cook 2 minutes longer or until the kale is tender. Stir in vinegar, lemon juice, zest, salt and pepper; cook 1-2 minutes longer. Remove from the heat and stir in the quinoa. Serve at room temperature.

NOTE: Look for quinoa in the cereal, rice or organic food aisle.

⅔ **CUP:** 190 cal., 7g fat (1g sat. fat), 0 chol., 164mg sod., 28g carb. (6g sugars, 3g fiber), 6g pro.

DIABETIC EXCHANGES: *2 starch, 1 fat.*

OAT DINNER ROLLS

These soft rolls are out of this world. The addition of oats makes them a little heartier than other dinner rolls.
—*Patricia Rutherford, Winchester, IL*

PREP: 30 MIN. + RISING • **BAKE:** 20 MIN.
MAKES: 2 DOZEN

2⅓ cups water, divided
1 cup quick-cooking oats
⅔ cup packed brown sugar
3 Tbsp. butter
1½ tsp. salt
2 pkg. (¼ oz. each) active dry yeast
5 to 5¾ cups all-purpose flour

1. In a large saucepan, bring 2 cups water to a boil. Stir in oats; reduce heat. Simmer, uncovered, for 1 minute. Stir in brown sugar, butter, salt and remaining water.

2. Transfer to a large bowl; let stand until mixture reaches 110°-115°. Stir in yeast. Add 3 cups flour; beat well. Add enough remaining flour to form a soft dough.

3. Turn onto a floured surface; knead until smooth and elastic, about 6-8 minutes. Place in a greased bowl; turn once to grease top. Cover and let rise in a warm place until doubled, about 1 hour.

4. Punch dough down; shape into 24 rolls. Place on greased baking sheets. Cover and let rise until doubled, about 30 minutes.

5. Bake at 350° for 20-25 minutes or until golden brown. Remove from pan and cool on wire racks.

1 ROLL: 132 cal., 1g fat (0 sat. fat), 0 chol., 150mg sod., 28g carb. (6g sugars, 1g fiber), 3g pro.

KALE QUINOA SALAD

Here's a holiday side dish you can feel good about serving. Kale packs a mighty punch of vitamins, while quinoa delivers a hearty serving of protein. Best of all, the flavor can't be beat!
—*Lisa Warren, Washington, DC*

PREP: 15 MIN. • **COOK:** 25 MIN.
MAKES: 6 SERVINGS

1½ cups water
½ cup tomato juice
1 cup quinoa, rinsed
1 small onion, chopped
1 Tbsp. olive oil
1 garlic clove, minced
½ tsp. crushed red pepper flakes
6 cups coarsely chopped fresh kale
¼ cup pine nuts
¼ cup dried currants
1 Tbsp. balsamic vinegar
1 tsp. lemon juice
1 tsp. grated lemon zest
¼ tsp. salt
⅛ tsp. pepper

1. In a large saucepan, bring the water and tomato juice to a boil. Add quinoa. Reduce heat; cover and simmer until the liquid is absorbed, 18-22 minutes. Remove pan from the heat; fluff with a fork.

BEETS IN ORANGE SAUCE

An irresistible orange glaze is just the thing to ensure that your family eats their veggies! The sweet and tangy glaze is a perfect complement to the earthy flavor of the beets.
—Taste of Home *Test Kitchen*

PREP: 15 MIN. • **COOK:** 35 MIN. • **MAKES:** 8 SERVINGS

- 8   whole fresh beets
- ¼   cup sugar
- 2   tsp. cornstarch
      Dash pepper
- 1   cup orange juice
- 1   medium navel orange, halved and sliced, optional
- ½   tsp. grated orange zest

1. Place beets in a large saucepan; cover with water. Bring to a boil. Reduce heat; cover and cook for 25-30 minutes or until tender. Drain and cool slightly. Peel and slice; place in a serving bowl and keep warm.

2. In a small saucepan, combine the sugar, cornstarch and pepper; stir in orange juice until smooth. Bring to a boil; cook and stir for 2 minutes or until thickened. Remove from the heat; stir in orange slices if desired and zest. Pour over beets.

NOTE: A 15-oz. can of sliced beets may be substituted for the fresh beets. Drain the beets and omit the first step of the recipe.

1 CUP: *63 cal., 0 fat (0 sat. fat), 0 chol., 39mg sod., 15g carb. (12g sugars, 1g fiber), 1g pro.*

HOLIDAY SALSA

When we offer this cream-cheesy salsa of fresh cranberries, cilantro and a little kick of jalapeno, everyone hovers around the serving dish until it's scraped clean.
—Shelly Pattison, Lubbock, TX

PREP: 20 MIN. + CHILLING • **MAKES:** 12 SERVINGS

- 1   pkg. (12 oz.) fresh or frozen cranberries
- 1   cup sugar
- 6   green onions, chopped
- ½   cup fresh cilantro leaves, chopped
- 1   jalapeno pepper, seeded and finely chopped
- 1   pkg. (8 oz.) cream cheese, softened
      Assorted crackers or tortilla chips

1. Pulse cranberries and sugar in a food processor until coarsely chopped. Stir together with onions, cilantro and jalapeno. Cover and refrigerate several hours or overnight.

2. To serve, place cream cheese on a serving plate. Drain salsa; spoon over cream cheese. Serve with crackers or chips.

NOTE: Wear disposable gloves when cutting hot peppers; the oils can burn skin. Avoid touching your face.

1 SERVING: *146 cal., 7g fat (4g sat. fat), 21mg chol., 71mg sod., 22g carb. (19g sugars, 2g fiber), 1g pro.*

SPICED PERSIMMON ICE CREAM

Developing new flavors of ice cream is a passion of mine, and there are very few ingredients that I won't experiment with. This creation was inspired by a great persimmon cookie recipe that I have.
—Cleo Gonske, Redding, CA

PREP: 20 MIN. + CHILLING
PROCESS: 15 MIN. + FREEZING
MAKES: 2 QT.

- 1 cup half-and-half cream
- 1 cup sugar
- 1 large egg, lightly beaten
- 3½ cups heavy whipping cream
- 2 cups mashed ripe persimmon pulp
- 1 pkg. (3.4 oz.) instant cheesecake pudding mix
- 2 tsp. ground cinnamon
- ¼ tsp. ground cloves
- ¼ tsp. ground nutmeg

1. In a large heavy saucepan, heat half-and-half cream and sugar until bubbles form around sides of pan. Whisk a small amount of the hot mixture into the egg. Return all to the pan, whisking constantly.
2. Cook and stir over low heat until the mixture is thickened and coats the back of a spoon. Quickly transfer to a bowl; place in ice water and stir for 2 minutes. Stir in heavy cream, persimmon, pudding mix and spices. Press plastic wrap onto the surface of custard. Refrigerate for several hours or overnight.

3. Fill the cylinder of ice cream freezer two-thirds full; freeze according to the manufacturer's directions. Refrigerate the remaining mixture until ready to freeze. Transfer ice cream to freezer containers, allowing headspace for expansion. Freeze 2-4 hours or until firm. Repeat with remaining ice cream mixture.
½ CUP: *294 cal., 21g fat (13g sat. fat), 78mg chol., 111mg sod., 24g carb. (22g sugars, 1g fiber), 3g pro.*

More Choices for Christmas Menus

Apple, Butternut & Sausage Dressing, p. 59

Company Shrimp & Crab Cakes, p. 60

Green Bean & Cauliflower Casserole, p. 61

Chicken-Prosciutto Pinwheels in Wine Sauce, p. 62

Meringue Pecan Pie, p. 63

And more!

PORK LOIN WITH STRAWBERRY-RHUBARB CHUTNEY

I love strawberry rhubarb pie, so I thought the same flavor combination could work as a chutney—and it does! It makes a delicious and festive accompaniment to a succulent pork roast. The chutney can be made a day ahead and kept in the refrigerator.
—Deborah Biggs, Omaha, NE

PREP: 20 MIN. • **BAKE:** 1 HOUR + STANDING
MAKES: 10 SERVINGS (1¾ CUPS SAUCE)

1   boneless pork loin roast (3 to 4 lbs.)
1   tsp. salt
½   tsp. pepper
2   Tbsp. canola oil
½   cup sugar
¼   cup red wine vinegar
1   cinnamon stick (3 in.)
½   tsp. grated lemon zest
2¼   cups chopped fresh or
     frozen rhubarb
⅔   cup sliced fresh strawberries
1½   tsp. minced fresh rosemary or
     ½ tsp. dried rosemary, crushed

1. Sprinkle roast with salt and pepper. In a large skillet, brown roast in oil on all sides.
2. Place roast on a rack in a shallow roasting pan. Bake, uncovered, at 350° until a thermometer reads 145°, 1 to 1½ hours. Remove roast to a serving platter; let stand for 15 minutes.
3. Meanwhile, in a large saucepan, combine the sugar, vinegar, cinnamon and lemon zest. Bring to a boil. Reduce heat; simmer, uncovered, until the sugar is dissolved, 2 minutes.
4. Add the rhubarb, strawberries and rosemary. Cook and stir over medium heat until rhubarb is tender and mixture is slightly thickened, 15-20 minutes. Discard the cinnamon stick and serve chutney with pork.

4 OZ. COOKED PORK WITH 3 TBSP. CHUTNEY: *243 cal., 9g fat (3g sat. fat), 68mg chol., 277mg sod., 13g carb. (11g sugars, 1g fiber), 27g pro.*
DIABETIC EXCHANGES: *3 lean meat, ½ fruit, ½ fat.*

ROASTED ASPARAGUS RISOTTO

This recipe's wow factor makes it perfect for special occasions. To save time, the asparagus and prosciutto can be roasting while the rice cooks on the stovetop. They'll be ready to stir into the risotto by the time the rice is done.
—Deonna Mazur, Buffalo, NY

PREP: 35 MIN. • **COOK:** 30 MIN.
MAKES: 8 SERVINGS

12   thin slices prosciutto
2   lbs. fresh asparagus, cut into
     1-in. pieces
5½   to 6 cups reduced-sodium
     chicken broth
1   shallot, chopped
2   garlic cloves, minced
2   tsp. olive oil
2   cups uncooked arborio rice
½   cup white wine
½   tsp. pepper
1   cup grated Parmesan cheese

1. Preheat oven to 400°. Place asparagus in an ungreased 15x10x1-in. baking sheet. Bake, uncovered, until crisp-tender, stirring occasionally, 20-25 minutes.
2. Meanwhile, place prosciutto in another ungreased baking pan. Bake until crisp, 10-12 minutes. Crumble prosciutto; set aside prosciutto and asparagus.
3. In a large saucepan, heat broth and keep warm. In a large skillet, saute shallot and garlic in oil until tender. Add rice; cook and stir for 2-3 minutes. Reduce the heat; stir in wine, pepper and salt. Cook and stir until all the liquid is absorbed.
4. Add heated broth, ½ cup at a time, stirring constantly. Allow the liquid to absorb between additions. Cook until risotto is creamy and rice is almost tender, 20 minutes.
5. Add the asparagus, prosciutto and cheese; cook and stir risotto until heated through. Serve immediately.

¾ CUP: *311 cal., 7g fat (3g sat. fat), 28mg chol., 962mg sod., 44g carb. (2g sugars, 2g fiber), 16g pro.*

BRIE MUSHROOM PASTRIES

You can use this recipe for parties as an appetizer or for dinner gatherings as the first course. The rustic and savory taste of the mushrooms is balanced by tangy Brie and delicate puff pastry.
—Vivi Taylor, Middleburg, FL

PREP: 45 MIN. • **BAKE:** 15 MIN.
MAKES: 1 DOZEN

- 2 tsp. olive oil
- 12 small baby portobello mushrooms (about 6 oz.), stems removed
- 3 oz. diced pancetta or bacon strips (about ½ cup)
- 1 lb. baby portobello mushrooms, finely chopped
- 2 shallots, finely chopped
- 3 garlic cloves, minced
- ¼ tsp. salt
- ⅛ tsp. pepper
- 1 sheet frozen puff pastry, thawed
- 1 large egg, lightly beaten
- 2 oz. Brie cheese, cut into 12 cubes (½ in.)

1. Preheat oven to 450°. In a large skillet, heat oil over medium heat. Place whole mushrooms in pan, stem side down; cook 3 minutes per side. Drain on paper towels.
2. In the same pan, saute pancetta over medium heat until browned, 3-4 minutes. Add chopped mushrooms; cook and stir 3 minutes. Add shallots and garlic; cook and stir until juices have evaporated, 3-4 minutes. Remove from heat; stir in salt and pepper.
3. On a lightly floured surface, roll pastry into a 15x12-in. rectangle. Cut 12 circles with a floured 3-in. round cookie cutter (save the scraps for another use). Press each circle into a greased muffin cup; prick bottoms with a fork. Brush lightly with beaten egg.

4. Fill whole mushrooms with cheese; place in pastry cups, cheese side up. Top with the pancetta mixture. Bake until the pastry is golden brown, 12-15 minutes. Serve warm or at room temperature. Refrigerate leftovers.

FREEZE OPTION: Cover and freeze unbaked pastries in muffin pan until firm. Transfer pastries to freezer containers, separating layers with waxed paper; return to freezer. To use, place pastries in oiled muffin pans; cover and thaw in refrigerator overnight. Bake as directed.

1 PASTRY: 148 cal., 8g fat (2g sat. fat), 26mg chol., 256mg sod., 13g carb. (4g sugars, 3g fiber), 10g pro.

APPLE, BUTTERNUT & SAUSAGE DRESSING

I'd heard about using squash in dressing, so I combined four things I love into one dish: apples, butternut squash, bacon and maple sausage! Now, it's one of my family's most requested dishes during the holidays.
—Brenda Crouch, Ansley, NE

PREP: 1¼ HOURS • **BAKE:** 45 MIN.
MAKES: 20 SERVINGS

- 1 medium butternut squash (about 3 lbs.), peeled and cubed
- 3 medium tart apples, peeled and cubed
- 2 Tbsp. olive oil
- 1 tsp. kosher salt
- 1 tsp. pepper
- 6 thick-sliced bacon strips, chopped
- 1 lb. maple pork sausage
- 4 celery ribs, chopped
- 2 medium onions, chopped
- 2 medium carrots, shredded
- 6 cups seasoned stuffing cubes, divided
- 2 cups crushed multigrain Club Crackers (2½x1 in.) (about 40 crackers)
- 1 can (12 oz.) evaporated milk
- 1 can (10½ oz.) condensed cream of celery soup, undiluted
- 6 large eggs, lightly beaten
- 1 cup cooked long grain rice
- 1 cup sour cream
- 1 tsp. garlic powder
- 1 tsp. poultry seasoning
- 1 tsp. rubbed sage
- ½ tsp. celery salt
- ½ tsp. ground cumin
- ¼ tsp. cayenne pepper
- ½ cup butter, cubed

1. Preheat oven to 425°. Place squash and apples on a rimmed baking sheet. Drizzle with oil; sprinkle with salt and pepper. Toss to coat. Roast until tender, about 25 minutes. Reduce oven setting to 375°.
2. Meanwhile, in a Dutch oven, cook the bacon over medium heat until crisp; stir occasionally. Remove bacon with a slotted spoon; drain on paper towels. Discard the drippings.
3. Add sausage, celery, onions and carrots to pot; cook over medium-high heat until sausage is no longer pink and vegetables are tender, 10-12 minutes, breaking up sausage into crumbles; drain.
4. Transfer to a large bowl. Add 5 cups stuffing cubes, crackers, evaporated milk, soup, eggs, rice, sour cream, seasonings and reserved squash mixture and bacon; toss. Transfer to two greased 13x9-in. baking dishes. Lightly crush the remaining 1 cup stuffing cubes. Sprinkle over top; dot with butter.
5. Bake, covered, for 30 minutes. Uncover and bake until bubbly and lightly browned, 15-20 minutes longer.

¾ **CUP:** *401 cal., 26g fat (10g sat. fat), 98mg chol., 793mg sod., 34g carb. (9g sugars, 5g fiber), 11g pro.*

Holiday Helper
You can make portions of this dish in advance to save time on feast day—roast the veggies and fruit and cook the bacon and sausage with the veggies a day or two ahead. On the morning of the feast, mix all the ingredients and bake!

NOTE: To toast nuts, bake in a shallow pan in a 350° oven for 5-10 minutes or cook in a skillet over low heat until lightly browned, stirring occasionally.

¾ CUP: 314 cal., 16g fat (5g sat. fat), 21mg chol., 482mg sod., 39g carb. (14g sugars, 7g fiber), 8g pro.

COMPANY SHRIMP & CRAB CAKES

The addition of shrimp gives crab cakes a new flavor. Using panko instead of flour makes the prep easier, plus the cakes stay together without tasting doughy. I love these crab cakes served with mango salsa!
—Regina Reynolds, Struthers, OH

PREP: 15 MIN. • **COOK:** 10 MIN./BATCH
MAKES: 6 SERVINGS

- 1 large egg, beaten
- ¼ cup dry bread crumbs
- ¼ cup mayonnaise
- 1 tsp. dried parsley flakes
- 2 Tbsp. finely chopped sweet red pepper
- 2 Tbsp. finely chopped sweet yellow pepper
- ½ lb. lump crabmeat, drained
- ½ lb. peeled and deveined cooked shrimp, finely chopped
- ½ cup panko (Japanese) bread crumbs
- ¼ cup olive oil

DIPPING SAUCE
- ½ cup Miracle Whip
- ¼ cup sour cream
- 2 Tbsp. minced fresh parsley
- 2 tsp. grated lemon peel
- 2 tsp. lemon juice

1. In a large bowl, combine the first 6 ingredients. Fold in the crab and shrimp. Shape into 12 patties; coat with the panko bread crumbs.

2. In a large skillet over medium heat, cook crab cakes in oil in batches until they are golden brown, 3-4 minutes on each side.

3. Meanwhile, in a small bowl, combine the sauce ingredients. Serve with crab cakes.

2 CAKES WITH 2 TBSP. SAUCE: 355 cal., 26g fat (5g sat. fat), 143mg chol., 462mg sod., 11g carb. (4g sugars, 1g fiber), 18g pro.

SPAGHETTI SQUASH WITH APPLES, BACON & WALNUTS

I've always loved spaghetti squash as an alternative to pasta and enjoy it in the classic marinara style, but I wanted a new recipe so my family and I could enjoy it more often. The savory, salty and sour flavors combine perfectly with a hint of sweet spice. While the squash is baking, prep the rest: It will take only minutes to finish after you shred the squash.
—Jeff Tori, Johnstown, CO

PREP: 1 HOUR • **COOK:** 20 MIN.
MAKES: 6 SERVINGS

- 1 medium spaghetti squash
- 1 tsp. ground cumin
- 8 bacon strips, chopped
- 8 green onions, sliced
- 2 Tbsp. butter
- 2 garlic cloves, minced
- ¼ tsp. crushed red pepper flakes
- 2 medium apple, peeled and chopped
- 1 cup apple cider or juice
- 2 Tbsp. maple syrup
- ½ tsp. salt
- 1 dash pepper
- ½ cup chopped walnuts, toasted
- 2 Tbsp. minced fresh parsley

1. Preheat oven to 400°. Cut the squash lengthwise in half; remove and discard the seeds. Sprinkle with ½ tsp. cumin. Place in a 15x10x1-in. baking pan, cut sides down. Bake until easily pierced with a fork, 35-45 minutes.

2. Cook bacon over medium heat until crisp, stirring occasionally. Remove with a slotted spoon; drain on paper towels. Discard the drippings.

3. Add green onions, 2 Tbsp. of butter, the garlic and pepper flakes; cook, stirring, over medium heat until tender, 2-3 minutes. Stir in apples, cider, syrup, salt, pepper and the remaining cumin. Bring to a boil; cook mixture until slightly thickened, 4-6 minutes.

4. When squash is cool enough to handle, use a fork to separate the strands. Add squash to the skillet; cook until liquid is absorbed, 2-3 minutes. Stir in the bacon, walnuts and parsley.

GREEN BEAN & CAULIFLOWER CASSEROLE

I like to make a savory homemade cream sauce for the timeless green bean casserole. This time I added another vegetable for a delicious twist that sets my casserole apart from the rest. You can omit the vermouth if you like by substituting another ½ cup of chicken broth.
—Ann Sheehy, Lawrence, MA

PREP: 45 MIN. • **BAKE:** 30 MIN.
MAKES: 10 SERVINGS

- 1 lb. fresh cauliflowerets, cut into 1-in. pieces
- 1 lb. fresh green beans, trimmed and cut into 2-in. pieces
- 4 tsp. olive oil, divided
- 1 cup panko (Japanese) bread crumbs
- 1 cup French-fried onions, crumbled
- 2 Tbsp. butter
- 8 oz. thinly sliced fresh mushrooms
- 1 shallot, finely chopped
- 2 garlic cloves, minced
- ¼ cup all-purpose flour
- ½ cup dry vermouth
- 1½ cups reduced-sodium chicken broth
- 1 tsp. salt
- 1 tsp. dried thyme
- ½ tsp. pepper
- ¼ tsp. ground nutmeg
- ½ cup cubed fully cooked ham
- ½ cup sour cream
- 1 cup plain Greek yogurt

1. Preheat oven to 375°. In a Dutch oven, bring 12 cups water to a boil. Add the cauliflower and beans; cook, uncovered, just until the beans turn bright green, 1-2 minutes. Drain and immediately drop into ice water. Drain and pat dry.

2. In a large skillet, heat 1 tsp. oil over medium-high heat. Add bread crumbs; cook and stir until lightly browned, 2-3 minutes. Stir in onions; remove from pan and set aside.

3. In the same skillet, heat butter and the remaining oil over medium heat. Add mushrooms and shallot; cook and stir until tender, 8-10 minutes. Add garlic; cook 1 minute longer. Stir in flour until blended. Gradually whisk in vermouth; cook, stirring, until most of the liquid is gone. Whisk in broth and seasonings. Bring to a boil, stirring constantly; cook and stir until thickened, 6-8 minutes. Remove from heat; stir in yogurt, sour cream, ham and the reserved vegetables. Transfer to a greased 13x9-in. baking dish.

4. Bake, uncovered, until bubbly, about 30-40 minutes. Sprinkle with the bread crumb mixture before serving.

NOTE: To make this a day ahead, assemble the casserole, cool to room temperature, then cover with foil and refrigerate. To use, bake, covered, about 45 minutes; uncover and bake until bubbly, 10 minutes longer.

1 CUP: *217 cal., 13g fat (6g sat. fat), 19mg chol., 539mg sod., 19g carb. (5g sugars, 3g fiber), 7g pro.*

CHICKEN-PROSCIUTTO PINWHEELS IN WINE SAUCE

We host a large group for holiday meals and these pinwheels always go over well alongside the regular dishes. I often double this recipe and use two 9x13-in. pans.
—Johnna Johnson, Scottsdale, AZ

PREP: 30 MIN. + CHILLING • **BAKE:** 30 MIN. • **MAKES:** 6 SERVINGS

6 boneless skinless chicken breast halves (6 oz. each)
6 thin slices prosciutto or deli ham
6 slices part-skim mozzarella cheese
2 large eggs, lightly beaten
½ cup Italian-style panko (Japanese) bread crumbs
½ cup butter, cubed
1 shallot, finely chopped
2 garlic cloves, minced
3 cups Madeira wine

1. Pound chicken breasts with a meat mallet to ¼-in. thickness; layer with prosciutto and mozzarella. Roll up chicken from a short side; secure with toothpicks.
2. Place eggs and bread crumbs in separate shallow bowls. Dip chicken in eggs, then roll in crumbs to coat. Cut each chicken breast crosswise into three slices; place in a greased 13x9-in. baking dish, cut side down. Refrigerate, covered, overnight.
3. Preheat oven to 350°. Remove chicken from refrigerator; uncover and let stand while the oven heats. In a small saucepan, heat butter over medium-high heat. Add shallot and garlic; cook and stir until tender, 1-2 minutes. Add wine. Bring mixture to a boil; cook until liquid is reduced to 1½ cups. Pour over chicken.
4. Bake pinwheels, uncovered, until chicken is no longer pink, 30-35 minutes. Discard toothpicks before serving.
3 PINWHEELS: *581 cal., 30g fat (15g sat. fat), 227mg chol., 827mg sod., 15g carb. (5g sugars, 0 fiber), 48g pro.*

CRUMB-TOPPED SWEET POTATO BAKE

With lots of spice and bright orange flavor, this heartwarming sweet potato dish is perfect for fall, winter and special holiday meals. The citrus and honey make for a delightful spin on a traditional sweet potato casserole.
—Billie Moss, Walnut Creek, CA

PREP: 15 MIN. • **BAKE:** 40 MIN. • **MAKES:** 6 SERVINGS

1 can (15¾ oz.) sweet potatoes, drained and mashed
1 cup crushed vanilla wafers (about 30 wafers)
3 large eggs, beaten
½ cup crushed pineapple
½ cup honey
⅓ cup orange juice
2 tsp. pumpkin pie spice
1 tsp. grated lemon zest
1 tsp. grated orange zest
1 cup chopped pecans
½ cup packed brown sugar
1 tsp. ground cinnamon
¼ tsp. ground nutmeg

In a large bowl, combine the first 9 ingredients. Transfer to a greased 2-qt. baking dish. In a small bowl, combine the pecans, brown sugar, cinnamon and nutmeg. Sprinkle over the sweet potato mixture. Bake, uncovered, at 350° until a knife inserted in the center comes out clean, 40-45 minutes.
¾ CUP: *505 cal., 20g fat (3g sat. fat), 107mg chol., 137mg sod., 81g carb. (65g sugars, 5g fiber), 7g pro.*

MERINGUE PECAN PIE

I only use this recipe on special occasions. It's an amazing variation on the pecan pie everyone knows—the filling is a custardy delight, and the meringue gives the whole thing a lightness that's the perfect ending to a multi-course feast.
—Therese Asche, Maple Grove, MN

PREP: 1 HOUR + CHILLING
BAKE: 15 MIN. + COOLING
MAKES: 8 SERVINGS

    Pastry for single-crust pie (9 in.)
¾ cup sugar
¼ cup all-purpose flour
1¾ cups 2% milk
6 Tbsp. butter, cubed
3 large egg yolks
1 cup chopped pecans, toasted
1 tsp. vanilla extract
MERINGUE
3 large egg whites, room temperature
½ tsp. vanilla extract
¼ tsp. cream of tartar
6 Tbsp. sugar

1. On a lightly floured surface, roll pastry to a ⅛-in.-thick circle; transfer to a 9-in. pie plate. Trim to ½ in. beyond rim of plate; flute edge. Refrigerate 30 minutes.
2. Preheat oven to 425°. Line unpricked pastry with a double thickness of foil. Fill with pie weights, dried beans or uncooked rice. Bake on a lower oven rack until edges are light golden brown, 12-15 minutes. Remove the foil and weights; bake until bottom is golden brown, for 3-6 minutes longer. Cool on a wire rack. Reduce oven setting to 350°.
3. In a large heavy saucepan, mix sugar and flour. Whisk in milk and butter. Cook and stir over medium heat until thickened and bubbly. Reduce heat to low; cook and stir 2 minutes longer. Remove from heat.
4. In a small bowl, whisk a small amount of hot mixture into egg yolks; return all to pan, whisking constantly. Bring to a gentle boil; cook and stir 2 minutes. Remove from heat. Stir in pecans and vanilla.
5. For meringue, beat egg whites, vanilla and cream of tartar on medium speed until foamy. Add sugar, 1 Tbsp. at a time, beating on high after each addition until the sugar is dissolved. Continue beating until soft glossy peaks form.

6. Transfer hot filling to the crust. Spread meringue evenly over the filling, sealing to edge of crust. Bake until the meringue is golden brown, 12-15 minutes. Cool for 1 hour on a wire rack. Refrigerate at least 6 hours before serving.
NOTE: Let pie weights cool before storing. Beans and rice may be reused for pie weights, but not for cooking.
1 PIECE: *522 cal., 33g fat (15g sat. fat), 126mg chol., 272mg sod., 51g carb. (32g sugars, 2g fiber), 8g pro.*
PASTRY FOR SINGLE-CRUST PIE (9 IN.): Combine 1¼ cups all-purpose flour and ¼ tsp. salt; cut in ½ cup cold butter until crumbly. Gradually add 3-5 Tbsp. ice water, tossing with a fork until dough holds together when pressed. Wrap and refrigerate for 1 hour.

PARSNIP POTATO GRATIN

Parsnips don't get much space in the produce section. But their subtle, earthy sweetness makes them worth the hunt!
—Kerry Dingwall, Wilmington, NC

PREP: 20 MIN. • **BAKE:** 50 MIN.
MAKES: 10 SERVINGS

4 large potatoes, peeled and thinly sliced
4 medium onions, thinly sliced
3 large parsnips, peeled and thinly sliced
1½ cups shredded Gruyere or Swiss cheese, divided
1 Tbsp. all-purpose flour
¾ tsp. salt
¼ tsp. pepper
2 cups heavy whipping cream

1. Preheat oven to 375°. Layer the potatoes, onions, parsnips and ¾ cup of cheese in a greased 13x9-in. baking dish; set aside. In a small saucepan, combine flour, salt, pepper; gradually whisk in the cream. Bring to a gentle boil, stirring occasionally. Remove from heat; pour over vegetables. Sprinkle with the remaining cheese.
2. Cover; bake for 30 minutes. Uncover and bake 20-25 minutes longer or until the vegetables are tender and the top is golden brown.
¾ CUP: *412 cal., 23g fat (14g sat. fat), 84mg chol., 268mg sod., 42g carb. (8g sugars, 5g fiber), 11g pro.*

FESTIVE BREADS

Nothing welcomes loved ones to the holidays like the delightful aroma of sweet home-baked treats at breakfast and tender rolls or savory crisp breads at dinner.

EGGNOG FRUIT BREAD

Presents from the pantry are a tradition in my family—and this moist, fruity quick bread is always a favorite. I wrap loaves in cellophane decorated with stickers and curly ribbons.
—Margo Stich, Rochester, MN

PREP: 25 MIN. • **BAKE:** 1 HOUR + COOLING
MAKES: 2 LOAVES

3	large eggs, room temperature
1	cup vegetable oil
1½	cups sugar
¾	tsp. vanilla extract
¾	tsp. rum extract
1½	cups eggnog
3	cups all-purpose flour, divided
2	tsp. baking powder
½	tsp. salt
½	tsp. ground nutmeg
1	cup candied fruit
½	cup chopped walnuts

1. Preheat oven to 350°. In a large bowl, beat the eggs and oil. Beat in the sugar, extracts and eggnog. Combine 2½ cups flour, the baking powder, salt and nutmeg; gradually add to the egg mixture. Toss the fruit with the remaining flour; stir into batter. Fold in the walnuts.
2. Pour into two greased 8x2-in. loaf pans. Bake 60-65 minutes or until a toothpick comes out clean. Cool for 10 minutes before removing from pans to wire racks to cool completely.
1 SERVING: *197 cal., 9g fat (2g sat. fat), 27mg chol., 82mg sod., 26g carb. (16g sugars, 1g fiber), 3g pro.*

RED VELVET CINNAMON ROLLS

Turn a box of red velvet cake mix into this easy dessert—or breakfast. Adding yeast to the mix is a clever trick, and the beautiful red rolls with their bright white icing are especially welcome at Christmastime.
—Erin Wright, Wallace, KS

PREP: 20 MIN. + RISING • **BAKE:** 15 MIN.
MAKES: 12 SERVINGS

1	pkg. red velvet cake mix (regular size)
2½	to 3 cups all-purpose flour
1	pkg. (¼ oz.) active dry yeast
1¼	cups warm water (120° to 130°)
½	cup packed brown sugar
1	tsp. ground cinnamon
¼	cup butter, melted

ICING

2	cups confectioners' sugar
2	Tbsp. butter, softened
1	tsp. vanilla extract
3	to 5 Tbsp. 2% milk

1. Combine the cake mix, 1 cup of flour and the yeast. Add water; beat on medium speed 2 minutes. Stir in enough of the remaining flour to form a soft dough (dough will be sticky). Turn onto a lightly floured surface; knead gently 6-8 times. Place in a greased bowl, turning once to grease the top. Cover and let rise in a warm place until doubled, about 2 hours. Meanwhile, in another bowl, mix brown sugar and cinnamon.
2. Punch down dough. Turn onto a lightly floured surface; roll the dough into an 18x10-in. rectangle. Brush with melted butter to within ¼ in. of edges; sprinkle with sugar mixture.
3. Roll up jelly-roll style, starting with a long side; pinch seam to seal. Cut roll crosswise into 12 slices. Place cut sides up in a greased 13x9-in. baking pan. Cover; let slices rise in a warm place until almost doubled, about 1 hour.
4. Preheat oven to 350°. Bake rolls until puffed and light brown, 15-20 minutes. Cool slightly.
5. Beat the confectioners' sugar, butter, vanilla and enough milk to reach a drizzling consistency. Drizzle icing over warm rolls.
1 CINNAMON ROLL: *429 cal., 10g fat (5g sat. fat), 16mg chol., 311mg sod., 81g carb. (48g sugars, 1g fiber), 5g pro.*

Holiday Helper
Make these morning beauties your own by swapping in your favorite flavor of cake mix. We particularly love spice cake, devil's food and orange.

GLAZED CRANBERRY SWEET POTATO BREAD

This distinctly different quick bread might just become one of your go-to holiday treats. Flavors of sweet potato, cranberry and orange come together so beautifully. Slices of the moist bread topped with an orange glaze make a sweet snack to enjoy anytime—and any season.
—Sweet Potato Festival Committee, Vardaman, MS

PREP: 15 MIN. • **BAKE:** 50 MIN. + COOLING
MAKES: 2 LOAVES (16 SERVINGS EACH)

3½ cups all-purpose flour
1⅔ cups sugar
2 tsp. baking soda
2 tsp. pumpkin pie spice
1 tsp. baking powder
¾ tsp. salt
4 large eggs, lightly beaten, room temperature
2 cups mashed cooked sweet potatoes
1 can (14 oz.) whole-berry cranberry sauce
⅔ cup canola oil
¾ cup chopped pecans
GLAZE
1 cup confectioners' sugar
¼ cup orange juice concentrate
⅛ tsp. ground allspice

1. In a large bowl, combine the flour, sugar, baking soda, pie spice, baking powder and salt. In another large bowl, combine the eggs, sweet potatoes, cranberry sauce and oil. Stir into dry ingredients just until moistened. Fold in the pecans.

2. Pour into 2 greased 9x5-in. loaf pans. Bake at 350° until a toothpick inserted in the center comes out clean, about 55-60 minutes. Cool for 10 minutes before removing from pans to wire racks to cool completely. In a small bowl, combine the glaze ingredients until smooth; drizzle over cooled loaves.

1 SLICE: *216 cal., 7g fat (1g sat. fat), 27mg chol., 161mg sod., 36g carb. (20g sugars, 1g fiber), 3g pro.*

BEST DINNER ROLLS

These classic dinner rolls are a perfect addition to any Christmas dinner table. If you can't decide which enticing topping to use, just make them all!
—Christina Pittman, Parkville, MO

PREP: 35 MIN. + RISING • **BAKE:** 10 MIN.
MAKES: 2 DOZEN

- ¼ cup sugar
- 1 pkg. (¼ oz.) active dry yeast
- 1¼ tsp. salt
- 4½ to 5 cups all-purpose flour
- 1 cup whole milk
- ½ cup water
- 2 Tbsp. butter
- 2 large eggs, room temperature
- 1 large egg, lightly beaten

FOR EVERYTHING DINNER ROLLS

- 1 tsp. kosher salt
- 1 tsp. dried minced garlic
- 1 tsp. dried minced onion
- 1 tsp. poppy seeds
- 1 tsp. sesame seeds

FOR PARMESAN-GARLIC DINNER ROLLS

- 2 Tbsp. grated Parmesan cheese
- ½ tsp. dried minced garlic

FOR ALMOND-HERB DINNER ROLLS

- 2 Tbsp. chopped sliced almonds
- ½ tsp. kosher salt
- ½ tsp. dried basil
- ½ tsp. dried oregano

1. In a large bowl, mix sugar, yeast, salt and 2 cups flour. In a small saucepan, heat milk, water and butter to 120°-130°. Add to dry ingredients; beat on medium speed 3 minutes. Add 2 eggs; beat on high for 2 minutes. Stir in enough remaining flour to form a soft dough (dough will be sticky).

2. Turn the dough onto a floured surface; knead until dough is smooth and elastic, 6-8 minutes. Place in a greased bowl, turning once to grease the top. Cover and let rise in a warm place until doubled, about 1 hour.

3. Punch down dough. Turn onto a lightly floured surface; divide and shape dough into 24 balls. Place in two greased 13x9-in. baking pans. Cover with kitchen towels; let rise in a warm place until doubled, about 30 minutes.

4. Preheat oven to 375°. Brush the tops of the rolls with the lightly beaten egg. Sprinkle with toppings of your choice. Bake until golden brown, 10-15 minutes. Remove from pans to wire racks to cool slightly; serve warm.

1 ROLL (CALCULATED WITHOUT TOPPINGS): *118 cal., 2g fat (1g sat. fat), 30mg chol., 143mg sod., 21g carb. (3g sugars, 1g fiber), 4g pro.*

THREE WAYS TO SHAPE DINNER ROLLS

A good basic dough can be shaped into any number of different rolls. Round rolls are a classic for a reason, but to try something a little different, here are three easy and elegant variations. Follow the recipe for the Best Dinner Rolls (left) or use your own favorite roll recipe.

CLOVERLEAF
Divide dough into 24 portions (or as many rolls as your recipe yields), then divide each portion into 3 equal pieces. Roll each piece into a ball. Place 3 balls in each cup of a greased muffin tin. Let rise, then top and bake as directed.

TWIST
Divide dough into 24 portions (or as many rolls as your recipe yields), roll each portion into a ball, then roll each ball into a 10-in. rope. Fold each rope in half and twist 2 or 3 times, holding both ends. Pinch the rope ends to seal. Let rise; top and bake as directed.

ROSETTE
Divide dough into 24 portions (or as many rolls as your recipe yields), roll each into a ball, then roll each ball into a 10-in. rope. Tie a loose knot in the center of the rope. Bring bottom end up and tuck into the center of the roll; wrap top end around and tuck under the roll. Let rise; top and bake as directed.

OVERNIGHT ROLLS

I'm pleased to share the recipe for these light and tender rolls, which I've made for 25 years. I once served them to a woman who'd been in the restaurant business for half a century. She said they were the best rolls she'd ever tasted.
—Dorothy Yagodich, Charlerio, PA

PREP: 25 MIN. + CHILLING • **BAKE:** 15 MIN. • **MAKES:** 20 ROLLS

- 1 pkg. (¼ oz.) active dry yeast
- ½ cup plus ¾ tsp. sugar, divided
- 1⅓ cups plus 3 Tbsp. warm water (110° to 115°), divided
- ⅓ cup canola oil
- 1 large egg, room temperature
- 1 tsp. salt
- 4¾ to 5¼ cups all-purpose flour
  Melted butter, optional

1. In a bowl, dissolve yeast and ¾ tsp. of sugar in 3 Tbsp. water. Add the remaining sugar and the water, oil, egg, salt and 2 cups of flour; mix well. Add enough of the remaining flour to form a soft dough.

2. Turn dough onto a floured surface; knead until smooth and elastic, about 6-8 minutes. Place in a greased bowl, turning once to grease top. Cover and let rise in a warm place until doubled, about 1 hour.

3. Punch dough down. Shape into 20 balls. Roll each into a 8-in. rope; tie into a loose knot. Place on a greased baking sheet; cover and refrigerate overnight. Allow the rolls to sit at room temperature for 45 minutes before baking.

4. Bake at 375° until lightly browned, about 12-15 minutes. Brush with butter if desired. Remove to wire racks to cool.

1 ROLL: *165 cal., 4g fat (1g sat. fat), 11mg chol., 122mg sod., 28g carb. (6g sugars, 1g fiber), 4g pro.*

MAPLE TWIST COFFEE CAKE

If you like the flavor of maple, you'll want to add this recipe to your keeper file. The coffee cake makes a pretty addition to a Christmas morning spread.
—Deanna Richter, Elmore, MN

PREP: 45 MIN. + RISING • **BAKE:** 20 MIN.
MAKES: 16 SERVINGS

- 1   pkg. (¼ oz.) active dry yeast
- ¾   cup warm milk (110° to 115°)
- ¼   cup butter, softened
- 3   Tbsp. sugar
- 1   large egg, room temperature
- 1   tsp. maple flavoring
- ½   tsp. salt
- 2¾   to 3 cups all-purpose flour

FILLING
- ½   cup sugar
- ⅓   cup chopped walnuts
- 1   tsp. ground cinnamon
- 1   tsp. maple flavoring
- ¼   cup butter, melted

GLAZE
- 1   cup confectioners' sugar
- 2   Tbsp. butter, melted
- 1   to 2 Tbsp. milk
- ½   tsp. maple flavoring

1. In a large bowl, dissolve yeast in warm milk. Add the butter, sugar, egg, maple flavoring, salt and 1½ cups of flour. Beat until smooth. Stir in enough of the remaining flour to form a soft dough.

2. Turn onto a floured surface; knead until smooth and elastic, about 6-8 minutes. Place in a greased bowl, turning once to grease top. Cover and let dough rise in a warm place until doubled, about 1 hour. Meanwhile, in a small bowl, combine the sugar, walnuts, cinnamon and maple flavoring; set aside.

3. Punch dough down. Turn onto a lightly floured surface; divide into thirds. Roll each portion into a 12-in. circle; place 1 circle on a greased baking sheet or a 12-in. pizza pan. Spread with a third of the butter; sprinkle with a third of the filling. Repeat layers twice. Pinch edges of dough to seal.

4. Carefully place a glass in the center of the circle. With scissors, cut the dough from its outside edge just to the glass, forming 16 wedges. Remove the glass; twist each wedge 5-6 times. Pinch the ends to seal and tuck under. Cover and let rise until doubled, about 30 minutes.

5. Bake at 375° until golden brown, 18-20 minutes. In a small bowl, combine glaze ingredients; set aside. Carefully remove coffee cake from pan by running a metal spatula under it to loosen; transfer to a wire rack. Drizzle with glaze.

1 PIECE: *236 cal., 10g fat (5g sat. fat), 33mg chol., 134mg sod., 34g carb. (17g sugars, 1g fiber), 4g pro.*

PISTACHIO QUICK BREAD

I love making many of these special loaves to give away as gifts for the holidays. They also freeze well, so it's easy to pull one out when unexpected guests stop by!
—Judy Fischer, Green Bay, WI

PREP: 20 MIN. • **BAKE:** 35 MIN. + COOLING
MAKES: 2 LOAVES (12 SLICES EACH)

- 1   pkg. white cake mix (regular size)
- 1   pkg. (3.4 oz.) instant pistachio pudding mix
- 4   large eggs, room temperature
- 1   cup sour cream
- ¼   cup water
- ¼   cup canola oil
- ⅓   cup sugar
- ¾   tsp. ground cinnamon

1. Preheat oven to 350°. In a large bowl, combine the cake and pudding mixes. Add eggs, sour cream, water and oil; beat until blended (batter will be thick).
2. Combine sugar and cinnamon. Spoon half of the batter into 2 greased 8x4-in. loaf pans; sprinkle each with 2 Tbsp. cinnamon sugar. Spread with remaining batter; sprinkle with remaining cinnamon sugar.
3. Bake for 35-40 minutes or until a toothpick inserted in the center comes out clean. Cool for 10 minutes before removing from pans to wire racks.
1 SLICE: *169 cal., 7g fat (2g sat. fat), 42mg chol., 218mg sod., 24g carb. (16g sugars, 0 fiber), 2g pro.*

CRANBERRY CORNBREAD

During the holidays, I make several pans of this sweet, cakelike cornbread for family and friends. Whole blueberries—coated in flour—can be used in place of the cranberries.
—Sylvia Gidwani, Milford, NJ

PREP: 15 MIN. • **BAKE:** 40 MIN. • **MAKES:** 9 SERVINGS

- ½   cup butter, softened
- 1   cup sugar
- 2   large eggs, room temperature
- 1½   cups all-purpose flour
- 1   cup cornmeal
- 2   tsp. baking powder
- ½   tsp. salt
- 1½   cups buttermilk
- 1   cup cranberries, halved

1. Preheat oven to 375°. In a bowl, cream butter and sugar until light and fluffy. Add eggs; mix well. Combine the flour, cornmeal, baking powder and salt. Add to the creamed mixture alternately with buttermilk. Fold in cranberries.
2. Transfer batter to a greased 9-in. square baking pan. Bake until a toothpick inserted in the center comes out clean, 40-45 minutes. Serve warm.
1 PIECE: *350 cal., 12g fat (7g sat. fat), 70mg chol., 414mg sod., 54g carb. (25g sugars, 1g fiber), 6g pro.*

CHRISTMAS MORNING POPOVERS

Popovers are a Christmas morning tradition my father-in-law started more than 30 years ago. Now I get up early to make them, then wake the family to begin opening gifts. When the popovers are ready, I serve them with lots of butter and assorted jams.
—Sue Jurack, Mequon, WI

PREP: 15 MIN. • **BAKE:** 35 MIN. • **MAKES:** 9 POPOVERS

- 1¼ cups whole milk
- 1 Tbsp. butter, melted and cooled
- 1 cup all-purpose flour
- ¼ tsp. salt
- 2 large eggs, room temperature

1. Preheat oven to 450°. In a small bowl, beat the milk, butter, flour and salt until blended. Add eggs, one at a time, beating well after each addition. Fill buttered popover pans or large custard cups three-fourths full.
2. Bake for 15 minutes. Reduce heat to 350° and bake until very firm, 20 minutes longer. Remove from the oven and prick each popover with a sharp knife to allow the steam to escape. Serve immediately.
1 POPOVER: *99 cal., 4g fat (2g sat. fat), 55mg chol., 109mg sod., 12g carb. (2g sugars, 0 fiber), 4g pro.*

Holiday Helper
Let the eggs and milk come to room temperature for about 30 minutes before preparing this recipe. Allowing them to warm up results in greater height in the popovers.

GINGERBREAD SCONES

These moist scones' gingerbread flavor make them just right for serving around Christmastime. Of course, they go great with a cozy, hand-warming drink, too.
—David Bostedt, Zephyrhills, FL

PREP: 20 MIN. • **BAKE:** 15 MIN. • **MAKES:** 1 DOZEN

- 2 cups all-purpose flour
- 3 Tbsp. brown sugar
- 2 tsp. baking powder
- 1 tsp. ground ginger
- ½ tsp. salt
- ½ tsp. baking soda
- ½ tsp. ground cinnamon
- ¼ cup cold butter, cubed
- ⅓ cup molasses
- ¼ cup milk
- 1 large egg, separated, room temperature
  Coarse sugar

1. Preheat the oven to 400°. In a large bowl, whisk the first 7 ingredients. Cut in butter until the mixture resembles coarse crumbs. In another bowl, whisk molasses, milk and egg yolk until blended; stir into crumb mixture just until moistened.
2. Turn onto a lightly floured surface; knead gently 6-8 times. Pat into an 8-in. circle. Cut into 12 wedges. Place wedges 1 in. apart on a greased baking sheet.
3. In a small bowl, beat egg white until frothy; brush over scones. Sprinkle with sugar. Bake until golden brown, 12-15 minutes. Serve warm.
1 SCONE: *157 cal., 5g fat (3g sat. fat), 29mg chol., 269mg sod., 26g carb. (9g sugars, 1g fiber), 3g pro.*

CANDY CANE CHOCOLATE LOAVES

Adding candy canes to a dense and delicious chocolate quick bread makes an amazing holiday treat. Coffee and cocoa intensify the appealing flavor.
—Shelly Platten, Amherst, WI

PREP: 25 MIN. • **BAKE:** 50 MIN. + COOLING
MAKES: 3 LOAVES (12 SLICES EACH)

¼ cup butter, softened
1⅔ cups packed brown sugar
4 large egg whites, room temperature
2 large eggs, room temperature
¾ cup strong brewed coffee
½ cup vanilla yogurt
¼ cup canola oil
1 Tbsp. vanilla extract
¼ tsp. peppermint extract
3½ cups all-purpose flour
¾ cup baking cocoa
1½ tsp. baking soda
½ tsp. salt
1½ cups buttermilk
1 cup (6 oz.) miniature semisweet chocolate chips

TOPPING
2 oz. white baking chocolate, melted
3 Tbsp. crushed candy canes

1. Preheat oven to 350°. Coat three 8x4-in. loaf pans with cooking spray. In a large bowl, beat butter and brown sugar until crumbly, about 2 minutes. Add the egg whites, eggs, coffee, yogurt, oil and the extracts until blended.
2. In another bowl, whisk the flour, cocoa, baking soda and salt; add to the brown sugar mixture alternately with buttermilk, beating well after each addition. Fold in chocolate chips.
3. Transfer to prepared pans. Bake until a toothpick inserted in center comes out clean, 50-55 minutes. Cool 10 minutes before removing from pans to wire racks to cool completely.
4. Drizzle melted white baking chocolate over the loaves. Sprinkle glazed loaves with crushed candies.

1 SLICE: *162 cal., 5g fat (2g sat. fat), 16mg chol., 124mg sod., 26g carb. (15g sugars, 1g fiber), 3g pro.*
DIABETIC EXCHANGES: *1½ starch, 1 fat.*

CRUNCHY BREADSTICKS

These thin, crisp breadsticks add a bit of elegance to a holiday dinner. Each bite is perfectly seasoned with thyme and a bit of coarse salt.
—Taste of Home *Test Kitchen*

PREP: 20 MIN. • **BAKE:** 20 MIN.
MAKES: 16 BREADSTICKS

  2 cups all-purpose flour
1½ tsp. baking powder
  ½ tsp. salt
  3 Tbsp. shortening
  ½ to ¾ cup ice water
  1 Tbsp. olive oil
  ¼ tsp. coarse salt
  ¼ tsp. dried thyme

1. Preheat oven to 350°. In a food processor, combine the flour, baking powder, salt and shortening; cover and process until mixture resembles coarse crumbs. While processing, gradually add water until dough forms a ball.
2. Transfer to a floured surface. Roll dough into a 10x8-in. rectangle. Cut into sixteen 10x½-in. strips. Twist each strip 4 times and place on baking sheets. Brush with oil. Combine coarse salt and thyme; sprinkle over breadsticks.
3. Bake until golden brown and crisp, 18-20 minutes. Cool on a wire rack.
1 BREADSTICK: *85 cal., 3g fat (1g sat. fat), 0 chol., 148mg sod., 12g carb. (0 sugars, 0 fiber), 2g pro.*

POTECA CAKE

My town is home to some 56 different nationalities, making us a true melting pot. This recipe showcases its Slavic heritage.
—Rachelle Stratton, Rock Springs, WY

PREP: 25 MIN. + CHILLING
BAKE: 1 HOUR
MAKES: 12 SERVINGS

  1 cup butter, cubed
  ½ cup 2% milk
  3 large egg yolks, beaten,
       room temperature
  2 pkg. (¼ oz. each) active dry yeast
  ¼ cup warm water (110° to 115°)
2½ cups all-purpose flour
  1 Tbsp. sugar
  ¼ tsp. salt

FILLING
  2 cups ground walnuts
  2 cups chopped dates
  ¼ cup 2% milk
  3 Tbsp. plus 1 cup sugar, divided
  ½ tsp. ground cinnamon
  3 large egg whites, room temperature
       Confectioners' sugar

1. In a small saucepan, melt the butter with the milk; cool. Stir in egg yolks until blended. In a small bowl, dissolve yeast in warm water.
2. In a large bowl, combine the flour, sugar and salt; add the butter mixture and the yeast mixture. Beat on medium speed for 3 minutes (dough will be sticky). Cover and refrigerate overnight.
3. In a small saucepan over medium heat, combine the nuts, dates, milk, 3 Tbsp. sugar and the cinnamon. Cook and stir until the mixture forms a paste. Transfer to a large bowl.

4. In a small bowl, beat the egg whites until soft peaks form. Gradually beat in the remaining sugar, 1 Tbsp. at a time, on high speed until stiff peaks form. Fold into the nut mixture.
5. Preheat oven to 350°. Cut dough in half; on a floured surface, roll 1 portion of dough into a 20-in. square. Spread with half the filling. Roll up tightly jelly-roll style. Place seam side up in a greased 10-in. tube pan. Repeat with the second portion; place seam side down over the first roll-up in the pan (layers will bake as one loaf).
6. Bake until golden brown, 60-70 minutes. Cool for 10 minutes before removing from the pan to a wire rack to cool completely. Sprinkle with confectioners' sugar.
1 SLICE: *509 cal., 26g fat (11g sat. fat), 92mg chol., 182mg sod., 66g carb. (41g sugars, 4g fiber), 8g pro.*

EVELYN'S SOUR CREAM TWISTS

These terrific flaky twists are good for breakfast, lunch or dinner—they're a touch sweet, but not too much. They also freeze well, so if you keep them in your freezer, you'll have them on hand when needed.
—Linda Welch, North Platte, NE

PREP: 40 MIN. + CHILLING • **BAKE:** 15 MIN.
MAKES: 4 DOZEN

- 1   pkg. (¼ oz.) active dry yeast
- ¼   cup warm water (110° to 115°)
- 3   cups all-purpose flour
- 1½ tsp. salt
- ½   cup cold butter
- ½   cup shortening
- 2   large eggs, room temperature
- ½   cup sour cream
- 3   tsp. vanilla extract, divided
- 1½ cups sugar

1. In a small bowl, dissolve yeast in water. In a bowl, combine flour and salt. Cut in butter and shortening until the mixture resembles coarse crumbs. Stir in eggs, sour cream, 1 tsp. vanilla and the yeast mixture; mix thoroughly. Cover the bowl and refrigerate overnight.
2. Combine sugar and remaining vanilla; lightly sprinkle ½ cup over a pastry cloth or countertop surface. On the sugared surface, roll half the dough into a 12x8-in. rectangle; refrigerate remaining dough. Sprinkle rolled dough with about 1 Tbsp. of the sugar mixture. Fold the dough rectangle into thirds.
3. Give dough a quarter turn and repeat rolling, sugaring and folding two more times. Roll into a 12x8-in. rectangle. Cut into 4x1-in. strips; twist each strip 2 or 3 times. Place on chilled ungreased baking sheets. Repeat with the remaining sugar mixture and dough.
4. Bake at 375° until lightly browned, 12-14 minutes. Immediately remove from pan and cool on wire racks.
1 TWIST: *97 cal., 5g fat (2g sat. fat), 16mg chol., 97mg sod., 12g carb. (6g sugars, 0 fiber), 1g pro.*

BRIE & CARAMELIZED ONION FLATBREAD

When planning a holiday party, saute the onions and garlic for this flatbread a day ahead so it's easy to put together on the big day. Prepared pizza dough makes it a snap.
—Trisha Kruse, Eagle, ID

PREP: 45 MIN. • **BAKE:** 20 MIN. + STANDING
MAKES: 1 FLATBREAD (12 PIECES)

- 2   Tbsp. butter
- 3   large sweet onions, halved and thinly sliced (about 6 cups)
- 2   garlic cloves, minced
- 1   Tbsp. brown sugar
- 1   Tbsp. balsamic vinegar
- ½   tsp. salt
- ¼   tsp. pepper
- 1   loaf (1 lb.) frozen pizza dough, thawed
- 8   oz. Brie cheese, cut into ½-in. pieces

1. Preheat the oven to 425°. Grease a 15x10x1-in. baking pan; set aside. Heat the butter in a large skillet over medium heat. Add onions; cook and stir 4-6 minutes or until softened. Reduce heat to medium-low; cook 25-30 minutes or until deep golden brown, stirring occasionally. Add garlic; cook and stir 1 minute longer.
2. Add brown sugar, vinegar, salt and pepper to the onion mixture. Cook and stir 5 minutes longer.
3. Press dough into a 12x10-in. rectangle onto prepared pan. Top with the onion mixture and cheese. Bake 20-25 minutes or until golden brown. Let the flatbread stand for 10 minutes before cutting.
1 PIECE: *206 cal., 9g fat (5g sat. fat), 24mg chol., 333mg sod., 25g carb. (6g sugars, 1g fiber), 8g pro.*

TROPICAL BUTTERHORN TREES

Coconut turns ordinary butterhorn rolls into a tropical treat! The tree shape makes this especially fun for Christmas.
—Carolyn Faust, Caldwell, TX

PREP: 40 MIN. + RISING • **BAKE:** 20 MIN.
MAKES: 2 TREES (11 ROLLS EACH) PLUS 2 EXTRA ROLLS

- 3 to 3½ cups all-purpose flour
- ¼ cup sugar
- 1 pkg. (¼ oz.) active dry yeast
- 1 tsp. salt
- ½ cup sour cream
- 6 Tbsp. butter, softened
- ¼ cup water
- 2 large eggs, room temperature

FILLING
- 2 Tbsp. butter, softened
- ¾ cup sweetened shredded coconut, toasted
- ½ cup sugar
- 2 tsp. grated orange zest

GLAZE
- ¼ cup sugar
- ¼ cup sour cream
- 2 Tbsp. orange juice
- 2 Tbsp. butter
- ¼ cup sweetened shredded coconut, toasted

1. In a large bowl, combine 1½ cups flour, sugar, yeast and salt. In a small saucepan, heat the sour cream, butter and water to 120°-130°; add to dry ingredients. Beat on medium speed for 2 minutes. Add eggs and ½ cup flour; beat 2 minutes longer. Stir in enough of the remaining flour to form a firm dough.

2. Turn the dough onto a lightly floured surface; knead until smooth and elastic, about 5-7 minutes. Place in a greased bowl, turning once to grease top. Cover and let rise in a warm place until doubled, about 1 hour.

3. Punch dough down. Turn onto a lightly floured surface; divide in half. Roll each portion into a 12-in. circle; spread each with 1 Tbsp. butter. Combine the coconut, sugar and orange zest; sprinkle over butter. Cut each circle into 12 wedges.

4. Start with the top of 1 tree: Roll up 1 wedge from the wide end and place point side down near the top center of a greased baking sheet. Roll up 2 wedges; place in the second row with sides touching. Repeat, adding 1 roll per row, until the tree has 4 rows. For the trunk, roll up another wedge and center it below the last row. Repeat to make the second tree on a second baking sheet, using 11 more wedges. Roll up the remaining 2 wedges; place one on each baking sheet.

5. Cover and let rise in a warm place until doubled, 40 minutes. Bake at 350° or until golden brown, 18-22 minutes. Remove to wire racks.

6. For glaze, in a small saucepan, combine the sugar, sour cream, orange juice and butter. Bring to a boil; cook and stir for 3 minutes. Spoon or brush the glaze over warm rolls; sprinkle with coconut.

1 ROLL: *173 cal., 8g fat (5g sat. fat), 35mg chol., 166mg sod., 23g carb. (10g sugars, 1g fiber), 3g pro.*

CHOCOLATE YEAST BREAD

Your family will be delighted by this tender loaf of chocolate bread. Toast slices and spread with butter, cream cheese or peanut butter—or whatever pleases you.
—Laura Cryts, Derry, NH

PREP: 30 MIN. + RISING • **BAKE:** 25 MIN.
MAKES: 2 LOAVES (16 SLICES EACH)

- 4½ cups all-purpose flour
- ⅓ cup baking cocoa
- 2 Tbsp. sugar
- 1 pkg. (¼ oz.) active dry yeast
- 1 tsp. salt
- ¼ tsp. baking soda
- 1 cup water
- ½ cup whole milk
- ½ cup semisweet chocolate chips
- 2 Tbsp. butter
- 1 large egg, room temperature
  Baking cocoa or confectioners' sugar, optional

1. In a bowl, combine 1¼ cups flour, the cocoa, sugar, yeast, salt and baking soda. In a saucepan, heat water, milk, chocolate chips and butter; stir until the chocolate is melted. Cool to 120°-130°. Add to the dry ingredients; beat on medium speed for 2 minutes. Add ½ cup flour and the egg; beat on high for 2 minutes. Stir in enough remaining flour to form a stiff dough.

2. Turn onto a floured surface; knead until smooth and elastic, about 6-8 minutes. Place in a greased bowl, turning once to grease top. Cover and let rise in a warm place until doubled, about 1 hour.

3. Punch dough down. Turn onto a lightly floured surface; divide in half. Shape into loaves. Place loaves in 2 greased 8x4-in. loaf pans. Cover and let rise until doubled, about 1 hour.

4. Bake at 375° until browned, about 25-30 minutes. Remove from pans to cool on wire racks. Dust with baking cocoa or confectioners' sugar if desired.

1 SLICE: *94 cal., 2g fat (1g sat. fat), 9mg chol., 95mg sod., 17g carb. (3g sugars, 1g fiber), 3g pro.*

CINNAMON ROLLS

My wife tells people that after I retired, I went from being the breadwinner to the bread baker! It started with a baking class at a nearby community college. Now my breads are favorites with friends and family.
—Ben Middleton, Walla Walla, WA

PREP: 20 MIN. + RISING • **BAKE:** 25 MIN.
MAKES: 2 DOZEN

- 2 pkg. (¼ oz. each) active dry yeast
- ½ cup sugar, divided
- 1 cup warm water (110° to 115°)
- 1 cup whole milk
- 6 Tbsp. butter
- 7 to 7½ cups all-purpose flour
- 3 large eggs, room temperature, beaten
- 1 tsp. salt

FILLING
- ¼ cup butter, softened
- 5 tsp. ground cinnamon
- ¾ cup packed brown sugar
- ¾ cup raisins or dried currants
  Vanilla frosting, optional

1. In a large bowl, dissolve the yeast and 1 Tbsp. sugar in water. In a saucepan, heat milk and butter to 110°-115°; add to the yeast mixture. Stir in 3 cups flour, the eggs, salt and remaining sugar. Stir in enough of the remaining flour to make a soft dough.

2. Turn out onto a lightly floured surface. Knead until smooth and elastic, 6-8 minutes. Place in a greased bowl, turning once to grease top. Cover and let rise in a warm place until doubled, about 1 hour.

3. Punch dough down and divide in half. Roll each half into a 15x12-in. rectangle. Brush with softened butter. Combine the cinnamon, sugar and raisins or currants; sprinkle evenly over dough. Roll up tightly, jelly-roll style, starting with the long side. Slice each roll into 12 pieces. Place pieces in 2 greased standard muffin pans or on 2 greased 13x9-in. baking pans. Cover and let rise until doubled, about 30 minutes.

4. Bake at 350° until golden brown, about 25-30 minutes. Cool in pans for 5 minutes; invert onto a wire rack. Frost with icing if desired. Serve warm.

1 CINNAMON ROLL: *248 cal., 6g fat (3g sat. fat), 41mg chol., 164mg sod., 43g carb. (15g sugars, 1g fiber), 5g pro.*

SWEET POTATO PAN ROLLS

These tender rolls are my brother's favorites, so I make them often. Spiced with cinnamon and nutmeg, they are super alongside a wide variety of dishes, from roast chicken to a bowl of steaming chili.
—Carly Curtin, Ellicott City, MD

PREP: 30 MIN. + RISING • **BAKE:** 20 MIN.
MAKES: 16 ROLLS

1. pkg. (¼ oz.) active dry yeast
½ cup warm water (110° to 115°)
½ cup mashed sweet potato
¼ cup butter, melted
3 Tbsp. honey
2 Tbsp. canola oil
1 large egg, room temperature
1 tsp. salt
½ tsp. sugar
¼ tsp. ground cinnamon
  Dash ground nutmeg
3½ to 4 cups bread flour

1. In a large bowl, dissolve yeast in warm water. Add sweet potato, butter, honey, oil, egg, salt, sugar, cinnamon, nutmeg and 1 cup of flour. Beat on medium speed until smooth. Stir in enough of the remaining flour to form a soft dough (the dough will be sticky).
2. Turn onto a floured surface; knead until smooth and elastic, about 6-8 minutes. Place in a greased bowl, turning once to grease the top. Cover and let rise in a warm place until doubled, about 1 hour.
3. Punch dough down. Turn onto a lightly floured surface; divide into 16 pieces. Shape each piece into a ball. Place balls in 2 greased 9-in. round baking pans. Cover and let rise until doubled, 30 minutes.
4. Bake at 375° until golden brown, 20-25 minutes.
1 ROLL: *154 cal., 5g fat (2g sat. fat), 21mg chol., 175mg sod., 25g carb. (4g sugars, 1g fiber), 4g pro.*
DIABETIC EXCHANGES: *1½ starch, 1 fat.*

APRICOT BUBBLE RING

Both of our daughters received ribbons for this recipe at the 4-H fair. The bubble ring is ideal for serving to a crowd at a special breakfast gathering.
—Lois Schlickau, Haven, KS

PREP: 25 MIN. + RISING • **BAKE:** 30 MIN.
MAKES: 20 SERVINGS

1 pkg. (¼ oz.) active dry yeast
¼ cup warm water (110° to 115°)
½ cup warm milk (110° to 115°)
⅓ cup butter, melted
⅓ cup sugar
2 large eggs, room temperature
1 tsp. salt
3¾ to 4 cups all-purpose flour
FILLING
¾ cup sugar
1 tsp. ground cinnamon
6 Tbsp. butter, melted, divided
⅔ cup apricot preserves
¾ cup finely chopped walnuts

1. In a large bowl, dissolve yeast in warm water. Add the milk, butter, sugar, eggs and salt; mix well. Add 2 cups flour; beat until smooth. Stir in enough remaining flour to form a soft dough.

2. Turn onto a floured surface; knead until smooth and elastic, 6-8 minutes. Place in a greased bowl, turning once to grease top. Cover and let rise in a warm place until doubled, about 1 hour.
3. Combine the sugar and cinnamon in a shallow bowl; set aside. Punch the dough down; cover and let rest for 10 minutes. Pour 2 Tbsp. melted butter into bottom of greased 10-in. fluted tube pan.
4. On a lightly floured surface, divide the dough into 20 pieces; form into balls. Dip each ball into remaining melted butter, then roll in cinnamon-sugar. Place 10 balls into prepared pan. Spoon half of the apricot preserves between the balls; sprinkle with half of the walnuts. Repeat. Cover and let rise until doubled, about 45 minutes.
5. Bake at 350° until browned, for about 30-35 minutes. Cool 5 minutes before inverting onto a serving plate. Serve the bubble ring warm.
1 PIECE: *252 cal., 10g fat (5g sat. fat), 37mg chol., 185mg sod., 37g carb. (16g sugars, 1g fiber), 4g pro.*

FLAVORS OF THE SEASON

Aroma and taste evoke some of our clearest and most meaningful memories—and some flavors are forever connected to Christmas.

Cranberry

Their deep red color and fruity tang make cranberries a perfect match for festive dishes.

DRIED CRANBERRY SCONES

I go on vacation with my best friend to Michigan every July. Her cousin is allowed, too—but only if she brings her special cherry scones. I make them with cranberries for the holidays. Don't try to double this recipe. If you need more than 12, make two separate batches of dough.
—Sherry Leonard, Whitsett, NC

PREP: 20 MIN. • **BAKE:** 15 MIN.
MAKES: 1 DOZEN

- 2 cups all-purpose flour
- ¼ cup sugar
- 2½ tsp. baking powder
- ½ tsp. salt
- 6 Tbsp. cold butter
- ¾ cup buttermilk
- 1 large egg, room temperature
- ¾ cup white baking chips
- ¾ cup dried cranberries
- 1 Tbsp. turbinado (washed raw) sugar

1. Preheat oven to 400°. In a large bowl, whisk flour, sugar, baking powder and salt. Cut in butter until mixture resembles coarse crumbs. In another bowl, whisk buttermilk and egg; stir into the crumb mixture just until moistened. Stir in the baking chips and cranberries.
2. Drop dough by ¼ cupfuls 2 in. apart onto parchment-lined baking sheet. Sprinkle with turbinado sugar. Bake until golden brown, 12-15 minutes.
1 SCONE: *247 cal., 10g fat (6g sat. fat), 34mg chol., 290mg sod., 36g carb. (20g sugars, 1g fiber), 4g pro.*

CRANBERRY WALNUT PIE

With its deep ruby-red color and golden lattice crust, this festive pie is perfect for Christmas and tastes as good as it looks.
—Diane Everett, Dunkirk, NY

PREP: 20 MIN. • **BAKE:** 50 MIN. + COOLING
MAKES: 8 SERVINGS

- 1 pkg. (12 oz.) fresh or frozen cranberries, thawed
- 1½ cups packed brown sugar
- 1 cup chopped walnuts
- ¼ cup butter, melted
- 4½ tsp. all-purpose flour

- 2 tsp. grated orange zest
  Dash salt
  Pastry for double-crust pie (9 in.)

1. Preheat oven to 375°. Place cranberries in a food processor; cover and process until finely chopped. Transfer to a large bowl; stir in brown sugar, walnuts, melted butter, flour, orange zest and salt.
2. On a lightly floured surface, roll one half of pastry dough to a ⅛-in.-thick circle; transfer to a 9-in. pie plate. Trim pastry to ½ in. beyond rim of plate. Add filling.
3. Roll remaining dough to a ⅛-in.-thick circle; cut into ½-in.-wide strips. Arrange over filling in a lattice pattern. Trim and seal strips to edge of bottom pastry; flute edge. Cover edges loosely with foil.

4. Bake for 30 minutes. Remove the foil; bake until the crust is golden brown and filling is bubbly, 20-25 minutes. Cool on a wire rack.
1 PIECE: *672 cal., 38g fat (19g sat. fat), 75mg chol., 391mg sod., 79g carb. (43g sugars, 4g fiber), 7g pro.*
PASTRY FOR DOUBLE-CRUST PIE (9-IN.): Combine 2½ cups all-purpose flour and ½ tsp. salt; cut in 1 cup cold butter until crumbly. Gradually add ⅓ to ⅔ cup ice water, tossing with a fork until the dough holds together when pressed. Divide dough in half and shape into disks; wrap disks separately and refrigerate 1 hour.

beat into the oil mixture. Stir in the dried chopped cranberries.

3. Transfer to prepared pan; sprinkle with almonds. Bake until a toothpick inserted in center comes out clean, 20-25 minutes.

4. Combine the glaze ingredients; pour over the warm cake. Cool for 10 minutes before serving. If desired, sprinkle with orange zest.

1 SLICE: *263 cal., 12g fat (1g sat. fat), 47mg chol., 182mg sod., 36g carb. (25g sugars, 1g fiber), 4g pro.*

SPICY CRANBERRY SALSA

This beautiful holiday dish is a big hit at our house; we serve it on wheat or other crispy crackers. Cranberries and various forms of chile peppers combine to make a very nice sweet-heat treat.
—*Diane Smith, Pine Mountain, GA*

PREP: 25 MIN. + CHILLING
MAKES: 24 SERVINGS

- 1 pkg. (12 oz.) fresh or frozen cranberries
- ¼ cup coarsely chopped green onions
- ¼ cup fresh cilantro leaves
- ¼ cup coarsely chopped green pepper
- 1 Tbsp. minced fresh gingerroot
- 2 to 3 tsp. ground chipotle pepper
- 1 medium lime
- 1 can (10 oz.) diced tomatoes and green chiles, drained
- ¾ cup sugar
- ½ tsp. kosher salt
- ⅛ tsp. cayenne pepper
- 3 pkg. (8 oz. each) cream cheese, softened
  Assorted crackers

1. Place the first 6 ingredients in a food processor. Finely grate enough zest from lime to measure 2 tsp. Cut lime crosswise in half; squeeze juice from lime. Add zest and juice to food processor. Process until coarsely chopped. Transfer to a bowl. Stir in diced tomatoes and green chiles, sugar, salt and cayenne. Refrigerate, covered, at least 4 hours.

2. Spread cream cheese onto a serving platter; top with cranberry salsa. Serve with crackers.

1 SERVING: *134 cal., 10g fat (6g sat. fat), 29mg chol., 184mg sod., 11g carb. (8g sugars, 1g fiber), 2g pro.*

TUSCAN SUN ORANGE CRANBERRY CAKE

Growing up, my family used farina flour in desserts; it lends a nice earthy texture to this cake. It's an old-world Italian-style cake, delicious but not too sweet—it's great in the morning, or as a snack served with strong coffee. The orange-cranberry combination is perfect!
—*Ninette Holbrook, Orlando, FL*

PREP: 25 MIN. • **BAKE:** 20 MIN. + COOLING
MAKES: 8 SERVINGS

- ⅓ cup sugar
- ⅓ cup canola oil
- 2 large eggs, room temperature
- 1 Tbsp. grated orange zest
- 1 Tbsp. orange juice
- ⅓ cup all-purpose flour
- ⅓ cup cream of wheat or farina flour
- ½ tsp. salt
- ¼ tsp. baking powder
- ⅓ cup dried cranberries, chopped
- ¼ cup sliced almonds

ORANGE GLAZE
- ¾ cup confectioners' sugar
- 1 Tbsp. orange juice
- 2 tsp. 2% milk
  Grated orange zest, optional

1. Preheat oven to 350°. Grease an 8-in. round baking pan.

2. In a large bowl, beat the sugar, oil, eggs, orange zest and juice until well blended. In another bowl, whisk the flour, cream of wheat, salt and baking powder; gradually

BOURBON PUNCH

Orange and cranberry form the base of this incredibly smooth holiday punch, hitting just the right seasonal note. Feel free to use less or more bourbon, change up the kind of alcohol you use—or leave it out entirely.
—Sharon Tipton, Casselberry, FL

TAKES: 10 MIN. • **MAKES:** 12 SERVINGS

- 4 cups cranberry juice, chilled
- 1 to 2 cups bourbon
- ¾ cup thawed lemonade concentrate
- ⅔ cup thawed orange juice concentrate
- 4 cups ginger ale, chilled
  Orange and lime slices, optional

Combine the cranberry juice, bourbon, and the lemonade and orange juice concentrates in a punch bowl. Stir in the ginger ale. If desired, garnish with orange and lime slices. Serve over ice.

¾ CUP: *143 cal., 0 fat (0 sat. fat), 0 chol., 8mg sod., 27g carb. (26g sugars, 0 fiber), 1g pro.*

CRACKLED CRANBERRY PECAN COOKIES

Cranberries, orange and nuts make one of my favorite flavor combinations, and this special drop cookie fits in particularly well with holiday potlucks. For a fruitcake-type cookie, use a mixture of dried fruits and substitute rum flavoring for half the vanilla.
—Deborah Biggs, Omaha, NE

PREP: 30 MIN. • **BAKE:** 10 MIN./BATCH
MAKES: 2 DOZEN

- ¼ cup boiling water
- ¼ cup orange juice
- ¾ cup dried cranberries
- ½ cup butter, softened
- ½ cup sugar
- ½ cup packed brown sugar
- 1 large egg, room temperature
- 1 tsp. grated orange zest
- 1 tsp. vanilla extract
- 1½ cups all-purpose flour
- ½ tsp. salt
- ½ tsp. cream of tartar
- ½ tsp. baking soda
- ¾ cup coarsely chopped pecans, toasted

1. Preheat oven to 350°. Pour the boiling water and orange juice over cranberries in a small bowl; let stand 5 minutes. Drain.
2. In a large bowl, cream butter and sugars until light and fluffy. Beat in egg, orange zest and vanilla. In another bowl, whisk flour, salt, cream of tartar and baking soda; gradually beat into the creamed mixture. Stir in pecans and cranberries.

3. Drop dough by tablespoonfuls 3 in. apart onto ungreased baking sheets. Bake until the edges begin to brown, about 10-12 minutes. Remove from pans to wire racks to cool. Store the cookies in an airtight container.

1 COOKIE: *139 cal., 7g fat (3g sat. fat), 18mg chol., 111mg sod., 20g carb. (13g sugars, 1g fiber), 1g pro.*

Orange

From Victorian gifts and decorations to modern stocking stuffers, oranges are a sweet Christmas tradition.

KUMQUAT, ORANGE & CHOCOLATE CHEESECAKE

We have a variety of fruit trees in our yard, including an orange and a kumquat tree. When I was thinking of what to make with the fruit, cheesecake came to mind. This treat has a classic Christmastime combination of chocolate and citrus.
—Johnna Johnson, Scottsdale, AZ

PREP: 45 MIN. + CHILLING
BAKE: 70 MIN. + COOLING
MAKES: 12 SERVINGS

- 2½ cups crushed gingersnap cookies (about 50 cookies)
- ⅓ cup butter, melted
- 7 oz. semisweet chocolate, chopped
- ⅔ cup heavy whipping cream
- 1 medium navel orange
- 2¾ cups whole-milk ricotta cheese
- ¼ cup packed dark brown sugar
- 1 tsp. vanilla extract
- 3 large eggs, lightly beaten
- 2 Tbsp. finely chopped kumquats (about 4)
  Semisweet chocolate curls, sliced kumquats

1. Preheat the oven to 350°. In a bowl, combine the gingersnaps and butter. Press onto the bottom of a greased 8-in. springform pan. Refrigerate while preparing the filling.
2. Place chopped chocolate in a small bowl. In a small saucepan, bring cream just to a boil. Pour over the chocolate; stir with a whisk until smooth. Cool slightly.
3. Finely grate enough zest from orange to measure 4 tsp. Cut the orange crosswise in half; squeeze juice from orange. In a large bowl, beat ricotta cheese and brown sugar until smooth. Beat in the chopped kumquats, orange juice, zest, vanilla and the cooled chocolate mixture. Add eggs; beat on low speed just until combined. Pour over crust.
4. Place pan on a baking sheet. Bake until the edges are lightly browned and the top is dry to the touch (the center will not be set), 70-80 minutes. Cool the cheesecake on a wire rack for 10 minutes. Loosen the sides from the pan with a knife. Cool 1 hour longer. Refrigerate overnight, covering when completely cooled.
5. Remove rim from pan. Top cheesecake with chocolate curls and thinly sliced kumquats.
1 SLICE: *435 cal., 25g fat (15g sat. fat), 98mg chol., 279mg sod., 36g carb. (18g sugars, 2g fiber), 11g pro.*

ORANGE MARMALADE BLUEBERRY BREAD

Juicy blueberries drenched in orange juice, orange zest and orange marmalade...this quick bread is perfect to serve as is, or spread individual slices with cream cheese. Sometimes, as a special treat, I stir a little additional marmalade into softened cream cheese to use as a topping.
—Darlene Brenden, Salem, OR

PREP: 15 MIN. • **BAKE:** 45 MIN. + COOLING
MAKES: 1 LOAF (16 SLICES)

- 2 cups all-purpose flour
- 1 cup sugar
- 2 tsp. grated orange zest
- 1 tsp. baking powder
- ½ tsp. salt
- ¼ tsp. baking soda
- 1 large egg, room temperature
- ¾ cup orange juice
- ¼ cup canola oil
- 1 cup fresh or frozen blueberries
- ¾ cup orange marmalade, divided

1. Preheat oven to 350°. In a large bowl, combine the flour, sugar, orange zest, baking powder, salt and baking soda. Whisk the egg, orange juice and oil; stir into the dry ingredients just until moistened. Fold in the blueberries and ½ cup of the marmalade.
2. Transfer to a greased 9x5-in. loaf pan. Bake until a toothpick inserted near the center comes out clean, 45-50 minutes. Cool for 15 minutes before removing from pan to a wire rack. Spoon the remaining marmalade over top.
NOTE: If using frozen blueberries, use without thawing to avoid discoloring the batter.
1 SLICE: *188 cal., 4 g fat (trace sat. fat), 13 mg chol., 132 mg sod., 37 g carb., 1g fiber, 2 g pro.*

A PROPERLY FILLED CHRISTMAS STOCKING

For much of its history, the orange was a luxury to most Europeans—an expensive and exotic fruit that came in the season with traveling merchants. Families gave them to children as gifts and used them as decorations, pierced with aromatic cloves. In the 19th century, oranges were placed in the toes of Christmas stockings, perhaps symbolizing the bags of gold Saint Nicholas is said to have given to three poor maidens to use as dowries.

In 1908, the mass marketing of oranges began, courtesy of the California Fruit Growers Association. Ads showed Santa delivering crates full of oranges; the industry publication, the *California Citrograph*, proclaimed "the Christmas stocking is really not properly filled without an orange in it." In the 1930s, the orange again became a luxury in Depression-era households. Perhaps not on quite the same level as the exotic, mysterious fruit that arrived along the Silk Road, the orange is still something sweet and special to celebrate the holidays.

SPICY CHOCOLATE ORANGE SNACK MIX

This munchable treat gets an extra zing from orange zest and a pop from cayenne pepper. Set out a bowl to snack on through the day or during a holiday movie night!
—Erica Wilson, Beverly, MA

PREP: 10 MIN. • **COOK:** 5 MIN. + COOLING
MAKES: 8 SERVINGS

- 5 cups Rice Chex
- 3 Tbsp. butter, cubed
- 1 Tbsp. orange juice
- ¼ tsp. cayenne pepper
- ¼ tsp. grated orange zest
- 1 cup semisweet chocolate chips

1. Place cereal in a large bowl. In a small microwave-safe bowl, combine butter, orange juice, cayenne and orange zest. Microwave, covered, on high for 45 seconds; stir. Cook 15-30 seconds longer or until the butter is melted; stir until smooth. Pour over the cereal.
2. Microwave in batches on high for 3 minutes, stirring every minute. Spread onto waxed paper to cool. Stir in chips. Store in an airtight container.

¾ **CUP:** 181 cal., 10g fat (6g sat. fat), 10mg chol., 154mg sod., 25g carb. (12g sugars, 1g fiber), 2g pro.

ORANGE GLAZE CAKE

Mom loved to bake—from the time I can remember, every Saturday she was in the kitchen creating another wonderful cake or pie. This tender orange cake bakes up deep golden brown and is a favorite of mine, my friends and my family. To make it an even more special treat, serve slices with ice cream or a drizzle of Curacao.
—Patricia Wright, Stratford, NJ

PREP: 25 MIN. • **BAKE:** 45 MIN. + COOLING
MAKES: 12 SERVINGS

- 1 cup butter, softened
- 2 cups sugar
- 2 Tbsp. grated orange zest
- 6 large eggs, room temperature
- 1 tsp. vanilla extract
- 3 cups all-purpose flour
- ¾ cup 2% milk
- 3 tsp. baking powder
- ⅛ tsp. salt

GLAZE
- ⅓ cup confectioners' sugar
- ¼ cup butter, melted
- ¼ cup orange juice
  Chopped candied orange peel, additional confectioners' sugar

1. Preheat oven to 350°. Grease and flour a 10-in. fluted tube pan.

2. In a large bowl, beat butter and sugar until crumbly, about 2 minutes. Add eggs, one at a time, beating well after each addition. Beat in orange zest and vanilla. In another bowl, whisk flour, baking powder and salt; add to the creamed mixture alternately with milk, beating well after each addition (the batter may appear curdled).
3. Transfer batter to prepared pan. Bake until a toothpick inserted in the center comes out clean, 45-50 minutes.
4. Poke holes in warm cake using a fork or wooden skewer. Mix confectioners' sugar, melted butter and orange juice; spoon slowly over cake. Cool for 15 minutes before removing from pan to a wire rack; cool completely. Serve topped with candied orange peel and sprinkle with additional confectioners' sugar.
NOTE: *To remove cakes easily, use solid shortening to grease plain and fluted tube pans.*
1 **SLICE:** *474 cal., 22g fat (13g sat. fat), 145mg chol., 341mg sod., 63g carb. (38g sugars, 1g fiber), 7g pro.*

SPARKLING CIDER SANGRIA

Adding orange and cranberry juices transforms apple cider into a holiday treat. This quick and easy alcohol-free beverage is absolutely delicious. A friend shared the recipe with me years ago; I made a few changes. It's a huge hit at holiday brunches.
—Joan Hallford, North Richland Hills, TX

PREP: 20 MIN. • **MAKES:** 8 SERVINGS

- 3 cups sparkling apple cider, chilled
- 1 cup unsweetened apple juice, chilled
- 1 cup orange juice, chilled
- 1 cup cranberry juice, chilled
- 1 small lemon, sliced
- 1 small navel orange, sliced
- 8 wooden skewers
- Assorted fresh fruit

In a large pitcher, combine sparking cider, juices, lemon slices and orange slices. Alternately thread fruit onto skewers. Serve in glasses with fruit skewers.

¾ CUP: *88 cal., 0 fat (0 sat. fat), 0 chol., 5mg sod., 22g carb. (20g sugars, 1g fiber), 1g pro.*

GRANDMA BRUBAKER'S ORANGE COOKIES

At least two generations of my family have enjoyed the recipe for these light, delicate, orange-flavored cookies.
—Sheri DeBolt, Huntington, IN

PREP: 20 MIN. • **BAKE:** 10 MIN./BATCH + COOLING
MAKES: 6 DOZEN

- 1 cup shortening
- 2 cups sugar
- 2 large eggs, room temperature, separated
- 1 cup buttermilk
- 5 cups all-purpose flour
- 2 tsp. baking powder
- 2 tsp. baking soda
- Pinch salt
- Juice and grated zest of 2 medium navel oranges

ICING
- 2 cups confectioners' sugar
- ¼ cup orange juice
- 1 Tbsp. butter
- 1 Tbsp. grated orange zest

1. Preheat oven to 325°. In a bowl, cream shortening and sugar. Beat in egg yolks and buttermilk. Sift together flour, baking powder, soda and salt; add to creamed mixture alternately with orange juice and zest. Add egg whites and beat until smooth.
2. Drop by rounded teaspoonfuls onto greased cookie sheets. Bake until set, about 10 minutes. Remove cookies to wire racks to cool completely.
3. For icing, combine all ingredients and beat until smooth. Frost cooled cookies.

1 COOKIE: *97 cal., 3g fat (1g sat. fat), 6mg chol., 58mg sod., 16g carb. (9g sugars, 0 fiber), 1g pro.*

Peppermint

The red-and-white striped, minty bite of peppermint is a perennial Christmas favorite!

PEPPERMINT CHOCOLATE ALMOND CRISPS

Peppermint, chocolate, lemon and almonds give these cookies a delightful holiday flavor. My husband's office staff love these cookies, and I make sure to send a plate every year.
—Jamie Seifert, Windermere, FL

PREP: 30 MIN. + STANDING
BAKE: 20 MIN. + COOLING
MAKES: 2 DOZEN

- 1 tube (16½ oz.) refrigerated sugar cookie dough
- ¼ cup all-purpose flour
- ¼ cup slivered almonds, coarsely chopped
- 1 Tbsp. grated lemon zest
- 1 tsp. peppermint extract
- 1 cup (6 oz.) semisweet chocolate chips
- 1 Tbsp. shortening
  Chopped candy canes and almond slivers, optional

1. Preheat oven to 325°. Place the cookie dough in a small bowl; let stand at room temperature 15-20 minutes to soften. Add the flour, almonds, zest and extract; beat until blended.
2. Divide dough in half. On a parchment-lined baking sheet, shape each portion into a 12x2-in. rectangle. Bake until golden brown and crisp, 20-25 minutes. Cool on pan 2 minutes. Remove to a wire rack to cool completely.
3. Transfer baked rectangles to a cutting board. Using a serrated knife, cut into 1-in. slices.
4. In a microwave-safe bowl, melt the chocolate chips and shortening; stir until smooth. Dip 1 end of each cookie into melted chocolate, allowing excess to drip off. If desired, sprinkle with candy cane pieces and almond slivers. Place on waxed paper; let stand until set. Store cookies between pieces of waxed paper in an airtight container.
1 COOKIE: *135 cal., 7g fat (2g sat. fat), 2mg chol., 65mg sod., 18g carb. (11g sugars, 1g fiber), 1g pro.*

CHOCOLATE CANDY CANE MARTINIS

A peppermint martini is perfect for a fun Christmas-time gathering of friends. Crushed candy canes on the rim add festive flair.
—Crystal Schlueter, Babbitt, MN

TAKES: 20 MIN. • **MAKES:** 12 SERVINGS

- 3 cups half-and-half cream
- 12 oz. cake-flavored vodka
- 12 oz. white chocolate liqueur
- 6 oz. cream cheese, softened
- ½ cup confectioners' sugar
- 2 cups heavy whipping cream
- 6 candy canes (regular size), finely crushed
- ¾ cup white baking chips
- 1½ tsp. shortening

1. In a pitcher, combine cream, vodka and liqueur. Refrigerate until serving.
2. In a large bowl, beat cream cheese and confectioners' sugar until smooth.

Gradually beat in cream until stiff peaks form. Fold in 3 Tbsp. of crushed candies; pour remaining candies onto a small plate. Refrigerate whipped cream mixture until serving.
3. In a microwave-safe bowl, melt chips and shortening; stir until smooth. Spread onto a small plate. Spin rims of 12 cocktail glasses into the melted chip mixture, then into the crushed candies. Pour the vodka mixture into the prepared glasses; dollop with whipped cream mixture. If desired, garnish with additional candy canes.
1 SERVING: *673 cal., 29g fat (18g sat. fat), 92mg chol., 104mg sod., 53g carb. (21g sugars, 0 fiber), 5g pro.*

Holiday Helper
White chocolate liqueur keeps things snowy-white, but you can use chocolate liqueur, too. If you want more minty flavor, add a splash of peppermint schnapps to the drink mixture.

SHORTCUT PEPPERMINT LAYER CAKE

When I first made this cake it was snowing outside, the entire family was home, and we enjoyed it all together. A perfectly pretty holiday cake for a perfect holiday moment! Be sure to measure the peppermint extract carefully—it's strong and a little bit goes a very long way.
—Mindie Hilton, Susanville, CA

PREP: 40 MIN. • **BAKE:** 15 MIN. + COOLING
MAKES: 12 SERVINGS

- 1 pkg. white cake mix (regular size)
- 2 Tbsp. baking cocoa, divided
- ¼ tsp. plus ⅛ tsp. peppermint extract, divided
- 1 tsp. red food coloring, optional, divided
- 2 cans (14 oz. each) whipped vanilla frosting, divided
- ¼ cup peppermint crunch baking chips

1. Preheat oven to 350°. Line bottoms of three greased 8-in. round baking pans with parchment; grease paper.
2. Prepare cake mix batter according to package directions. Remove 1⅓ cups of the batter to a small bowl; stir in 1 Tbsp. cocoa, ¼ tsp. extract and if desired, ½ tsp. food coloring until blended.
3. Transfer plain batter to prepared pans. Top with red batter. Cut through batter with a knife to swirl. Bake until a toothpick inserted in the center comes out clean, 15-18 minutes. Cool in pans 10 minutes before removing to wire racks; remove paper. Cool completely.
4. Mix 1 cup frosting with the remaining 1 Tbsp. cocoa, ⅛ tsp. of extract and, if desired, ½ tsp. food coloring. Place 1 cake layer on a serving plate; spread with 1 cup plain frosting. Repeat layers. Top with the remaining cake layer. Frost the sides of the cake with the remaining plain frosting. Spread red frosting over top of the cake. Gently press baking chips into frosting on the top of the cake. Refrigerate leftovers.
1 SLICE: *506 cal., 23g fat (7g sat. fat), 0 chol., 357mg sod., 76g carb. (57g sugars, 1g fiber), 3g pro.*

MINI PEPPERMINT COFFEE CAKES

I like these cute little muffins because they're easy to prepare and are wonderful as little snacks or gifts during the holidays. They're a little different from your typical Christmas cookie. And they're great for a festive breakfast, too.
—Ethel Lambert, Baltimore, MD

PREP: 30 MIN. • **BAKE:** 15 MIN. + COOLING
MAKES: 20 SERVINGS

- 1 pkg. funfetti cake mix (regular size)
- ½ cup water
- ½ cup sour cream
- ⅓ cup butter, melted
- 3 large eggs, room temperature
- ½ cup crushed peppermint candies
- ½ cup sugar
- ½ cup pecan halves, finely chopped
- 1 tsp. ground cinnamon

1. Preheat oven to 350°. Line 20 muffin cups with paper liners. In a large bowl, combine the cake mix, water, sour cream, butter and eggs; beat on low speed for 30 seconds. Beat on medium 2 minutes. Stir in peppermint candies. Fill prepared cups three-fourths full. In a small bowl, combine sugar, pecans and cinnamon; sprinkle over tops.
2. Bake until a toothpick inserted in center comes out clean, 15-18 minutes. Cool in pans for 10 minutes before removing to wire racks to cool completely.
1 MINI COFFEE CAKE: *183 cal., 8g fat (4g sat. fat), 37mg chol., 212mg sod., 27g carb. (17g sugars, 1g fiber), 2g pro.*

PERFECT PEPPERMINT PATTIES

I make lots of different candy at Christmas to give as gifts. It can be time consuming, but it's worth it to see the delight it brings to people. Calling for just a few ingredients, this is one candy that's simple to prepare.
—Joanne Adams, Bath, ME

PREP: 20 MIN. + CHILLING • **MAKES:** 5 DOZEN

- 3¾ cups confectioners' sugar
- 3 Tbsp. butter, softened
- 2 to 3 tsp. peppermint extract
- ½ tsp. vanilla extract
- ¼ cup evaporated milk
- 2 cups (12 oz.) semisweet chocolate chips
- 2 Tbsp. shortening

1. In a large bowl, combine the first 4 ingredients. Add milk and mix well. Roll into 1-in. balls and place on a waxed paper-lined baking sheet. Flatten each with a glass into a ¼-in. patty. Cover and freeze for 30 minutes.

2. Microwave the chocolate chips and shortening on high until melted; stir until smooth. Dip patties in the chocolate, allowing the excess to drip off. Place on waxed paper; let stand until set.

1 PATTY: *67 cal., 3g fat (1g sat. fat), 2mg chol., 7mg sod., 11g carb. (10g sugars, 0 fiber), 0 pro.*

CREAMY COCONUT PEPPERMINT PIE

Garnished with toasted coconut and more peppermint candy, this creamy dessert welcomes the holidays! Look for premade shortbread crusts in the baking aisle of the grocery store.
—Cheryl Perry, Hertford, NC

PREP: 15 MIN. + CHILLING • **MAKES:** 8 SERVINGS

- 1 envelope unflavored gelatin
- ½ cup coconut milk
- 2½ cups peppermint ice cream, melted
- ¼ cup crushed peppermint candies, divided
- ¼ tsp. coconut extract
- 1 cup flaked coconut, toasted, divided
- 1 shortbread crust (9 in.)

1. In a large microwave-safe bowl, sprinkle gelatin over coconut milk; let stand 1 minute. Microwave on high for 30-40 seconds. Stir until the gelatin is completely dissolved, about 1 minute.

2. Stir ice cream, 2 Tbsp. crushed candies and the extract into the gelatin mixture; fold in ½ cup coconut. Pour into the crust. Sprinkle with the remaining coconut. Refrigerate the pie for at least 2 hours.

3. Just before serving, top with remaining crushed candies.

1 SLICE: *281 cal., 15g fat (10g sat. fat), 18mg chol., 165mg sod., 33g carb. (22g sugars, 1g fiber), 4g pro.*

Ginger

The intoxicating aroma, the tongue-teasing flavor—it isn't quite the holidays without this beloved spice!

GINGERBREAD CINNAMON ROLLS WITH SPICED FROSTING

These cinnamon rolls are sure to please anyone who has a sweet tooth. They're just the thing for a Christmas morning treat. Be sure to eat them while they're still warm—they're best that way. The dough for these rolls is sticky, so don't worry if your fingers get messy.
—Andrea Price, Grafton, WI

PREP: 30 MIN. + RISING • **BAKE:** 25 MIN.
MAKES: 1 DOZEN

- 1 pkg. (¼ oz.) active dry yeast
- ½ cup warm 2% milk (110° to 115°)
- ¼ cup warm water (110° to 115°)
- ⅓ cup molasses
- ¼ cup packed brown sugar
- 1 large egg, room temperature
- 2 Tbsp. canola oil
- ½ tsp. salt
- 3½ to 4 cups all-purpose flour

FILLING
- ¼ cup packed brown sugar
- 2 Tbsp. sugar
- 1 tsp. ground cinnamon
- ½ tsp. ground ginger
- ¼ tsp. ground cloves
- 2 Tbsp. butter, softened

SPICED GLAZE
- 1½ cups confectioners' sugar
- ½ tsp. ground cinnamon
- ½ tsp. vanilla extract
- 6 to 7 tsp. 2% milk

1. In a small bowl, dissolve yeast in warm milk and water. In a large bowl, combine molasses, brown sugar, egg, oil, salt, the yeast mixture and 1½ cups flour; beat on medium speed until smooth. Stir in enough of the remaining flour to form a soft, sticky dough.
2. Turn dough onto a floured surface; knead 6-8 minutes (dough will remain sticky and will not be smooth). Place in a greased bowl, turning once to grease the top. Cover and let rise in a warm place until doubled, about 1 hour.
3. For filling, mix sugars and spices. Punch down dough. Turn onto a lightly floured surface. Press the dough into a 12x8-in. rectangle. Brush with butter to within ½ in. of edges; sprinkle with the sugar mixture. Roll up jelly-roll style, starting with a long side; pinch seam to seal. Cut into 12 slices.
4. Place in a greased 13x9-in. baking pan, cut side down. Cover; let rise in a warm place until almost doubled, about 1 hour.
5. Preheat oven to 350°. Bake until golden brown, 20-25 minutes. In a small bowl, mix confectioners' sugar, cinnamon, vanilla and enough of the milk to reach desired consistency; spread over warm rolls.

1 ROLL: *315 cal., 5g fat (2g sat. fat), 22mg chol., 133mg sod., 62g carb. (33g sugars, 2g fiber), 5g pro.*

HOT GINGER COFFEE

This warm winter drink is wonderful after shoveling, skiing or sledding!
—Audrey Thibodeau, Gilbert, AZ

TAKES: 25 MIN. • **MAKES:** 6 SERVINGS

- 6 Tbsp. ground coffee (not instant)
- 1 Tbsp. grated orange zest
- 1 Tbsp. chopped crystallized ginger
- ½ tsp. ground cinnamon
- 6 cups cold water
  Whipped cream, cinnamon sticks and/or additional orange zest, optional

Combine coffee, orange zest, ginger and cinnamon; pour into a coffee filter. Brew according to manufacturer's directions. Pour into mugs; if desired, garnish with whipped cream, cinnamon sticks and orange zest.

1 CUP: *22 cal., 0 fat (0 sat. fat), 0 chol., 3mg sod., 5g carb. (2g sugars, 0 fiber), 1g pro.*

creamed mixture alternately with milk, beating well after each addition (batter may appear curdled).

3. Transfer batter to the prepared pan. Bake until a toothpick inserted in center comes out clean, 50-55 minutes. Cool in pan for 10 minutes before removing to a wire rack; remove paper. Cool completely. If desired, serve with whipped cream and additional maple syrup.

1 SLICE: *368 cal., 14g fat (8g sat. fat), 68mg chol., 224mg sod., 57g carb. (38g sugars, 1g fiber), 6g pro.*

SPICED WALNUTS

I pick my walnuts from a local tree, clean them and crack them myself—this recipe is worthy of my hard-won walnuts! The rich, buttery taste will fool you, as there's not a drop of butter in them. Not overly sweet, the nuts get nice and crispy from the egg bath. They work well as an appetizer and are an always-welcome hostess gift. They also freeze well, so you can enjoy them any time of year.
—Sherri Starkin, Lyle, WA

PREP: 15 MIN. • **BAKE:** 45 MIN. + COOLING
MAKES: 5 CUPS

1	**large egg white**
1	**Tbsp. water**
1	**pkg. (16 oz.) walnut halves**
⅔	**cup sugar**
2	**tsp. ground cinnamon**
1	**tsp. salt**
¾	**tsp. ground ginger**
¾	**tsp. ground allspice**
½	**tsp. ground coriander**

1. Preheat oven to 275°. In a bowl, beat egg white and water until foamy. Add walnuts. In a large bowl, combine the remaining ingredients. Add the nut mixture; toss to coat.

2. Transfer to greased baking sheets. Bake until toasted and crisp, 45-50 minutes, stirring every 15 minutes. Cool on a wire rack. Store spiced nuts in an airtight container.

⅓ CUP: *235 cal., 20g fat (2g sat. fat), 0 chol., 162mg sod., 14g carb. (10g sugars, 2g fiber), 5g pro.*

GINGER SPICE CAKE

I make this spice cake every year during the holidays. It has such lovely rich ginger flavor and dense texture, you can simply dust it with confectioner's sugar and call it done. To make it extra-special, top it with some fresh whipped cream and a drizzle of real maple syrup.
—Christine Campbell, Manitowoc, WI

PREP: 25 MIN. • **BAKE:** 50 MIN. + COOLING
MAKES: 12 SERVINGS

10	**Tbsp. butter, softened**
1	**cup maple syrup**
3	**Tbsp. brown sugar**
2	**large eggs, room temperature**
2	**cups all-purpose flour**
2	**Tbsp. ground ginger**
2	**Tbsp. ground cinnamon**
1	**tsp. baking powder**
½	**tsp. ground allspice**
½	**tsp. ground nutmeg**
¼	**tsp. salt**
1	**can (14 oz.) sweetened condensed milk**
	Whipped cream and additional maple syrup, optional

1. Preheat oven to 350°. Line the bottom of a greased 9-in. round baking pan with parchment; grease paper.

2. In a large bowl, beat butter, maple syrup and brown sugar until blended. Add the eggs, one at a time, beating well after each addition. In another bowl, whisk the flour, ginger, cinnamon, baking powder, allspice, nutmeg and salt; add dry mixture to the

OLD-FASHIONED GINGERBREAD

My dad would always tell me his mother made gingerbread with hot water and that it was dense and rich with molasses. Over the years I looked for such a recipe, to no avail. Then one day I was given a book compiled by an elderly woman who recalled recipes from her childhood in Virginia, and there it was! I made one slight change, substituting shortening for lard. For gingerbread lovers, this classic version is wonderful, whether you eat it hot and dripping with butter or at room temperature.
— CJWKAT from tasteofhome.com

PREP: 25 MIN. • **BAKE:** 35 MIN. + COOLING • **MAKES:** 9 SERVINGS

½   cup butter, cubed
¼   cup shortening, cubed
1   cup boiling water
2   large eggs, room temperature
1½   cups molasses
2   cups all-purpose flour
1   Tbsp. ground ginger
2   tsp. baking powder
1   tsp. ground cinnamon
½   tsp. salt
¼   tsp. baking soda
    Confectioners' sugar, optional

1. Preheat oven to 350°. Grease a 9-in. square baking pan; set aside. In a large bowl, mix butter, shortening and boiling water until smooth; cool slightly. Beat in eggs and molasses until well blended. In another bowl, whisk flour, ginger, baking powder, cinnamon, salt and baking soda; gradually beat into molasses mixture. Transfer to prepared pan.
2. Bake until a toothpick inserted in center comes out clean, 35-40 minutes. Cool completely on wire rack. If desired, sprinkle with confectioners' sugar before serving.
1 PIECE: *414 cal., 17g fat (8g sat. fat), 68mg chol., 390mg sod., 62g carb. (40g sugars, 1g fiber), 4g pro.*

GINGER CRINKLES

I came up with these cookies by combining ingredients from two different recipes. They're the perfect ginger cookie—crispy on the outside and chewy in the middle. I send them to my son and he shares them with his employees. Whenever I ask what kind of cookies to send, these are at the very top of the list.
—Judy Wilson, Sun City West, AZ

PREP: 25 MIN. + CHILLING • **BAKE:** 10 MIN./BATCH
MAKES: 2½ DOZEN

¾   cup butter-flavored shortening
1½   cups sugar, divided
1   large egg, room temperature
¼   cup molasses
2   cups all-purpose flour
2   tsp. baking soda
1½   tsp. ground ginger
1   tsp. ground cinnamon
½   tsp. salt
½   tsp. ground cloves

1. In a large bowl, cream shortening and 1 cup sugar until light and fluffy. Beat in egg and molasses. In another bowl, whisk flour, baking soda, ginger, cinnamon, salt and cloves; gradually beat into creamed mixture. Refrigerate, covered, until firm, about 1 hour.
2. Preheat oven to 350°. Place the remaining ½ cup sugar in a shallow bowl. Shape dough into 1-in. balls; roll in sugar. Place 2 in. apart on parchment-lined baking sheets.
3. Bake until set and tops are cracked, 10-12 minutes. Cool on pans for 2 minutes. Remove to wire racks to cool completely.
1 COOKIE: *118 cal., 5g fat (1g sat. fat), 6mg chol., 127mg sod., 17g carb. (10g sugars, 0 fiber), 1g pro.*

CHRISTMAS FAST & SLOW

Perfect for the busy holiday season, these satisfying dishes can be prepped and cooked to suit your schedule. They all can be made either in an electric pressure cooker or a slow cooker—instructions are given for both!

CARIBBEAN CHIPOTLE PORK SLIDERS

One of our favorite pulled pork recipes combines the heat of chipotle peppers with cool tropical coleslaw. The robust flavors make these sliders a big hit with guests.
—Kadija Bridgewater, Boca Raton, FL

PREP: 35 MIN. • **COOK:** 75 MIN. + RELEASING
MAKES: 20 SERVINGS

1 large onion, quartered
1 (3 to 4 lb.) boneless pork shoulder butt roast
2 chipotle peppers in adobo sauce, finely chopped
3 Tbsp. adobo sauce
¾ cup honey barbecue sauce
¼ cup water
4 garlic cloves, minced
1 Tbsp. ground cumin
1 tsp. salt
¼ tsp. pepper

COLESLAW
2 cups red cabbage, finely chopped
1 medium mango, peeled and chopped
1 cup pineapple tidbits, drained
¾ cup chopped fresh cilantro
1 Tbsp. lime juice
¼ tsp. salt
⅛ tsp. pepper
20 Hawaiian sweet rolls, split and toasted

1. Place onion in a 6-qt. electric pressure cooker. Cut roast in half; place over onion. In a small bowl, combine chipotle peppers, adobo sauce, barbecue sauce, water, garlic, cumin, salt and pepper; pour over meat. Lock lid; close pressure-release valve. Adjust to pressure-cook on high for 75 minutes. Allow pressure to naturally release for 10 minutes, then quick-release any remaining pressure.
2. Remove roast; cool slightly. Skim fat from cooking juices. If desired, press cancel, then select saute setting and adjust for low heat; simmer, stirring constantly, until the juices are slightly thickened. Press cancel.
3. Shred pork with 2 forks. Return pork to pressure cooker; stir to heat through.
4. For coleslaw, in a large bowl, combine cabbage, mango, pineapple, cilantro, lime juice, salt and pepper. Place ¼ cup pork mixture on each roll bottom; top with 2 Tbsp. coleslaw. Replace tops.
1 SANDWICH: *265 cal., 10g fat (4g sat. fat), 55mg chol., 430mg sod., 27g carb. (15g sugars, 2g fiber), 16g pro.*

COOK IT SLOW
PREP: 35 MIN. • **COOK:** 8 HOURS

Place onion in a 5-qt. slow cooker. Cut roast in half; place over onion. In a small bowl, combine chipotle peppers, adobo sauce, barbecue sauce, water, garlic, cumin, salt and pepper; pour over the meat. Cook, covered, on low for 8-10 hours or until the meat is tender. Follow directions in Steps 2, 3 and 4 to shred pork and make coleslaw.

APPLE BALSAMIC CHICKEN

I love the sweet and tart flavor that balsamic vinegar gives this dish. It's easy to prepare and the chicken is tender and flavorful.
—Juli Snaer, Enid, OK

PREP: 15 MIN. • **COOK:** 15 MIN. + RELEASING
MAKES: 4 SERVINGS

- ½   cup chicken broth
- ¼   cup apple cider or juice
- ¼   cup balsamic vinegar
- 2   Tbsp. lemon juice
- ½   tsp. salt
- ½   tsp. garlic powder
- ½   tsp. dried thyme
- ½   tsp. paprika
- ½   tsp. pepper
- 4   bone-in chicken thighs (about 1½ lbs.), skin removed
- 2   Tbsp. butter
- 2   Tbsp. all-purpose flour

1. Combine the first 9 ingredients. Place chicken in a 6-qt. electric pressure cooker; pour broth mixture over the meat. Lock lid; close pressure-release valve. Adjust to pressure-cook on high for 10 minutes. Allow pressure to naturally release for 10 minutes, then quick-release any remaining pressure.

2. Remove chicken; keep warm. Skim fat from cooking liquid. In a small saucepan, melt butter; whisk in flour until smooth. Gradually add cooking liquid. Cook and stir until sauce is thickened, 2-3 minutes. Serve with chicken.

1 CHICKEN THIGH WITH ⅓ CUP SAUCE: *277 cal., 15g fat (6g sat. fat), 103mg chol., 536mg sod., 9g carb. (4g sugars, 0 fiber), 25g pro.*

> ### COOK IT SLOW
> **PREP:** 15 MIN. • **COOK:** 4 HOURS
>
> Place chicken in a 1½-qt. slow cooker. Combine broth ingredients and pour over meat. Cover and cook on low for 4-5 hours or until chicken is tender. Make sauce as directed in Step 2.

LENTIL PUMPKIN SOUP

Plenty of herbs and spices brighten up my hearty pumpkin soup. It's just the thing we need on nippy days and nights.
—Laura Magee, Houlton, WI

TAKES: 25 MIN.
MAKES: 6 SERVINGS (2¼ QT.)

- 1   lb. medium red potatoes (about 4 medium), cut into ½-in. pieces
- 1   can (15 oz.) canned pumpkin
- 1   cup dried lentils, rinsed
- 1   medium onion, chopped
- 3   garlic cloves, minced
- ½   tsp. ground ginger
- ½   tsp. pepper
- ⅛   tsp. salt
- 2   cans (14½ oz. each) vegetable broth
- 1½ cups water
      Minced fresh cilantro, optional

In a 6-qt. electric pressure cooker, combine the first 10 ingredients. Lock the lid; close pressure-release valve. Adjust to pressure-cook on high for 12 minutes. Quick-release pressure. If desired, sprinkle servings with cilantro.

1½ CUPS: *210 cal., 1g fat (0 sat. fat), 0 chol., 463mg sod., 42g carb. (5g sugars, 7g fiber), 11g pro.*
DIABETIC EXCHANGES: *3 starch, 1 lean meat.*

> ### COOK IT SLOW
> **PREP:** 15 MIN. • **COOK:** 7 HOURS
>
> In a 3- or 4-qt. slow cooker, combine all ingredients except cilantro. Cook, covered, on low for 7-9 hours or until potatoes and lentils are tender. Top with cilantro if desired.

BEEF OSSO BUCCO

Our beef osso bucco boasts a thick, savory sauce complemented by the addition of gremolata, a chopped herb condiment made of lemon zest, garlic and parsley.
—Taste of Home *Test Kitchen*

PREP: 45 MIN.
COOK: 40 MIN./BATCH + RELEASING
MAKES: 6 SERVINGS

- ½ cup all-purpose flour
- ¾ tsp. salt, divided
- ½ tsp. pepper
- 6 beef shanks (14 oz. each)
- 2 Tbsp. butter
- 1 Tbsp. olive oil
- ½ cup white wine or beef broth
- 1 can (14½ oz.) diced tomatoes, undrained
- 1½ cups beef broth
- 2 medium carrots, chopped
- 1 medium onion, chopped
- 1 celery rib, sliced
- 1 tsp. dried thyme
- 1 tsp. dried oregano
- 2 bay leaves
- 2 Tbsp. cornstarch
- ¼ cup cold water

GREMOLATA
- ⅓ cup minced fresh parsley
- 1 Tbsp. grated lemon zest
- 1 Tbsp. grated orange zest
- 2 garlic cloves, minced
  Polenta, optional

1. In a large shallow dish, combine flour, ½ tsp. salt and pepper. Pat beef dry with paper towels. Add beef to dish, 1 piece at a time; turn to coat.

2. Select saute setting on a 6-qt. electric pressure cooker and adjust for medium heat. Add 1 Tbsp. butter and 1½ tsp. oil; brown 3 beef shanks. Remove from pressure cooker; repeat with remaining butter, oil and beef shanks. Add ¼ cup wine, stirring to loosen browned bits. Press cancel. In a large bowl, combine the tomatoes, broth, vegetables, seasonings and remaining salt. Return browned beef shanks to cooker; pour in half of the tomato mixture.

3. Lock lid; close pressure-release valve. Adjust to pressure-cook on high for 40 minutes. Allow pressure to naturally release for 10 minutes, then quick-release

any remaining pressure. Remove meat and vegetables from pressure cooker; keep warm. Make second batch with remaining ingredients, repeating the previous procedure. Press cancel.

4. After removing all meat and vegetables, discard bay leaves. Skim fat from cooking juices. Select saute setting and adjust for medium heat. Bring to a boil. In a bowl, mix cornstarch and water until smooth; stir into juices. Return to a boil, stirring constantly; cook and stir until thickened, about 2 minutes. Press cancel.

5. In a small bowl, combine gremolata ingredients. Serve beef with gremolata and sauce. If desired, serve over polenta.

1 SHANK WITH 1 CUP SAUCE AND 4 TSP. GREMOLATA: *398 cal., 15g fat (6g sat. fat), 112mg chol., 640mg sod., 17g carb. (5g sugars, 4g fiber), 47g pro.*

COOK IT SLOW

PREP: 30 MIN. • **COOK:** 7 HOURS

Coat beef as directed. Brown in a large skillet, in batches if needed, then transfer meat and drippings to a 6-qt. slow cooker. Add wine to skillet, stirring to loosen browned bits from pan; pour over meat. Add tomatoes, broth, carrots, onion, celery, thyme, oregano, bay leaves and remaining salt. Cover and cook on low for 7-9 hours or until meat is tender. Discard bay leaves. Make the sauce in a saucepan following the directions in Step 4; make gremolata as directed in Step 5.

CRANBERRY-MUSTARD PORK LOIN

This dressed-up pork loin is a family favorite because it's so tasty, and a favorite of mine because it's so fast and easy!
—Laura Cook, Wildwood, MO

PREP: 15 MIN. • **COOK:** 30 MIN. + RELEASING
MAKES: 8 SERVINGS

- 1 boneless pork loin roast (2 lbs.)
- 1 can (14 oz.) whole-berry cranberry sauce
- ¼ cup Dijon mustard
- 3 Tbsp. packed brown sugar
- 3 Tbsp. lemon juice
- 1 Tbsp. cornstarch
- ¼ cup cold water

1. Place roast in a 6-qt. electric pressure cooker. Combine cranberry sauce, mustard, brown sugar and lemon juice; pour over roast. Lock lid; close pressure-release valve. Adjust to pressure-cook on high for 25 minutes. Allow pressure to naturally release for 10 minutes, then quick-release any remaining pressure. Remove roast; keep warm. Press cancel.
2. Strain cooking juices into a 2-cup measuring cup; add enough water to measure 2 cups. Return juices to the pressure cooker. Select saute setting and adjust for medium heat; bring liquid to a boil. In a small bowl, mix cornstarch and water until smooth; gradually stir into cooking juices. Cook and stir until sauce is thickened, 1-2 minutes. Press cancel. Serve sauce with pork.

3 OZ. COOKED PORK: *255 cal., 6g fat (2g sat. fat), 56mg chol., 236mg sod., 28g carb. (19g sugars, 1g fiber), 22g pro.*

COOK IT SLOW
PREP: 15 MIN. • **COOK:** 4 HOURS

Place roast in a 3-qt. slow cooker. Combine the cranberry sauce, mustard, brown sugar and lemon juice; pour over roast. Cover and cook on low for 4-5 hours or until the meat is tender. Remove roast and keep warm. Make sauce in a saucepan following directions in Step 2.

BEEF BRISKET IN BEER

One bite of this super tender brisket and your family will be hooked! The rich gravy is perfect for spooning over a side of creamy mashed potatoes.
—Eunice Stoen, Decorah, IA

PREP: 15 MIN. • **COOK:** 70 MIN. + RELEASING
MAKES: 6 SERVINGS

- 1   fresh beef brisket (2½ to 3 lbs.)
- 2   tsp. liquid smoke, optional
- 1   tsp. celery salt
- ½   tsp. pepper
- ¼   tsp. salt
- 1   large onion, sliced
- 1   can (12 oz.) beer or nonalcoholic beer
- 2   tsp. Worcestershire sauce
- 2   Tbsp. cornstarch
- ¼   cup cold water

1. Cut brisket in half; rub with liquid smoke if desired, celery salt, pepper and salt. Place the brisket fatty side up in a 6-qt. electric pressure cooker. Top with onion. Combine beer and Worcestershire sauce; pour over meat. Lock lid; close pressure-release valve. Adjust to pressure-cook on high for 70 minutes. Allow pressure to naturally release for 10 minutes, then quick-release any remaining pressure. If the brisket isn't fork-tender, reseal cooker and cook for an additional 10-15 minutes. Press cancel.

2. Remove the brisket; cover with foil and keep warm. Strain cooking juices, then return juices to pressure cooker. Select saute setting and adjust for medium heat; bring to a boil. In a small bowl, mix cornstarch and water until smooth; gradually stir into juices. Cook and stir until thickened, about 2 minutes. Press cancel. Serve sauce with the beef.

NOTE: This is a fresh beef brisket, not corned beef.

5 OZ. COOKED BRISKET: 285 cal., 8g fat (3g sat. fat), 80mg chol., 430mg sod., 7g carb. (3g sugars, 0 fiber), 39g pro.
DIABETIC EXCHANGES: 5 lean meat, ½ starch.

COOK IT SLOW

PREP: 15 MIN. • **COOK:** 8 HOURS

Cut brisket and rub with seasonings as directed, then place in a 3-qt. slow cooker. Top with onion and beer mixture as directed. Cover and cook on low for 8-9 hours or until tender. After removing brisket from cooker, strain cooking juices and transfer to a small saucepan; follow directions in Step 2 to thicken.

Holiday Helper
Liquid smoke is a gratifying addition to this recipe as it adds depth of flavor. Be careful not to overdo it; a small amount goes a long way. Look for liquid smoke in the grocery store near the spices and marinades.

PROVENCAL HAM & BEAN SOUP

There is nothing quite like the wonderful aroma of this delicious soup bubbling away!
—Lyndsay Wells, Ladysmith, BC

PREP: 15 MIN. + SOAKING
COOK: 10 MIN. + RELEASING
MAKES: 10 SERVINGS (3½ QT.)

- 2 cups assorted dried beans for soup
- 1 can (28 oz.) whole plum tomatoes, undrained
- 2 cups cubed fully cooked ham
- 1 large Yukon Gold potato, peeled and chopped
- 1 medium onion, chopped
- 1 cup chopped carrot
- 1 celery rib, chopped
- 2 garlic cloves, minced
- 2 tsp. herbes de Provence
- 1½ tsp. salt
- 1 tsp. pepper
- 1 carton (32 oz.) unsalted chicken stock
  French bread

1. Rinse and sort beans; soak according to package directions. Drain and rinse beans, discarding liquid.
2. Transfer beans to a 6-qt. electric pressure cooker. Add tomatoes; crush with a wooden spoon until chunky. Stir in ham, vegetables, garlic, seasonings and stock. Lock lid; close pressure-release valve. Adjust to pressure-cook on high for 10 minutes. Allow pressure to naturally release for 10 minutes, then quick-release any remaining pressure. Serve with bread.
1⅓ CUPS: 212 cal., 2g fat (0 sat. fat), 17mg chol., 887mg sod., 33g carb. (5g sugars, 9g fiber), 17g pro.

> ### COOK IT SLOW
> **PREP:** 15 MIN. + SOAKING
> **COOK:** 7 HOURS
>
> Prepare beans as directed in Step 1; transfer to a 6-qt. slow cooker. Add remaining ingredients as directed in Step 2; cook, covered, on low for 7-9 hours or until beans are tender.

MEDITERRANEAN CHICKEN ORZO

Orzo pasta with chicken, olives and herbes de Provence has the bright flavors of Mediterranean cuisine. Here's a bonus: Leftovers reheat well.
—Thomas Faglon, Somerset, NJ

PREP: 15 MIN. • **COOK:** 15 MIN. + STANDING
MAKES: 6 SERVINGS

- 6 boneless skinless chicken thighs (about 1½ lbs.), cut into 1-in. pieces
- 2 cups reduced-sodium chicken broth
- 2 medium tomatoes, chopped
- 1 cup sliced pitted green olives, drained
- 1 cup sliced pitted ripe olives, drained
- 1 large carrot, halved lengthwise and chopped
- 1 small red onion, finely chopped
- 1 Tbsp. grated lemon zest
- 3 Tbsp. lemon juice
- 2 Tbsp. butter
- 1 Tbsp. herbes de Provence
- 1 cup uncooked orzo pasta

1. In a 6-qt. electric pressure cooker, combine the first 11 ingredients; stir to combine. Lock lid; close pressure-release valve. Adjust to pressure-cook on high for 8 minutes. Quick-release pressure.
2. Add orzo. Lock lid; close pressure-release valve. Adjust to pressure-cook on low for 3 minutes. Allow pressure to naturally release for 4 minutes, then quick-release any remaining pressure. Let stand 8-10 minutes before serving.
1⅓ CUPS: 415 cal., 19g fat (5g sat. fat), 86mg chol., 941mg sod., 33g carb. (4g sugars, 3g fiber), 27g pro.

> ### COOK IT SLOW
> **PREP:** 15 MIN. • **COOK:** 4 HOURS
>
> In a 3- or 4-qt. slow cooker, combine first 11 ingredients. Cook, covered, on low for 4-5 hours or until the chicken, pasta and vegetables are tender, adding orzo during the last 30 minutes of cooking.

1 Tbsp. sugar
½ tsp. salt
½ tsp. Italian seasoning
⅛ to ¼ tsp. cayenne pepper
1 bay leaf
1 cup uncooked orzo or other small pasta
1 lb. peeled and deveined cooked shrimp (31-40 per lb.)

1. Select saute setting on a 6-qt. electric pressure cooker and adjust for medium heat. Add 1 Tbsp. oil. When oil is hot, brown chicken in batches, adding oil as needed. Press cancel. Stir in next 11 ingredients. Lock lid; close pressure-release valve. Adjust to pressure-cook on high for 8 minutes. Quick-release pressure. Press cancel.

2. Discard bay leaf. Select saute setting and adjust for medium heat. Stir in orzo. Cook until al dente, stirring often. Stir in shrimp; cook until shrimp are heated through, about 2 minutes more. Press cancel.

1½ CUPS: 418 cal., 12g fat (2g sat. fat), 165mg chol., 611mg sod., 40g carb. (10g sugars, 4g fiber), 36g pro. DIABETIC EXCHANGES: 4 lean meat, 2 starch, 2 vegetable, 1 fat.

COOK IT SLOW
PREP: 20 MIN. • **COOK:** 7½ HOURS

Brown chicken in oil in a skillet, then transfer to a 3-qt. slow cooker. Stir in tomatoes, celery, green pepper, onion, garlic, sugar and seasonings. Eliminate the 1½ cups water. Cook, covered, on low for 7-8 hours or until the chicken is just tender. Discard bay leaf. Stir in pasta; cook, covered, on high 15 minutes or until the pasta is tender. Stir in shrimp; cook, covered, 5 minutes longer or until heated through.

ITALIAN SHRIMP & PASTA
This dish will remind you a bit of classic shrimp Creole, but it has a surprise Italian twist.
—Karen Edwards, Sanford, ME

PREP: 20 MIN. • **COOK:** 20 MIN.
MAKES: 6 SERVINGS

2 Tbsp. canola oil
4 boneless skinless chicken thighs (about 1 lb.), cut into 2x1-in. strips
1 can (28 oz.) crushed tomatoes
1½ cups water
2 celery ribs, chopped
1 medium green pepper, cut into 1-in. pieces
1 medium onion, coarsely chopped
2 garlic cloves, minced

 Holiday Helper
Orzo is rice-shaped pasta. You can find it in the pasta aisle of the grocery store.

CHICKEN MARBELLA

This sweet, briny, savory and herbal recipe packs a big punch of garlic. The Mediterranean flavors make me think of dinner on the patio with family or friends.
—Beth Jacobson, Milwaukee, WI

PREP: 30 MIN. • **COOK:** 10 MIN. + RELEASING
MAKES: 6 SERVINGS

1 cup reduced-sodium chicken broth (¼ cup for slow-cooked method)
1 cup pitted green olives, divided
1 cup pitted dried plums, divided
2 Tbsp. dried oregano
2 Tbsp. packed brown sugar
2 Tbsp. capers, drained
2 Tbsp. olive oil
4 garlic cloves, minced
½ tsp. salt
½ tsp. pepper
6 bone-in chicken thighs, skin removed (about 2 lbs.)
1 Tbsp. minced fresh parsley
1 Tbsp. white wine
1 Tbsp. lemon juice
Hot cooked couscous

1. Place broth, ½ cup olives, ½ cup dried plums, oregano, brown sugar, capers, oil, garlic, salt and pepper in a food processor; process until smooth. Transfer mixture to a 6-qt. electric pressure cooker. Place chicken in pressure cooker. Lock lid; close pressure-release valve. Adjust to pressure-cook on high for 10 minutes. Allow pressure to naturally release for 10 minutes, then quick-release any remaining pressure.
2. Chop remaining olives and dried plums. Remove chicken; keep warm. Stir parsley, wine, lemon juice, and remaining olives and plums into olive mixture. Serve with chicken and couscous.

1 SERVING: *352 cal., 17g fat (3g sat. fat), 77mg chol., 908mg sod., 26g carb. (13g sugars, 2g fiber), 23g pro.*

COOK IT SLOW
PREP: 30 MIN. • **COOK:** 4 HOURS

1. Place ½ cup olives, ½ cup dried plums, oregano, brown sugar, capers, oil, garlic, salt and pepper in a food processor; process until smooth. Transfer mixture to a 4-qt. slow cooker. Place chicken in slow cooker. Cook, covered, on low for 4-5 hours or until chicken is tender.
2. Chop remaining olives and dried plums. Remove chicken from slow cooker; keep warm. Stir ¼ cup chicken broth, the parsley, wine, lemon juice, and remaining olives and plums into olive mixture. Serve with chicken and couscous.

1 SERVING: *372 cal., 18g fat (3g sat. fat), 87mg chol., 845mg sod., 26g carb. (13g sugars, 2g fiber), 25g pro.*

WHITE BEAN CHICKEN CHILI

My sister shared this chili recipe with me. The jalapeno adds just enough heat to notice but not too much for my children.
—Kristine Bowles, Rio Rancho, NM

- ¾ lb. boneless skinless chicken breasts, cut into 1¼-in. pieces
- ¼ tsp. salt
- ¼ tsp. pepper
- 2 Tbsp. olive oil, divided
- 1 medium onion, chopped
- 1 jalapeno pepper, seeded and chopped
- 4 garlic cloves, minced
- 2 tsp. dried oregano
- 1 tsp. ground cumin
- 2 cans (15 oz. each) cannellini beans, rinsed and drained, divided
- 2½ cups chicken broth, divided
- 1½ cups shredded cheddar cheese
  Optional toppings: sliced avocado, quartered cherry tomatoes and chopped fresh cilantro

PREP: 25 MIN. • **COOK:** 20 MIN.
MAKES: 6 SERVINGS (1½ QT.)

1. Toss chicken with salt and pepper. Select saute setting on a 6-qt. electric pressure cooker and adjust for medium heat. Heat 1 Tbsp. olive oil. Add chicken; brown on all sides. Remove chicken.

2. Add the remaining oil to the pressure cooker. Saute onion until tender. Add jalapeno, garlic, oregano and cumin; cook and stir 2 minutes. Press cancel. Return chicken to pressure cooker.

3. In a bowl, mash 1 cup beans; stir in ½ cup broth. Stir bean mixture and remaining whole beans and broth into the chicken mixture.

4. Lock lid; close pressure-release valve. Adjust to pressure-cook on high for 10 minutes. Quick-release pressure. Stir chili before serving. Sprinkle with cheese; add toppings if desired.

FREEZE OPTION: Freeze cooled chili in freezer containers. To use, partially thaw in refrigerator overnight. Heat through in a saucepan; stir occasionally and add a little broth or water if necessary.

NOTE: Wear disposable gloves when cutting hot peppers; the oils can burn skin. Avoid touching your face.

1 CUP: 344 cal., 16g fat (6g sat. fat), 62mg chol., 894mg sod., 23g carb. (1g sugars, 6g fiber), 25g pro.

COOK IT SLOW
PREP: 25 MIN. • **COOK:** 3 HOURS

Use a skillet to brown the seasoned chicken as directed in Step 1 and to saute the vegetable mixture as directed in Step 2. Transfer chicken to a 3-qt. slow cooker; top with vegetable mixture. Follow Step 3 as directed. Cook, covered, on low until chicken is tender, 3-3½ hours. Stir before serving. Sprinkle with cheese; add toppings if desired.

Holiday Helper
Reserve the drained bean liquid—it's a perfect thinner for chili, and it won't water down the dish.

CHAR SIU PORK

I based this juicy pork on the Asian influence here in Hawaii. It's tasty as it is, in a bun or over rice, with fried rice, ramen and salads.
—Karen Naihe, Kamuela, HI

- ½ cup honey
- ½ cup hoisin sauce
- ¼ cup soy sauce
- ¼ cup ketchup
- 4 garlic cloves, minced
- 4 tsp. minced fresh gingerroot
- 1 tsp. Chinese five-spice powder
- 1 boneless pork shoulder butt roast (3 to 4 lbs.)
- ½ cup chicken broth
  Fresh cilantro leaves

PREP: 25 MIN. + MARINATING
COOK: 1¼ HOURS + RELEASING
MAKES: 8 SERVINGS

1. Combine the first 7 ingredients; pour into a large resealable plastic bag. Cut roast in half; add to bag and turn to coat. Refrigerate overnight.
2. Transfer pork and marinade to a 6-qt. electric pressure cooker. Add chicken broth. Lock lid; close pressure-release valve. Adjust to pressure-cook on high for 75 minutes. Allow pressure to naturally release for 10 minutes, then quick-release any remaining pressure. Press cancel.
3. Remove pork; when cool enough to handle, shred meat using 2 forks. Skim fat from cooking juices. Return pork to pressure cooker. Select saute setting and adjust for low heat; heat through. Press cancel. Top pork with fresh cilantro.
4 OZ. COOKED PORK: *392 cal., 18g fat (6g sat. fat), 102mg chol., 981mg sod., 27g carb. (24g sugars, 1g fiber), 31g pro.*

COOK IT SLOW
PREP: 25 MIN. + MARINATING
COOK: 5 HOURS

Marinate pork as directed in Step 1, then transfer meat and marinade to a 4-qt. slow cooker; do not add chicken broth. Cook, covered, 5-6 hours on low or until tender. Remove; when cool enough to handle, shred meat using 2 forks. Skim fat from cooking juices; stir in chicken broth. Return pork to slow cooker and heat through. Top with fresh cilantro.

pressure-cook on high for 40 minutes. Quick-release pressure. Add carrots; bring back to full pressure and cook 7 minutes. Quick-release pressure. Press cancel.

3. Remove ribs and vegetables; keep warm. Skim fat from the cooking liquid. Discard thyme and bay leaf. Select saute setting and adjust for medium heat; bring cooking juices to a boil. In a small bowl, mix cornstarch and water until smooth; stir into juices. Cook and stir until thickened, 1-2 minutes; press cancel. If desired, sprinkle with additional salt and pepper. Serve with ribs and vegetables.

1 SERVING: *250 cal., 13g fat (5g sat. fat), 55mg chol., 412mg sod., 12g carb. (4g sugars, 2g fiber), 20g pro.*

COOK IT SLOW
PREP: 30 MIN. • **COOK:** 6¼ HOURS

Brown seasoned ribs in a large skillet; transfer to a 4- or 5-qt. slow cooker. Add carrots, broth, thyme and bay leaf to ribs. Add onions to the skillet; cook and stir over medium heat for 8-9 minutes or until tender. Add garlic and tomato paste; cook and stir 1 minute longer. Stir in wine. Bring to a boil; cook 8-10 minutes or until liquid is reduced by half. Add to slow cooker. Cook, covered, on low for 6-8 hours or until the meat is tender. After removing ribs and vegetables, transfer cooking juices to a small saucepan; follow directions for Step 3 to thicken gravy.

 Holiday Helper
Short ribs can be an expensive cut of beef, but they are perfect for a special occasion—and make the holidays a bit more of an event!

SHORT RIBS

These short ribs, exploding with flavor and tenderness, are an easy alternative to braised short ribs. Serve with egg noodles, rice or polenta.
—Rebekah Beyer, Sabetha, KS

PREP: 30 MIN. • **COOK:** 50 MIN.
MAKES: 6 SERVINGS

- 3 lbs. bone-in beef short ribs
- ½ tsp. salt
- ½ tsp. pepper
- 1 Tbsp. canola oil
- 2 large onions, cut into ½-in. wedges
- 6 garlic cloves, minced
- 1 Tbsp. tomato paste
- 1 cup beef broth
- 2 cups dry red wine or beef broth
- 4 fresh thyme sprigs
- 1 bay leaf
- 4 medium carrots, cut into 1-in. pieces
- 4 tsp. cornstarch
- 3 Tbsp. cold water
  Additional salt and pepper, optional

1. Sprinkle ribs with salt and pepper. Select saute setting on a 6-qt. electric pressure cooker; adjust for medium heat. Add oil. Working in batches, brown the ribs on all sides; transfer to a plate and keep warm.

2. Add onions to cooker; cook and stir until tender, 8-9 minutes. Add garlic and tomato paste; cook and stir 1 minute more. Stir in beef broth, wine, thyme and bay leaf. Bring to a boil; cook 8-10 minutes or until liquid is reduced by half. Add ribs back to cooker, partially but not fully submerging them. Lock lid; close the pressure-release valve. Adjust to

ITALIAN SAUSAGE & KALE SOUP

The first time I made this colorful soup, our home smelled wonderful. We knew it was a keeper to see us through cold winter days.
—Sarah Stombaugh, Chicago, IL

- 1 lb. bulk hot Italian sausage
- 6 cups chopped fresh kale
- 2 cans (15½ oz. each) great northern beans, rinsed and drained
- 1 can (28 oz.) crushed tomatoes
- 4 large carrots, finely chopped (about 3 cups)
- 1 medium onion, chopped
- 3 garlic cloves, minced
- 1 tsp. dried oregano
- ¼ tsp. salt
- ⅛ tsp. pepper
- 5 cups chicken stock
  Grated Parmesan cheese

PREP: 20 MIN. • **COOK:** 15 MIN.
MAKES: 8 SERVINGS (3½ QT.)

1. Select saute setting on a 6-qt. electric pressure cooker and adjust for medium heat. Add the sausage. Cook and stir, crumbling meat, until no longer pink. Press cancel. Remove sausage; drain. Return sausage to pressure cooker.
2. Add next 10 ingredients. Lock lid; close pressure-release valve. Adjust to pressure-cook on high for 10 minutes. Allow pressure to naturally release for 5 minutes, then quick-release any remaining pressure.
3. Top each serving with cheese.

1¾ CUPS: 297 cal., 13g fat (4g sat. fat), 31mg chol., 1105mg sod., 31g carb. (7g sugars, 9g fiber), 16g pro.

COOK IT SLOW
PREP: 20 MIN. • **COOK:** 8 HOURS

Use a large skillet to cook sausage as directed in Step 1. Drain and transfer to a 5-qt. slow cooker. Add kale, beans, tomatoes, carrots, onion, garlic, seasonings and stock to slow cooker. Cook, covered, on low 8-10 hours or until vegetables are tender. Top each serving with cheese.

RED CLAM SAUCE

This recipe tastes as if it's taken a whole day's work. What a classy way to jazz up pasta sauce!
—JoAnn Brown, Latrobe, PA

1 Tbsp. canola oil
1 medium onion, chopped
2 garlic cloves, minced
2 cans (6½ oz. each) chopped clams, undrained
1 can (14½ oz.) diced tomatoes, undrained
1 can (6 oz.) tomato paste
¼ cup minced fresh parsley
1 bay leaf
1 tsp. sugar
1 tsp. dried basil
½ tsp. dried thyme
6 oz. hot cooked linguine, drained
Additional fresh parsley, optional

PREP: 20 MIN. • **COOK:** 5 MIN.
MAKES: 4 SERVINGS

1. Select saute setting on a 6-qt. electric pressure cooker; adjust for medium heat. Add oil. When hot, add onion; saute until tender. Add garlic; cook 1 minute longer. Press cancel.
2. Stir in the next 8 ingredients. Lock lid; close pressure-release valve. Adjust to pressure-cook on high for 3 minutes. Allow pressure to naturally release for 5 minutes, then quick-release any remaining pressure. Discard bay leaf. Serve with linguine and, if desired, additional minced parsley.

FREEZE OPTION: Omit additional parsley. Cool before placing in a freezer container. Cover and freeze for up to 3 months. To use, thaw in the refrigerator overnight. Place in a large saucepan; heat through, stirring occasionally. Serve with linguine and, if desired, minced parsley.

1 CUP SAUCE WITH ¾ CUP COOKED LINGUINE: *305 cal., 5g fat (0 sat. fat), 15mg chol., 553mg sod., 53g carb. (14g sugars, 7g fiber), 15g pro.*

> ### COOK IT SLOW
> **PREP:** 25 MIN. • **COOK:** 3 HOURS
>
> Use a small skillet to saute the onion and garlic in oil; transfer to a 1½- or 2-qt. slow cooker. Stir in the clams, tomatoes, tomato paste, parsley, bay leaf, sugar, basil and thyme. Cover and cook on low until heated through, 3-4 hours. Discard bay leaf; serve sauce with linguine.

TURKEY WITH BERRY COMPOTE

This delicious dish gives you that yummy turkey flavor without taking up oven space. The berries make a perfect chutney all year round. For a browner turkey, broil it for a few minutes before serving.
—Margaret Bracher, Robertsdale, AL

PREP: 15 MIN.
COOK: 45 MIN. + RELEASING
MAKES: 12 SERVINGS (3¼ CUPS COMPOTE)

- 1 tsp. salt
- ½ tsp. garlic powder
- ½ tsp. dried thyme
- ½ tsp. pepper
- 2 boneless skinless turkey breast halves (2 lbs. each)
- ⅓ cup water

COMPOTE
- 2 medium apples, peeled and finely chopped
- 2 cups fresh raspberries
- 2 cups fresh blueberries
- 1 cup white grape juice
- ¼ tsp. crushed red pepper flakes
- ¼ tsp. ground ginger

1. Mix salt, garlic powder, thyme and pepper; rub over turkey breasts. Place in a 6-qt. electric pressure cooker. Pour water around turkey. Lock lid; close pressure-release valve. Adjust to pressure-cook on high for 30 minutes. Allow the pressure to naturally release for 10 minutes, then quick-release any remaining pressure. A thermometer inserted in turkey breasts should read at least 165°. Press cancel.

2. Remove turkey and cooking juices from pressure cooker; tent with foil. Let stand 10 minutes before slicing.

3. Select the saute setting and adjust for low heat. Add compote ingredients; simmer, uncovered, until the mixture is slightly thickened and the apples are tender, 15-20 minutes, stirring occasionally. Press cancel. Serve turkey with compote.

5 OZ. COOKED TURKEY WITH ¼ CUP COMPOTE: *215 cal., 1g fat (0 sat. fat), 94mg chol., 272mg sod., 12g carb. (8g sugars, 2g fiber), 38g pro.*
DIABETIC EXCHANGES: *5 lean meat, 1 starch.*

Holiday Helper
When fresh fruit is out of season, you can use frozen fruit in this recipe—it's just as delicious!

COOK IT SLOW
PREP: 35 MIN. + STANDING
COOK: 3 HRS.

Place herb-rubbed turkey breasts in a 5- or 6-qt. slow cooker. Pour water around turkey. Cook, covered, on low for 3-4 hours (a thermometer inserted in turkey should read at least 165°). Use a large saucepan to make the compote, following the directions in Step 3.

JOY TO
THE SWIRLED

Rolls and pinwheels, spirals and twists, these beautiful dishes add a distinct elegance to your holiday table— from appetizer to main course to dessert!

CRAB CRESCENTS

These elegant little spiral-wrapped bites are delicious, decadent and easy to make—the perfect combination for a holiday party!
—Stephanie Howard, Oakland, CA

TAKES: 25 MIN. • **MAKES:** 16 APPETIZERS

1 tube (8 oz.) refrigerated crescent rolls
3 Tbsp. prepared pesto
½ cup fresh crabmeat

1. Preheat oven to 375°. Unroll crescent dough; separate into 8 triangles. Cut each triangle in half lengthwise, forming 2 triangles. Spread ½ tsp. of pesto over each triangle; place 1 rounded tsp. of crab along the wide end of each triangle.
2. Roll up each triangle from the wide end; place triangles point side down 1 in. apart on an ungreased baking sheet.
3. Bake until golden brown, 10-12 minutes. Serve warm.

1 CRESCENT: *74 cal., 4g fat (1g sat. fat), 5mg chol., 144mg sod., 6g carb. (1g sugars, 0 fiber), 2g pro.*

GINGERBREAD WITH FIG-WALNUT SAUCE

PICTURED ON P. 114
I experimented with aniseed this past holiday season and fell in love with the flavor. It really enhances the gingerbread spices and fig sauce in this extraordinary fluted tube cake.
—Shelly Bevington, Hermiston, OR

PREP: 30 MIN. • **BAKE:** 40 MIN. + COOLING
MAKES: 12 SERVINGS

1 cup unsalted butter, softened
1 cup packed brown sugar
3 large eggs, room temperature
1 cup molasses
2½ cups all-purpose flour
2 tsp. baking soda
2 tsp. ground ginger
1½ tsp. aniseed, crushed
1 tsp. salt
1 tsp. ground cinnamon
½ tsp. ground allspice
¼ tsp. ground cloves
1 cup buttermilk
1 Tbsp. lemon juice
Confectioners' sugar, optional

SAUCE
12 oz. Calimyrna dried figs, cut into eighths
1 cup finely chopped walnuts
2 Tbsp. walnut or canola oil
1 Tbsp. aniseed, crushed
1 tsp. ground cinnamon
½ tsp. ground cloves
1¾ cups water
1 cup sugar
2 Tbsp. lemon juice
¼ tsp. salt

1. Preheat oven to 350°. In a large bowl, cream butter and brown sugar until light and fluffy. Add eggs, one at a time, beating well after each addition. Beat in molasses (the mixture will appear curdled).
2. In a small bowl, combine flour, baking soda, ginger, aniseed, salt, cinnamon, allspice and cloves. Add to the creamed mixture alternately with buttermilk and lemon juice; beat well after each addition.
3. Pour the batter into a well-greased and floured 10-in. fluted tube pan. Bake until a toothpick inserted in the center comes out clean, 40-50 minutes.
4. Cool 10 minutes before removing from pan to a wire rack to cool completely. Dust with confectioners' sugar if desired.
5. For the sauce, in a large skillet, cook figs and walnuts in oil over medium heat for 4 minutes. Stir in aniseed, cinnamon and cloves; cook until aromatic, about 1-2 minutes longer.
6. Stir in water, sugar, lemon juice and salt. Bring to a boil. Reduce heat; simmer, uncovered, until thickened, 8-12 minutes, stirring occasionally. Cool sauce to room temperature. Serve with gingerbread.
1 SLICE WITH ⅓ CUP SAUCE: *629 cal., 26g fat (11g sat. fat), 88mg chol., 534mg sod., 97g carb. (70g sugars, 5g fiber), 8g pro.*

PUFF PASTRY CHRISTMAS PALMIERS

Traditional French palmiers (pronounced palm-YAY) are usually a sweet pastry. To make them into savory appetizers, I swirl in pesto, feta and sundried tomatoes.
—Darlene Brenden, Salem, OR

PREP: 15 MIN. + CHILLING • **BAKE:** 15 MIN.
MAKES: 2 DOZEN

- 1 pkg. (17.30 oz.) frozen puff pastry, thawed
- 1 large egg
- 1 Tbsp. water
- ¼ cup prepared pesto
- ½ cup feta or goat cheese, crumbled
- ¼ cup oil-packed sun-dried tomatoes, patted dry and finely chopped

1. Preheat oven to 400°. Unfold one sheet of puff pastry. Whisk the egg and water; brush over pastry. Spread with half the pesto. Sprinkle with half the feta and half the sun-dried tomatoes.

2. Roll up the left and right sides toward the center, jelly-roll style, until rolls meet in the middle. Repeat with the remaining pastry sheet and ingredients. Freeze until firm, about 30 minutes.

3. Cut each roll crosswise into 12 slices. On baking sheets lined with parchment, bake palmiers until golden and crisp, about 15 minutes.

1 APPETIZER: *121 cal., 7g fat (2g sat. fat), 9mg chol., 126mg sod., 12g carb. (0 sugars, 2g fiber), 2g pro.*

FLANK STEAK PINWHEELS

The secret to these pretty pinwheels lies in their butterfly treatment. Because the steaks are flattened, they don't need marinade. Instead, they're filled with colorful, holiday-appropriate red pepper and green spinach and topped with a flavorful, homemade blue cheese sauce.
—Taste of Home *Test Kitchen*

PREP: 30 MIN. • **GRILL:** 10 MIN.
MAKES: 4 SERVINGS

- 8 bacon strips
- 1 beef flank steak (1½ lbs.)
- 4 cups fresh baby spinach
- 1 jar (7 oz.) roasted sweet red peppers, drained

CREAM CHEESE SAUCE

- 3 oz. cream cheese, softened
- ¼ cup 2% milk
- 1 Tbsp. butter
- ¼ tsp. pepper
- ½ cup crumbled blue cheese

1. Place bacon strips on a microwave-safe plate lined with paper towels. Cover with another paper towel; microwave on high for 2-3 minutes or until partially cooked.

2. Meanwhile, cut the steak horizontally from a long side to within ½ in. of the opposite side. Open the meat so it lies flat; cover with plastic wrap. Use a meat mallet to flatten steak to ¼-in. thickness. Remove plastic. Place spinach over the steak to within 1 in. of edges; top with red peppers.

3. With the grain of the meat going from left to right, roll up steak jelly-roll style. Wrap the bacon strips around the beef; secure with toothpicks. Cut beef across the grain into eight slices.

4. Grill slices, covered, over medium heat for about 5-7 minutes on each side or until the meat reaches desired doneness (for medium-rare, a thermometer should read 135°; medium, 140°; medium-well, 145°). Discard toothpicks.

5. In a small saucepan, combine cream cheese, milk, butter and pepper. Cook and stir over low heat just until smooth (do not boil). Stir in blue cheese. Serve with pinwheels.

2 PINWHEELS: *509 cal., 34g fat (17g sat. fat), 138mg chol., 812mg sod., 5g carb. (3g sugars, 1g fiber), 43g pro.*

THE STAR ATTRACTION

This Christmas Star Twisted Bread looks intricate, but it's easy to do. Layer dough and jam (left), ending with dough. Use a cookie cutter as guide; cut into strips (center). Twist 2 strips away from each other, twice (right); pinch ends together. Change the flavor by using blueberry jam and 1 tsp. lemon zest, or blackberry jam and ½ tsp. cardamom.

GREEK PINWHEELS

I love Greek-style food and appetizers, so I made up this simple combination of puff pastry, cream cheese and tasty fillings to share at a baby shower.
—Veronica Worlund, Pasco, WA

TAKES: 30 MIN. • **MAKES:** 20 APPETIZERS

- 1 sheet frozen puff pastry, thawed
- 1 Tbsp. beaten egg
- ¾ tsp. water
- 4 oz. cream cheese, softened
- ⅓ cup marinated quartered artichoke hearts, drained and finely chopped
- ¼ cup crumbled feta cheese
- 1 Tbsp. finely chopped drained oil-packed sun-dried tomatoes
- 3 Greek olives, finely chopped
- 1 tsp. Greek seasoning

1. Preheat oven to 425°. Unfold the puff pastry. Whisk together the egg and water; brush over pastry. Combine the remaining ingredients; spread over pastry to within ½ in. of the edges. Roll up jelly-roll style. Cut into twenty ½-in. slices.
2. Place slices 2 in. apart on greased baking sheets. Bake until puffed and golden brown, 9-11 minutes. Serve warm.
1 SERVING: *92 cal., 6g fat (2g sat. fat), 9mg chol., 142mg sod., 7g carb. (0 sugars, 1g fiber), 2g pro.*

CHRISTMAS STAR TWISTED BREAD

This gorgeous sweet bread swirled with jam may look tricky, but it's not. The best part is opening the oven to find the star-shaped beauty in all its glory.
—Darlene Brenden, Salem, OR

PREP: 45 MIN. + RISING
BAKE: 20 MIN.
MAKES: 16 SERVINGS

- 1 pkg. (¼ oz.) active dry yeast
- ¼ cup warm water (110° to 115°)
- ¾ cup warm whole milk (110° to 115°)
- 1 large egg, room temperature
- ¼ cup butter, softened
- ¼ cup sugar
- 1 tsp. salt
- 3¼ to 3¾ cups all-purpose flour
- ¾ cup seedless raspberry jam
- 2 Tbsp. butter, melted
  Confectioners' sugar

1. Dissolve yeast in warm water until foamy. In another bowl, combine milk, egg, butter, sugar and salt; add yeast mixture and 3 cups flour. Beat on medium speed until smooth, about 1 minute. Stir in enough of the remaining flour to form a soft dough.
2. Turn dough onto a floured surface; knead until smooth and elastic, about 6-8 minutes. Place in a greased bowl, turning once to grease top. Cover and let rise in a warm place until doubled, about 1 hour.
3. Punch down dough. Turn onto a lightly floured surface; divide into 4 portions. Roll 1 portion into a 12-in. circle. Place on a greased or parchment-lined 14-in. pizza pan. Spread with one-third of the jam to within ½ in. from edge. Repeat twice, layering dough and jam, and ending with the final portion of dough.
4. Place a 2½-in. round cookie cutter in the center of the dough (do not press down). With a sharp knife, make 16 evenly spaced cuts from the cutter to the edge of dough, forming a starburst. Remove the cutter; grasp 2 adjacent strips and twist twice outward. Pinch the ends together. Repeat with remaining strips.
5. Cover and let rise until almost doubled, about 30 minutes. Bake at 375° until golden brown, 18-22 minutes. (Watch during final 5 minutes for any dripping.) Remove from oven; brush with melted butter, avoiding areas where jam is visible. Cool completely on a wire rack. Dust with confectioners' sugar.
1 PIECE: *193 cal., 5g fat (3g sat. fat), 24mg chol., 192mg sod., 33g carb. (13g sugars, 1g fiber), 4g pro.*

EGGPLANT ROLLATINI

These authentic eggplant roll-ups may take some time to prepare, but the end result is restaurant-quality and just right for a special occasion. Your family will request this dish time and again.
—Nancy Sousley, Lafayette, IN

PREP: 1 HOUR • **BAKE:** 30 MIN.
MAKES: 5 SERVINGS

- 1   large eggplant
- 1   Tbsp. salt

SAUCE
- 1   small onion, chopped
- ¼   cup olive oil
- 2   garlic cloves, minced
- 1   can (15 oz.) tomato sauce
- 1   can (14½ oz.) diced tomatoes
- ½   cup chicken broth
- ¼   cup tomato paste
- 2   Tbsp. minced fresh parsley
- 2   tsp. sugar
- ½   tsp. salt
- ½   tsp. dried basil
- ¼   tsp. pepper
- ⅛   tsp. crushed red pepper flakes

FILLING
- 1   carton (15 oz.) ricotta cheese
- 1   cup shredded part-skim mozzarella cheese
- ½   cup grated Parmesan cheese
- ¼   cup minced fresh parsley
- 1   large egg, lightly beaten
- ⅛   tsp. pepper

COATING
- 3   large eggs, lightly beaten
- 1   cup seasoned bread crumbs
- 1   cup grated Parmesan cheese, divided
- 2   garlic cloves, minced
- 2   Tbsp. minced fresh parsley
     Dash each salt and pepper

1. Peel and slice eggplant lengthwise into fifteen ⅛-in.-thick slices. Place in a colander over a plate; sprinkle with salt and toss. Let stand 30 minutes.

2. Meanwhile, for the sauce, in a large saucepan, saute onion in oil. Add garlic; cook 1 minute longer. Stir in the remaining sauce ingredients. Bring to a boil. Reduce heat; simmer, uncovered, until the flavors are blended, stirring occasionally, 20-25 minutes. Rinse and drain eggplant.

3. In a large bowl, combine the filling ingredients; set aside.

4. Place the eggs in a shallow bowl. In a second shallow bowl, combine the bread crumbs, ½ cup of Parmesan cheese, the garlic, parsley, salt and pepper. Dip the eggplant in the eggs, then in the bread crumb mixture.

5. In an electric skillet, heat ½ in. of oil to 375°. Fry the eggplant in batches until golden brown, 2-3 minutes on each side. Drain on paper towels.

6. Preheat oven to 375°. Spoon 1 cup sauce into an ungreased 13x9-in. baking dish. Spread 2 rounded Tbsp. filling over each eggplant slice. Carefully roll up eggplant slices; place seam side down in baking dish. Spoon the remaining sauce over roll-ups. Sprinkle with the remaining Parmesan cheese. Cover and bake until bubbly, 30-35 minutes.

3 ROLLS: *726 cal., 48g fat (15g sat. fat), 181mg chol., 3182mg sod., 44g carb. (19g sugars, 7g fiber), 35g pro.*

HERB-STUFFED PORK LOIN

This stunning pork roast is one of my favorite recipes when I'm entertaining company. It's especially good with garden-fresh herbs, but dried ones work nicely as well.
—Michele Montgomery, Lethbridge, AB

PREP: 20 MIN.
BAKE: 1 HOUR 20 MIN. + STANDING
MAKES: 12 SERVINGS

- 1 boneless pork loin roast (3 lbs.)
- ¼ cup Dijon mustard
- 4 garlic cloves, minced
- ⅓ cup minced chives
- ¼ cup minced fresh sage or 4 tsp. rubbed sage
- 2 Tbsp. minced fresh thyme or 2 tsp. dried thyme
- 1 Tbsp. minced fresh rosemary or 1 tsp. dried rosemary, crushed
- 2¾ tsp. pepper, divided
- 1 tsp. salt, divided
- 1 Tbsp. olive oil

1. Starting about a third in from one side, make a lengthwise slit down the roast to within ½ in. of the bottom. Turn roast over and make another lengthwise slit, starting about a third in from the opposite side. Open roast so it lies flat; cover with plastic wrap. Flatten to ¾-in. thickness; remove the plastic wrap.

2. Combine the mustard and garlic; rub two-thirds of the mixture over the roast. Combine chives, sage, thyme, rosemary, ¾ tsp. pepper and ½ tsp. salt. Sprinkle two-thirds of the herb mixture over the roast. Roll up jelly-roll style, starting with a long side; tie several times with kitchen string. Rub oil over roast; sprinkle with the remaining salt and pepper.

3. On an oiled grill rack over a drip pan, grill roast, covered, over indirect medium heat or bake roast, uncovered, at 350° for 1 hour.

4. Brush the remaining mustard mixture over roast; sprinkle with remaining herb mixture. Grill or bake until a thermometer reads 160°, 20-25 minutes longer. Let stand for 10 minutes before slicing.

3 OZ. COOKED PORK: *199 cal., 10g fat (3g sat. fat), 69mg chol., 372mg sod., 2g carb. (0 sugars, 1g fiber), 25g pro.*

RUGELACH WITH A TWIST

Once I read about making rugelach using ice cream, I just had to try it. And once my family tasted the tender, flaky cookies, I had to bake more right away!
—Diane Fuqua, Baltimore, MD

PREP: 25 MIN. + CHILLING
BAKE: 20 MIN./BATCH • **MAKES:** 32 COOKIES

- 1 cup butter, softened
- 2¾ cups all-purpose flour
- 1 cup vanilla ice cream, melted
- ¾ cup finely chopped pecans
- ¾ cup miniature semisweet chocolate chips
- ¼ cup sugar
- ¼ cup firmly packed brown sugar
- 2 tsp. ground cinnamon
- 1 large egg
- 1 Tbsp. water

1. Beat butter and flour until blended. Beat in ice cream. Divide dough into four portions; shape each portion into a disk. Wrap each disk; refrigerate for 1 hour.

2. Preheat oven to 350°. Mix pecans and chocolate chips. In another bowl, mix sugars and cinnamon. Roll each portion of dough into a 10-in. circle; sprinkle each circle with 2 Tbsp. of the sugar mixture and about ⅓ cup of the pecan mixture. Gently press the pecan mixture into the dough. Cut each circle into 8 wedges; roll up each wedge from the wide end. Place rolls 1 in. apart on parchment-lined baking sheets, point side down. Whisk together egg and water; brush over pastries.

3. Bake until golden brown, 18-22 minutes. Remove from pans to wire racks to cool.

1 COOKIE: *151 cal., 10g fat (5g sat. fat), 23mg chol., 52mg sod., 16g carb. (6g sugars, 1g fiber), 2g pro*

CRANBERRY SWIRL LOAF

This is my variation on Mother's beloved swirled date bread. The slightly tart filling balances the sweet streusel topping, and every slice reveals that enticing ruby swirl. Sometimes I add a simple glaze.
—Darlene Brenden, Salem, OR

PREP: 30 MIN. + RISING
BAKE: 40 MIN.
MAKES: 1 LOAF (16 SLICES)

- ⅓ cup sugar
- 1 pkg. (¼ oz.) quick-rise yeast
- ½ tsp. salt
- 3 to 3½ cups all-purpose flour
- ½ cup water
- ½ cup milk
- ⅓ cup butter, cubed

FILLING

- 1 cup chopped fresh or frozen cranberries
- ¼ cup packed brown sugar
- ¼ cup water
- 1 Tbsp. butter
- 1 Tbsp. lemon juice
- ½ cup chopped walnuts, optional

TOPPING

- 2 Tbsp. all-purpose flour
- 2 Tbsp. sugar
- 2 Tbsp. cold butter, divided

1. Mix sugar, yeast, salt and 1 cup flour. In a small saucepan, heat water, milk and butter to 120°-130°. Add to the dry ingredients; beat on medium speed for 2 minutes. Stir in enough of the remaining flour to form a soft dough.
2. Turn onto a floured surface; knead until smooth and elastic, about 6-8 minutes. Place in a greased bowl, turning once to grease the top. Cover and let rise in a warm place until doubled, about 1 hour.
3. Meanwhile, in a small saucepan, combine cranberries, brown sugar and water. Cook over medium heat until cranberries are soft, about 15 minutes. Remove from heat; stir in butter, lemon juice and, if desired, walnuts. Cool.
4. Punch down dough. Turn onto a lightly floured surface; roll into a 20x10-in. rectangle. Spread filling to within ½ in. of edges. Roll up jelly-roll style, starting with a long side; pinch seam to seal. Transfer to a greased 9x5-in. loaf pan, arranging in a slight zigzag fashion to fit.

5. Combine flour and sugar; cut in 1 Tbsp. butter until crumbly. Melt remaining butter; brush over dough. Sprinkle with crumb mixture. Cover with a towel; let rise in a warm place until doubled, about 40 minutes. Preheat oven to 350°.
6. Bake until golden brown and dough is cooked through, 40-45 minutes. Carefully remove from pan to a wire rack to cool.
1 SLICE: *210 cal., 9g fat (4g sat. fat), 17mg chol., 140mg sod., 30g carb. (10g sugars, 1g fiber), 4g pro.*

CHRISTMAS PARTY PINWHEELS

These festive appetizers look so special and pretty that folks can't resist! Refreshing ranch dressing and crisp colorful vegetables make these pinwheels a pleasure to serve to holiday guests.
—Janis Plourde, Smooth Rock Falls, ON

PREP: 15 MIN. + CHILLING
MAKES: ABOUT 6½ DOZEN

- 2 pkg. (8 oz. each) cream cheese, softened
- 1 pkg. (0.4 oz.) ranch salad dressing mix
- ½ cup minced sweet red pepper
- ½ cup minced celery
- ¼ cup sliced green onions
- ¼ cup sliced pimiento-stuffed olives
- 4 flour tortillas (10 in.)

In a bowl, beat cream cheese and dressing mix until smooth. Add the red pepper, celery, onions and olives; mix well. Spread about ¾ cup of filling on each tortilla. Roll up each tortilla tightly; wrap each individually in plastic. Refrigerate for at least 2 hours. Cut into ½-in. slices.
1 PINWHEEL: *34 cal., 2g fat (1g sat. fat), 6mg chol., 84mg sod., 2g carb. (0 sugars, 0 fiber), 1g pro.*

4. Combine cornstarch and water until smooth; stir into the sauce. Bring to a boil; cook and stir until thickened, about 2 minutes. Drain the meat loaf; serve with sauce.

1 SLICE: *319 cal., 17g fat (7g sat. fat), 124mg chol., 732mg sod., 8g carb. (2g sugars, 1g fiber), 32g pro.*

RED & GREEN COOKIE TWIRLS

For the holidays, my mom would make red and green cookie dough, then roll them together for a twirly effect. Seeing these peppermint-flavored cookies, so colorful, brings back lots of happy memories.
—Jill Heatwole, Pittsville, MD

PREP: 30 MIN. + CHILLING
BAKE: 10 MIN./BATCH • **MAKES:** 6 DOZEN

10 Tbsp. butter, softened
½ cup packed brown sugar
¼ cup sugar
1 large egg, room temperature
½ tsp. peppermint extract
2 cups all-purpose flour
½ tsp. baking powder
½ tsp. salt
⅛ tsp. baking soda
½ tsp. red gel food coloring
¼ tsp. green gel food coloring

1. Cream butter and sugars until light and fluffy; beat in egg and extract. In another bowl, whisk together flour, baking powder, salt and baking soda; gradually add to the creamed mixture, blending well.
2. Divide dough in half. Tint one half red and the other green. Divide each portion in half, for a total of 4 portions. Roll out each portion between sheets of waxed paper into a 9x6-in. rectangle. Refrigerate for 15 minutes. Preheat oven to 375°.
3. Remove waxed paper. Place 1 green rectangle on a red rectangle. Roll up tightly jelly-roll style, starting with a long side; wrap in plastic. Repeat. Refrigerate until firm, about 1 hour. Unwrap rolls and cut crosswise into ¼-in. slices. Place slices 1 in. apart on ungreased baking sheets. Bake until set, 7-9 minutes. Remove to wire racks to cool.
1 COOKIE: *36 cal., 2g fat (1g sat. fat), 7mg chol., 36mg sod., 5g carb. (2g sugars, 0 fiber), 0 pro.*

FESTIVE SWIRLED MEAT LOAF

Dress up meat loaf for a dinner during the holiday week when company's in town! This crowd-sized pinwheel features ham, Swiss cheese and a homemade tomato sauce.
—Vera Sullivan, Amity, OR

PREP: 20 MIN. • **BAKE:** 1¼ HOURS
MAKES: 20 SERVINGS

3 large eggs
1 cup dry bread crumbs
½ cup finely chopped onion
½ cup finely chopped green pepper
¼ cup ketchup
2 tsp. minced fresh parsley
1 tsp. dried basil
1 tsp. dried oregano
1 garlic clove, minced
2 tsp. salt
½ tsp. pepper
5 lbs. lean ground beef (90% lean)
¾ lb. thinly sliced deli ham
¾ lb. thinly sliced Swiss cheese
TOMATO PEPPER SAUCE
½ cup finely chopped onion
2 celery ribs, chopped
½ cup chopped green pepper
1 garlic clove, minced
1 to 2 tsp. olive oil
2 cups chopped fresh tomatoes
1 cup beef broth
1 bay leaf
1 tsp. sugar
¼ tsp. salt
¼ tsp. dried thyme
1 Tbsp. cornstarch
2 Tbsp. cold water

1. Preheat oven to 350°. In a large bowl, combine the first 11 ingredients. Crumble ground beef over the mixture; mix well. On a piece of heavy-duty foil, pat the beef mixture into a 17x15-in. rectangle. Cover with ham and cheese slices to within ½ in. of edges.
2. Roll up tightly jelly-roll style, starting with a short side. Place roll seam side down in a roasting pan. Bake, uncovered, until a thermometer reads 160°, about 1¼-1½ hours.
3. In a large saucepan, saute the onion, celery, green pepper and garlic in oil until tender, 3-5 minutes. Add tomatoes, broth, bay leaf, sugar, salt and thyme. Simmer, uncovered, for 30 minutes. Discard the bay leaf.

GIANT CINNAMON ROLL

This must-try cinnamon roll is all about the pillowy texture, the sweet spices and the homemade caramel drizzle.
—Leah Rekau, Milwaukee, WI

PREP: 30 MIN. + RISING • **BAKE:** 30 MIN.
MAKES: 12 SERVINGS

- 1 pkg. (¼ oz.) active dry yeast
- ½ cup warm water (110° to 115°)
- ½ cup heavy whipping cream, warmed (110° to 115°)
- ½ cup sugar
- ½ tsp. sea salt
- 3 to 4 cups all-purpose flour
- 1 large egg, beaten, room temperature
- 3 Tbsp. butter, melted

FILLING

- ¼ cup butter, softened
- ¼ cup sugar
- 1 Tbsp. ground cinnamon

TOPPING

- 1 cup sugar
- 2 Tbsp. water
- 6 Tbsp. butter
- ½ cup heavy whipping cream
- 1 tsp. sea salt

1. Dissolve yeast in warm water and whipping cream until foamy. In another bowl, combine sugar and salt; add 3 cups of flour, the yeast mixture, egg and melted butter. Stir until moistened. Add enough remaining flour to form a soft dough.
2. Turn dough onto a lightly floured surface; knead until smooth and elastic, 3-4 minutes. Place in a greased bowl, turning once. Cover; let rise in a warm place until doubled, about 30 minutes.
3. Punch down dough. Turn onto a lightly floured surface; roll into a 15x12-in. rectangle. Spread softened butter over dough. Sprinkle with sugar and cinnamon. Using a pizza cutter, cut into 2-in.-wide strips. Roll up one strip and place upright in the center of a greased 9-in. deep-dish pie plate; wrap remaining strips around center core to form one giant roll. Cover with greased foil; let rise until doubled, about 1 hour.
4. Bake at 350° until golden brown, 30-40 minutes. If dough starts browning too quickly, cover lightly with foil. Cool on a wire rack.

5. For the topping, combine sugar and water in a small saucepan; cook over medium heat until mixture turns light amber. Add butter, stirring vigorously. Remove from heat and add cream; continue to stir vigorously. Cool slightly. Pour ¾ cup sauce over warm roll; sprinkle with salt. Serve with remaining sauce.
1 SERVING: *416 cal., 21g fat (13g sat. fat), 76mg chol., 354mg sod., 55g carb. (30g sugars, 1g fiber), 5g pro.*

Holiday Helper
Reduce proofing (rising) times by giving the yeast a toasty place to hang out. If your kitchen is cold, microwave a bit of water to create a sauna, then put the bowl of dough into the microwave and close the door. Happy yeast, happy roll!

CREME DE MENTHE CUPCAKES

Creme de menthe (which means "mint cream" in French) liqueur adds a cool flavor to these mascarpone-frosted cupcakes; use green food coloring to add a lovely swirl to both the cake and frosting. For a thick layer of frosting as pictured, double the frosting ingredients listed.
—Keri Whitney, Castro Valley, CA

PREP: 30 MIN. • **BAKE:** 15 MIN. + COOLING
MAKES: 1 DOZEN

- ¾ cup butter, softened
- 1 cup sugar
- 2 large eggs, room temperature
- ½ tsp. mint extract
- 1½ cups cake flour
- 1½ tsp. baking powder
- ¼ tsp. salt
- ⅔ cup 2% milk
- 2 Tbsp. white (clear) creme de menthe
  Green paste food coloring

FROSTING
- 1 carton (8 oz.) mascarpone cheese
- ⅓ cup heavy whipping cream
- ¼ cup confectioners' sugar
- 4 tsp. white (clear) creme de menthe
  Green paste food coloring

1. Preheat oven to 350°. Cream butter and granulated sugar until light and fluffy. Add eggs, 1 at a time, beating well after each addition. Add the mint extract. In another bowl, whisk flour, baking powder and salt; add to the creamed mixture alternately with milk and creme de menthe, beating well after each addition. Transfer 2 cups of batter to a separate bowl. Mix food coloring into the remaining batter.
2. Spoon the batters alternately into a pastry bag with a #12 round tip. Pipe the batter into 12 paper-lined muffin cups until three-fourths full. Bake until a toothpick comes out clean, 15-20 minutes. Cool 10 minutes; remove from pan to a wire rack to cool completely.
3. For the frosting, stir the mascarpone and whipping cream until smooth. Add the confectioners' sugar and creme de menthe; stir until blended. Transfer half the frosting to a separate bowl; mix food coloring into remaining frosting. Stir each portion vigorously until stiff peaks form (do not overmix).
4. Spoon the frostings alternately into a pastry bag fitted with a #12 round tip. Pipe frosting onto cupcakes. Refrigerate any leftovers.
1 CUPCAKE: *372 cal., 24g fat (14g sat. fat), 95mg chol., 222mg sod., 35g carb. (21g sugars, 0 fiber), 5g pro.*

CHIVE PINWHEEL ROLLS

These light, pleasant-tasting dinner rolls complement almost any entree. With the chive filling swirled through a golden bread, they're suited for special occasions and holiday gatherings alike.
—Ann Niemela, Ely, MN

PREP: 25 MIN. + RISING • **BAKE:** 30 MIN.
MAKES: 15 ROLLS

- 3½ cups all-purpose flour
- 3 Tbsp. sugar
- 1 pkg. (¼ oz.) active dry yeast
- 1½ tsp. salt
- 1 cup whole milk
- ⅓ cup canola oil
- ¼ cup water
- ¼ cup mashed potatoes (without added milk and butter)
- 1 large egg, room temperature

CHIVE FILLING
- 1 cup sour cream
- 1 cup minced chives
- 1 large egg yolk
  Butter, melted

1. In a large bowl, combine 2½ cups of flour, the sugar, yeast and salt. In a small saucepan, heat the milk, oil, water and mashed potatoes to 120°-130°. Add to the dry ingredients; beat just until moistened. Add egg; beat until smooth. Stir in enough remaining flour to form a soft dough.
2. Turn dough onto a floured surface; knead until smooth and elastic, 6-8 minutes. Place in a greased bowl; turn once to grease top. Cover and let rise in a warm place until doubled, about 1 hour.
3. Turn dough onto a floured surface. Roll into a 15x10-in. rectangle. In a small bowl, combine sour cream, chives and egg yolk. Spread sour cream mixture over dough to within ½ in. of edges.
4. Roll up dough jelly-roll style, starting with a long side; pinch seam to seal. Cut into 1-in. slices. Place slices cut side down in a 13x9-in. baking pan. Cover and let rise until doubled, about 1 hour.
5. Bake at 350° for 30-35 minutes or until golden brown. Brush with butter. Cool on a wire rack. Refrigerate any leftovers.
1 ROLL: *214 cal., 9g fat (3g sat. fat), 41mg chol., 258mg sod., 27g carb. (4g sugars, 1g fiber), 5g pro.*

BUDAPEST ROLL

If you're a fan of Yule logs and pumpkin rolls, taste my Swedish specialty made from hazelnut meringue. Make this gorgeous cake your own by using 1 cup maraschino cherries, chocolate chips or toasted nuts in place of the oranges.
—Catherine Walbridge, Boise, ID

PREP: 25 MIN. + STANDING
BAKE: 20 MIN.
MAKES: 12 SERVINGS

- 6 **large egg whites**
- ⅔ **cup finely ground hazelnuts**
- 6 **Tbsp. instant vanilla pudding mix**
- 1⅓ **cups sugar**

FILLING
- 1⅓ **cups heavy whipping cream**
- 1 **Tbsp. sugar**
- ½ **tsp. vanilla extract**
- 1 **can (11 oz.) mandarin oranges, drained**
- 1 **oz. bittersweet chocolate, chopped**

1. Let the egg whites stand at room temperature 30 minutes. Meanwhile, combine nuts and pudding mix. Line a 15x10-in. baking pan with parchment.

2. Preheat oven to 350°. Beat egg whites on medium speed until foamy. Gradually add sugar, 1 Tbsp. at a time, beating on high after each addition until sugar is dissolved. Continue beating until stiff glossy peaks form. Fold in nut mixture.

3. Pipe meringue in long strips or spread over prepared pan until the entire pan is covered. Bake until set and dry, about 20 minutes. Cool completely. Cover meringue with parchment; place another baking pan on top. Flip the pans. Remove top pan; carefully peel parchment from the meringue.

4. Beat cream until it begins to thicken. Add sugar and vanilla; beat until stiff peaks form. Spread cream over the meringue and top with oranges; roll up jelly-roll style, starting with a long side and peeling paper away while rolling.

5. Microwave chocolate on high until melted, stirring occasionally. Drizzle melted chocolate over meringue roll.

1 SLICE: *256 cal., 13g fat (7g sat. fat), 37mg chol., 68mg sod., 33g carb. (31g sugars, 1g fiber), 3g pro.*

SEASONAL GET-TOGETHERS

A fun sleepover for the kids, an old-fashioned Christmas dinner or a post-holiday indulgence party just for the ladies—try out these ideas for holiday gatherings!

Farmhouse Christmas

Warming, satisfying and comforting—
these down-home dishes are just
the thing to greet family and friends
during the holiday season.

ABERDEEN BEEF PIE

Set in the middle of the table, this hearty beef pie will be the center of attention. With chunks of tender beef and tasty vegetables under a flaky pastry crust, this is pure comfort food to welcome your family home for the holidays.
—Peggy Goodrich, Enid, OK

PREP: 1½ HOURS
BAKE: 35 MIN. + STANDING
MAKES: 12 SERVINGS

- ¼ lb. sliced bacon, diced
- 3 lbs. beef stew meat, cut into 1-in. cubes
- 1 cup chopped onion
- 1½ cups halved fresh baby carrots
- 6 Tbsp. all-purpose flour
- 1 cup beef broth
- 1 Tbsp. Worcestershire sauce
- 1 pkg. (10 oz.) frozen peas
- ½ tsp. salt
- ½ tsp. pepper
- 1 refrigerated pie pastry
- 1 large egg, lightly beaten, optional

1. In a Dutch oven, cook bacon over medium heat until crisp. Remove to paper towels to drain. Brown beef in the drippings in batches; drain and set the beef aside. Add onion to the pan; saute until crisp-tender. Add carrots, bacon and beef.

2. Meanwhile, in a small bowl, combine flour, broth and Worcestershire sauce until smooth; add to the beef mixture. Bring to a boil. Reduce heat; cover and simmer until meat is tender, 1-1½ hours. Stir in the peas, salt and pepper. Transfer to an ungreased 11x7-in. baking dish.

3. Preheat oven to 375°. On a lightly floured surface, roll out crust into a 12x8-in. rectangle. Cut slits in the crust. Place over filling; trim and seal edges. If desired, brush with beaten egg. Bake until crust is golden and the filling is bubbly, 35-40 minutes. Let stand for 15 minutes before serving. Refrigerate leftovers.

1 SERVING: *308 cal., 14g fat (6g sat. fat), 76mg chol., 389mg sod., 18g carb. (3g sugars, 2g fiber), 25g pro.*

CHIPOTLE CHICKEN SOUP WITH CORNMEAL DUMPLINGS

I combined two of my favorite soup recipes to come up with this filling soup that has a Tex-Mex flair. The cornmeal dumplings are the perfect finishing touch.
—Nancy Granaman, Burlington, IA

PREP: 20 MIN. • **COOK:** 30 MIN.
MAKES: 6 SERVINGS

- 1 can (15 oz.) black beans, rinsed and drained
- 1 can (14½ oz.) no-salt-added stewed tomatoes, cut up
- 1 can (14½ oz.) reduced-sodium chicken broth
- 1¾ cups water
- 1 tsp. ground cumin
- 1 tsp. minced chipotle pepper in adobo sauce
- 2 cups cubed cooked chicken breast
- 1 large egg
- 1 large egg white
- 1 pkg. (8½ oz.) cornbread/muffin mix
- ⅓ cup reduced-fat biscuit/baking mix
- 1 Tbsp. fat-free milk
- ¼ cup minced fresh cilantro, optional

1. In a small bowl, mash half of the beans. Transfer the mashed and remaining whole beans to a Dutch oven. Add tomatoes, broth, water, cumin and chipotle pepper. Bring to a boil. Reduce heat; cover and simmer for 15 minutes. Add chicken.

2. For dumplings, in a small bowl, combine egg, egg white, muffin mix and baking mix; stir in milk. Drop by tablespoonfuls onto simmering soup. Cover and simmer until a toothpick inserted in a dumpling comes out clean (do not lift the cover while simmering), 10-12 minutes. Ladle soup into bowls. Sprinkle each individual serving with cilantro if desired.

1⅓ CUPS: *356 cal., 7g fat (2g sat. fat), 80mg chol., 808mg sod., 48g carb. (13g sugars, 5g fiber), 24g pro.*

ROASTED PUMPKIN SALAD WITH ORANGE DRESSING

Roasted pumpkin surrounded by dried fruits makes this beautiful seasonal salad a natural match for holiday recipes. The dressing is a light, tasty mix of honey, olive oil and balsamic vinegar. Top it all off with crumbled goat cheese for that final tangy touch.
—Sasha King, Westlake Village, CA

PREP: 45 MIN. • **BAKE:** 45 MIN.
MAKES: 16 SERVINGS

- 1 medium pie pumpkin or butternut squash (about 3 lbs.)
- ¼ cup plus 6 Tbsp. olive oil, divided
- ¼ cup plus 2 Tbsp. honey, divided
- ¾ tsp. salt, divided
- ¼ tsp. pepper, divided
- ½ cup orange juice
- ¼ cup balsamic vinegar
- 1 Tbsp. chopped shallot
- 1 garlic clove, minced
- 2 tsp. grated orange peel
- 10 oz. fresh arugula or 1 lb. fresh baby spinach
- 1 cup dried apricots, thinly sliced
- 1 cup dried cranberries
- 1 pkg. (5.3 oz.) fresh goat cheese, crumbled

1. Preheat oven to 350°. Peel pumpkin and cut into 1-in. cubes, reserving seeds. Place pumpkin cubes in a large bowl. Toss with ¼ cup oil, ¼ cup honey, ½ tsp. salt and ⅛ tsp. pepper. Place pumpkin in a greased 15x10x1-in. baking pan; bake until tender, 30-35 minutes.

2. Place the seeds on a baking sheet. Bake until golden brown, 8-10 minutes.

3. Place orange juice, vinegar, shallot, garlic, orange peel and the remaining 2 Tbsp. honey in a small saucepan. Bring to a boil; cook until the liquid is reduced by half, 15-20 minutes. Strain into a small bowl. Gradually whisk in the remaining 6 Tbsp. oil, ¼ tsp. salt and ⅛ tsp. pepper until blended.

4. In a large bowl, combine arugula, apricots, cranberries and the roasted pumpkin. Sprinkle with goat cheese and the pumpkin seeds. Drizzle with dressing before serving.

1½ CUPS: *195 cal., 10g fat (2g sat. fat), 6mg chol., 157mg sod., 27g carb. (20g sugars, 3g fiber), 2g pro.*
DIABETIC EXCHANGES: *2 fat, 1½ starch, 1 vegetable.*

APPLESAUCE SWEET POTATOES

During the holidays, using your slow cooker not only frees up oven space, but time, too! Sweet potatoes are a must on our family menu, and this no-fuss version will have everyone thinking you spent hours in the kitchen.
—Pamela Allen, Marysville, OH

PREP: 15 MIN. • **COOK:** 4 HOURS • **MAKES:** 8 SERVINGS

- 3 lbs. sweet potatoes (about 5 medium), peeled and sliced
- 1½ cups unsweetened applesauce
- ⅔ cup packed brown sugar
- 3 Tbsp. butter, melted
- 1 tsp. ground cinnamon
- ½ cup glazed pecans, chopped, optional

1. Place sweet potatoes in a 4-qt. slow cooker. In a small bowl, mix applesauce, brown sugar, melted butter and cinnamon; pour over the potatoes.
2. Cook, covered, on low for 4-5 hours or until the potatoes are tender. If desired, sprinkle with pecans before serving. Serve with a slotted spoon.
¾ CUP: *303 cal., 5g fat (3g sat. fat), 11mg chol., 57mg sod., 65g carb. (39g sugars, 6g fiber), 3g pro.*

CRUNCHY WHITE BAKED MACARONI & CHEESE

This creamy, bubbly, indulgent classic is down-home comfort food at its finest. The topping is made with panko bread crumbs for an extra bit of crunch.
—Nicole Duffy, New Haven, CT

PREP: 25 MIN. • **BAKE:** 30 MIN. + STANDING • **MAKES:** 8 SERVINGS

- 1 pkg. (16 oz.) uncooked elbow macaroni
- 1 can (12 oz.) evaporated milk
- 1 cup milk
- 1 lb. process white deli cheese, cubed
- 8 oz. cubed white cheddar cheese
- 1½ cups panko (Japanese) bread crumbs
- ½ cup grated Parmesan cheese
- ½ tsp. dried parsley flakes

1. Preheat oven to 350°. In a large saucepan, cook macaroni according to the package directions. Drain and set aside.
2. In the same saucepan, combine evaporated milk, milk, process cheese and cheddar cheese. Cook and stir until the cheeses are melted and the mixture is smooth. Stir in the macaroni; heat through. Transfer to a greased 13x9-in. baking dish. Combine bread crumbs, Parmesan cheese and parsley flakes; sprinkle over the macaroni mixture. Cover and bake for 20 minutes. Uncover; bake until bubbly and golden brown, 10-15 minutes longer. Let stand 10 minutes before serving.
1 CUP: *639 cal., 31g fat (18g sat. fat), 104mg chol., 1091mg sod., 61g carb. (11g sugars, 2g fiber), 30g pro.*

CINNAMON CHOCOLATE CAKE

A healthy hint of cinnamon gives this chocolate cake an extra step up over the expected sheet cake. Its sweet frosting is full of crunchy pecans.
—Victor Clifford, San Jose, CA

PREP: 30 MIN. • **BAKE:** 35 MIN.
MAKES: 15 SERVINGS

- ½ cup butter
- ½ cup vegetable oil
- 2 oz. unsweetened chocolate
- 1 cup water
- 2 large eggs, room temperature
- 2 cups sugar
- 2 tsp. vanilla extract
- 2 cups all-purpose flour
- 2 tsp. ground cinnamon
- 1 tsp. baking soda
- ½ tsp. salt
- ½ cup buttermilk

FROSTING
- ½ cup butter
- 6 Tbsp. whole milk
- 2 oz. unsweetened chocolate
- 3¾ cups confectioners' sugar
- 2 tsp. vanilla extract
- 1 cup chopped pecans
  Additional chopped pecans, optional

1. Preheat oven to 350°. In a small saucepan, combine butter, oil and chocolate. Cook and stir over low heat until the chocolate is melted. Remove from the heat. Add water; pour into a mixing bowl. Cool to room temperature.
2. Beat in the eggs, sugar and vanilla. Combine flour, cinnamon, baking soda and salt; add to the chocolate mixture alternately with buttermilk. Pour into a greased 13x9-in. baking dish. Bake until a toothpick comes out clean, 30-35 minutes. Move to a wire rack.
3. In a small saucepan, combine butter, milk and chocolate. Cook and stir over low heat until chocolate is melted. Remove from heat. Stir in confectioners' sugar and vanilla until smooth; fold in pecans. Spread over warm cake. Sprinkle with additional chopped pecans if desired.
1 SLICE: *575 cal., 30g fat (12g sat. fat), 58mg chol., 291mg sod., 74g carb. (57g sugars, 3g fiber), 5g pro.*

HERBED BRUSSELS SPROUTS

I love Brussels sprouts and wanted my children to love them, too! Topped with a tangy sauce and mixed with mushrooms, these are so tasty my kids eat them right up. Chopped pimientos add a splash of red to the green sprouts, so this dish fits right in on a Christmas table.
—Debbie Marrone, Warner Robins, GA

PREP: 20 MIN. • **BAKE:** 15 MIN.
MAKES: 8 SERVINGS

- 8 cups fresh Brussels sprouts (about 2½ lbs.)
- 1 cup sliced fresh mushrooms
- ¼ cup packed brown sugar
- ¼ cup cider vinegar
- 2 Tbsp. butter, melted
- ½ tsp. salt
- ½ tsp. dried tarragon
- ½ tsp. dried marjoram
- ½ tsp. pepper
- ¼ cup chopped pimientos

1. Preheat oven to 350°. Trim Brussels sprouts and cut an "X" in the base of each. Place sprouts in a steamer basket; place basket in a large saucepan over 1 in. water. Bring to a boil; cover and steam 9-11 minutes or until crisp-tender.
2. Transfer sprouts to a 13x9-in. baking dish coated with cooking spray. Top with mushrooms. In a small bowl, combine the brown sugar, vinegar, butter, salt, tarragon, marjoram and pepper. Drizzle mixture over the vegetables. Sprinkle with pimientos.
3. Bake, uncovered, 15-20 minutes or until the vegetables are tender.
¾ CUP: *94 cal., 3g fat (2g sat. fat), 8mg chol., 203mg sod., 16g carb. (9g sugars, 4g fiber), 3g pro.*
DIABETIC EXCHANGES: *2 vegetable, ½ starch, ½ fat.*

PJ's & Pancakes

With school holidays, it's the right time for a sleepover party! Knock their socks off with a breakfast buffet.

SET UP A PANCAKE BAR

To set up the perfect pancake and waffle bar, give kids lots of options! Make sure you handle the cooking—whether it's on a stovetop griddle, in an electric skillet or in a waffle iron, you can "take orders" and let each child pick a favorite. Many of the toppings can be added to the batter—especially chocolate chips, nuts and fruit.

SPREADS

Butter
Peanut butter
Nutella
Marshmallow fluff
Jam or preserves
Pie filling
Yogurt
Lemon curd

TOPPINGS

Fresh fruits: blueberries,
strawberries or bananas
Toasted nuts
Shredded sweetened coconut
Sprinkles
Mini chocolate chips
Mini marshmallows
Granola
Dried fruit: cherries or cranberries
Bacon, cooked and crumbled

FINISHING TOUCHES

Honey
Maple syrup
Caramel sauce
Chocolate sauce
Whipped cream
Cinnamon sugar

ORANGE CREAM

I learned this recipe from a fellow teacher when I was living in West Virginia. It's a standout for a morning party, since it's even better when made the night before, so the flavors have time to mix. Plus, kids love it— it tastes like a Creamsicle in a bowl!
—Georgeanna Wellings, Dacula, GA

PREP: 15 MIN. + CHILLING
MAKES: 8 SERVINGS

1½ cups cold 2% milk
1 pkg. (3.4 oz.) instant vanilla pudding mix
¾ cup sour cream
⅓ cup thawed orange juice concentrate
2 cans (11 oz. each) mandarin oranges, drained
1 can (20 oz.) unsweetened pineapple tidbits, drained
1 can (15 oz.) sliced peaches in extra-light syrup, drained
2 large red apples, chopped

In a large bowl, whisk the milk and dry pudding mix for 2 minutes. Stir in sour cream and orange juice concentrate. Gently stir in fruit. Refrigerate, covered, at least 1 hour before serving.

¾ CUP: *194 cal., 5g fat (3g sat. fat), 7mg chol., 91mg sod., 38g carb. (33g sugars, 2g fiber), 3g pro.*

THE BEST EVER PANCAKES

PICTURED ON P. 136

I'm not joking when I say I make pancakes every weekend. I love them in any form and variation, and this is one of my favorite pancake recipes.
—James Schend, Pleasant Prairie, WI

PREP: 15 MIN. • **COOK:** 5 MIN./BATCH
MAKES: 12 PANCAKES

1½ cups (6.75 oz./190g) all-purpose flour
2 Tbsp. sugar
1 tsp. baking powder
½ tsp. baking soda
½ tsp. salt
1 cup buttermilk
2 large eggs
¼ cup butter, melted
1 tsp. vanilla extract

1. In a large bowl, whisk together the first 5 ingredients. In another bowl, whisk the remaining ingredients; stir into the dry ingredients just until moistened.
2. Preheat griddle over medium heat. Lightly grease griddle. Pour batter by ¼ cupfuls onto the griddle; cook until bubbles on top begin to pop and the bottoms are golden brown. Turn; cook until the second side is golden brown.

3 PANCAKES: *360 cal., 15g fat (8g sat. fat), 126mg chol., 817mg sod., 45g carb. (10g sugars, 1g fiber), 10g pro.*

CHOCOLATE LOVER'S PANCAKES

These indulgent chocolate pancakes are fluffy on the inside, with a rich but not-too-sweet flavor from the cocoa and a nice tang from the buttermilk. They're delicious with either maple or chocolate syrup—and even better with both swirled together on the plate!
—Harland Johns, Leesburg, TX

PREP: 15 MIN. • **COOK:** 5 MIN./BATCH • **MAKES:** 4 SERVINGS

- 1 cup all-purpose flour
- ¼ cup baking cocoa
- 2 Tbsp. sugar
- 1 tsp. baking powder
- ½ tsp. baking soda
- ½ tsp. salt
- 1 cup buttermilk
- 1 large egg
- 2 Tbsp. butter, melted
- 1 tsp. vanilla extract
  Maple syrup and chocolate syrup

1. In a large bowl, whisk flour, cocoa, sugar, baking powder, baking soda and salt. In another bowl, whisk the buttermilk, egg, melted butter and vanilla until blended. Add to the dry ingredients, stirring just until moistened.
2. Place a greased large nonstick skillet over medium heat. Pour batter by ¼ cupfuls onto skillet; cook until bubbles on top begin to pop and bottoms are golden brown. Turn; cook until the second side is golden brown. Serve with syrups.
2 PANCAKES: *271 cal., 8g fat (4g sat. fat), 64mg chol., 753mg sod., 42g carb. (16g sugars, 2g fiber), 8g pro.*

HOME FRIES

When I was little, my dad and I would get up early on Sundays and make these for the family. The rest of the gang would be awakened by the tempting aroma.
—Teresa Koide, Manchester, CT

PREP: 25 MIN. • **COOK:** 15 MIN./BATCH • **MAKES:** 8 SERVINGS

- 1 lb. bacon, chopped
- 8 medium potatoes (about 3 lbs.), peeled and cut into ½ in. pieces
- 1 large onion, chopped
- 1 tsp. salt
- ½ tsp. pepper

1. In a large skillet, cook chopped bacon over medium-low heat until crisp. Remove bacon from pan with slotted spoon; drain on paper towels. Remove bacon drippings from the pan; reserve.
2. Working in batches, add ¼ cup bacon drippings, the potatoes, onion, salt and pepper to pan; toss to coat. Cook and stir over medium-low heat until the potatoes are golden brown and tender, 15-20 minutes, adding more drippings as needed. Stir in cooked bacon; serve immediately.
1 CUP: *349 cal., 21g fat (8g sat. fat), 33mg chol., 681mg sod., 31g carb. (3g sugars, 2g fiber), 10g pro.*

TROPICAL BERRY SMOOTHIES

This fruity, healthy smoothie is a big hit with kids and adults alike because it tastes like a treat while delivering the vitamins. The recipe is easy to increase based on the number of people you'll be serving.
—Hillary Engler, Cape Girardeau, MO

TAKES: 10 MIN. • **MAKES:** 2 SERVINGS

- 1 cup pina colada juice blend
- 1 container (6 oz.) vanilla yogurt
- ¼ cup frozen mango chunks
- ¼ cup frozen unsweetened blueberries
- ⅓ cup frozen unsweetened strawberries

In a blender, combine all the ingredients; cover and process for 30 seconds or until smooth. Pour into chilled glasses; serve immediately.

1¼ CUPS: 172 cal., 2g fat (1g sat. fat), 4mg chol., 62mg sod., 35g carb. (32g sugars, 2g fiber), 5g pro.

OVERNIGHT YEAST WAFFLES

Whip up this crowd-sized batch of batter the night before your big brunch. In the morning, it's quick and easy to turn out enough for the whole crew. What a delicious way to get the party started!
—Mary Balcomb, Florence, OR

PREP: 15 MIN. + CHILLING • **COOK:** 5 MIN./BATCH
MAKES: 10 SERVINGS

- 1 pkg. (¼ oz.) active dry yeast
- ½ cup warm water (110° to 115°)
- 1 tsp. sugar
- 2 cups warm whole milk (110° to 115°)
- ½ cup butter, melted
- 2 large eggs, lightly beaten
- 2¾ cups all-purpose flour
- 1 tsp. salt
- ½ tsp. baking soda

1. In a large bowl, dissolve yeast in warm water. Add sugar; let stand for 5 minutes. Add milk, butter and eggs; mix well. Combine flour and salt; stir into the milk mixture. Cover and refrigerate overnight.
2. Stir batter; add baking soda and stir well. Bake waffles in a preheated waffle iron according to manufacturer's directions until golden brown.
2 WAFFLES: 220 cal., 12g fat (7g sat. fat), 74mg chol., 366mg sod., 22g carb. (3g sugars, 1g fiber), 6g pro.

BANANA BLENDER PANCAKES

This mouthwatering recipe is a hit with banana lovers! Whipping up the batter in the blender makes it simple and easy to mix, pour and wash up. Feel free to experiment with different favorite fruits. Serve with butter and syrup.
—Lorraine Caland, Shuniah, ON

PREP: 15 MIN. • **COOK:** 5 MIN./BATCH
MAKES: 5 SERVINGS

- 1 cup all-purpose flour
- ¼ cup whole wheat flour
- ¼ cup cornmeal
- 1 Tbsp. sugar
- 1½ tsp. baking powder
- ¼ tsp. salt
- 1¼ cups 1% milk
- 1 large egg
- 1 Tbsp. canola oil
- 1 medium banana, coarsely mashed
  Honey, sliced banana and cinnamon, optional

1. In a blender, combine ½ cup flour, the whole wheat flour, cornmeal, sugar, baking powder, salt, milk, egg and oil; cover and process just until smooth. Gently stir in the remaining ½ cup flour and the mashed banana.

2. Place a greased large nonstick skillet over medium heat. In batches, pour batter by ¼ cupfuls onto the skillet; cook until bubbles on top begin to pop and bottoms are golden brown. Turn; cook until second side is golden brown. If desired, serve with honey, sliced banana and cinnamon.

2 PANCAKES: *236 cal., 5g fat (1g sat. fat), 40mg chol., 304mg sod., 41g carb. (9g sugars, 2g fiber), 8g pro.*

Post-Holiday Night In

With the holidays past, it's time for Mom and her friends to kick back for some post-Christmas indulgence. This is the time for grown-ups to relax—you've earned it!

FESTIVE COCKTAIL CRANBERRY COLADA

I had to do a lot of coaxing to get this recipe from a chef I knew, but my persistence paid off. Since it contains cranberry juice, it is wonderful at Thanksgiving and Christmas, but I like it on hot days, too.
—Susan Kieboam, Amherstburg, ON

TAKES: 10 MIN. • **MAKES:** 10 SERVINGS

- 5 cups cranberry juice
- 2½ cups unsweetened pineapple juice
- 2½ cups orange juice
- 1¼ cups cream of coconut
  Assorted fresh fruit, optional

Working in batches, place all ingredients in a blender; cover and process until well combined. Serve over ice. If desired, garnish with fresh fruit.

1 CUP: *229 cal., 5g fat (4g sat. fat), 0 chol., 19mg sod., 47g carb. (44g sugars, 0 fiber), 1g pro.*

GRUYERE & CRAB PALMIERS

I keep these little bursts of flavor in my freezer so they can be pulled out and popped into the oven whenever needed. Crab, pancetta and Gruyere make a sophisticated, elegant app—and you can make your own variations on the filling. Try chicken and pesto, or a Mediterranean version with spinach and feta.
—Grace Voltolina, Westport, CT

PREP: 30 MIN. + CHILLING • **BAKE:** 15 MIN.
MAKES: 3 DOZEN

- 1 large egg, lightly beaten
- 1 Tbsp. mayonnaise
- 1 tsp. minced fresh thyme
  or ¼ tsp. dried thyme
- 1 tsp. Dijon mustard
- ½ tsp. pepper
- ½ tsp. smoked paprika
- ½ tsp. prepared horseradish
- ¼ tsp. Worcestershire sauce
- 1 can (6 oz.) lump crabmeat, drained
- 4 oz. sliced pancetta, chopped
- 1 pkg. (17.3 oz.) frozen
  puff pastry, thawed
- ½ cup shredded Gruyere
  or Swiss cheese

1. Preheat oven to 400°. Combine the first 8 ingredients; fold in crab. In a small skillet, cook pancetta over medium heat until partially cooked but not crisp; drain on paper towels.
2. Unfold 1 sheet puff pastry. Spread half the crab mixture to within ½ in. of edges. Sprinkle with half the cheese and half the pancetta.
3. Roll up the left and right sides toward the center, jelly-roll style, until rolls meet in the middle. Repeat with remaining pastry and ingredients. Refrigerate until firm enough to slice, about 30 minutes.
4. Cut each roll crosswise into ½-in. slices. Place 2 in. apart on parchment-lined baking sheets. Bake until golden and crisp,

15-20 minutes. Cool on pans 2 minutes. Remove to wire racks to cool.
FREEZE OPTION: Cover and freeze unbaked sliced palmiers on waxed paper-lined baking sheets until firm. Transfer to freezer containers; close tightly and return to freezer. To use, bake as directed.
1 PALMIER: *93 cal., 6g fat (2g sat. fat), 14mg chol., 149mg sod., 8g carb. (0 sugars, 1g fiber), 3g pro.*

STEAK & PROSCIUTTO SKEWERS WITH CREAMY BASIL-TARRAGON SAUCE

These flavorful bites of marinated steak layered with prosciutto can be cooked on the grill or under the broiler, so they're ideal for holiday parties no matter what climate you live in! The thick sauce is lovely and creamy—use it as a dip, or smear it on a plate and set the skewers over the top.
—Elizabeth Nutt, Alpharetta, GA

PREP: 25 MIN. + MARINATING
GRILL: 10 MIN.
MAKES: 7 KABOBS (1 CUP SAUCE)

- ½ cup minced fresh gingerroot
- ½ cup Worcestershire sauce
- ¼ cup cider vinegar
- ¼ cup dry red wine or beef broth
- 2 garlic cloves, minced
- 1 beef flank steak (1¼ lbs.), cut into ½-in. strips
- 1 pkg. (3 oz.) thinly sliced prosciutto, cut into ½-in. strips
- 2 Tbsp. olive oil
- ¼ tsp. salt
- ¼ tsp. pepper

SAUCE
- ⅔ cup cream cheese, softened
- ¼ cup heavy whipping cream
- 2 Tbsp. lemon juice
- 2 Tbsp. minced fresh basil
- 2 Tbsp. minced fresh tarragon
- 1 Tbsp. minced fresh parsley

1. In a bowl or shallow dish, combine the first 5 ingredients. Add beef and turn to coat. Refrigerate at least 4 hours.

2. Drain beef, discarding marinade. Layer 1 slice steak and 1 slice prosciutto; roll up. Repeat with remaining slices of meat.

3. Thread onto metal or soaked wooden skewers. Brush with oil; sprinkle with salt and pepper. Grill, covered, over medium-high heat or broil 4 in. from heat until beef reaches desired doneness, 10-12 minutes, turning occasionally.

4. In a small bowl, beat cream cheese and cream until blended. Stir in lemon juice and herbs. Serve with kabobs.

1 KABOB WITH 2 TBSP. SAUCE: *298 cal., 22g fat (10g sat. fat), 81mg chol., 502mg sod., 4g carb. (2g sugars, 0 fiber), 21g pro.*

SPICED APPLE CIDER JELLY SHOTS

These spiced, spiked gelatin squares always get the party started. If you're going for the more traditional shot-style look, pour the mixture into 2-ounce plastic cups and refrigerate until set.
—Rachel Bernard Seis, Milwaukee, WI

PREP: 10 MIN. • **COOK:** 5 MIN. + CHILLING
MAKES: 64 SQUARES

- 1½ cups cold apple cider or juice
- 4 envelopes unflavored gelatin
- 1 cup sugar
- 1½ cups ginger-flavored vodka
- 2 tsp. Angostura bitters
- 2 Tbsp. cinnamon sugar
  Thinly sliced apple, optional

1. Pour apple cider into a large saucepan and sprinkle gelatin over top; let stand, without stirring, until gelatin softens, about 5 minutes. Whisk in sugar. Heat and stir over low heat until sugar and gelatin are completely dissolved, 8-10 minutes (do not boil); remove from heat. Stir in vodka; pour mixture into a 9-in. square baking pan coated with cooking spray. Refrigerate, uncovered, until mixture is firm, about 2 hours.

2. To unmold, run a sharp knife along edges of gelatin; invert onto a cutting board and lift off pan. Cut into 64 squares; brush tops with bitters and sprinkle with cinnamon sugar. If desired, garnish with apple slices.

1 SQUARE: *28 cal., 0 fat (0 sat. fat), 0 chol., 1mg sod., 4g carb. (4g sugars, 0 fiber), 0 pro.*

ROASTED BEETROOT & GARLIC HUMMUS

This tasty beetroot hummus is the prettiest pink snack I've ever seen. The healthy recipe is handy to make in large batches for a party or to keep in the fridge for lunches and snacks throughout the week.
—Elizabeth Worndl, Toronto, ON

PREP: 25 MIN. • **BAKE:** 45 MIN.
MAKES: 4 CUPS

- 3 fresh medium beets (about 1 lb.)
- 1 whole garlic bulb
- ½ tsp. salt, divided
- ½ tsp. coarsely ground pepper, divided
- 1 tsp. plus ¼ cup olive oil, divided
- 1 can (15 oz.) garbanzo beans or chickpeas, rinsed and drained
- 3 to 4 Tbsp. lemon juice
- 2 Tbsp. tahini
- ½ tsp. ground cumin
- ½ tsp. cayenne pepper
- ¼ cup plain Greek yogurt, optional
  Minced fresh dill weed or parsley
  Assorted fresh vegetables
  Sliced or torn pita bread

1. Preheat oven to 375°. Pierce beets with a fork; place in a microwave-safe bowl and cover loosely. Microwave on high for 4 minutes, stirring halfway. Cool slightly. Wrap beets in individual foil packets.
2. Remove the papery outer skin from garlic bulb, but do not peel or separate cloves. Cut in half crosswise. Sprinkle halves with ¼ tsp. salt and ¼ tsp. pepper; drizzle with 1 tsp. oil. Wrap in individual foil packets. Roast the beets and garlic until the garlic cloves are soft, about 45 minutes.
3. Remove beets and garlic from oven; unwrap. Rinse beets with cold water; peel when cool enough to handle. Squeeze garlic from skins. Place beets and garlic in a food processor. Add garbanzo beans, lemon juice, tahini, cumin, cayenne pepper and the remaining olive oil, salt and ground pepper. Process until smooth.
4. If desired, pulse 2 Tbsp. Greek yogurt with the beet mixture, dolloping the remaining yogurt over finished hummus. Sprinkle with dill or parsley. Serve with assorted vegetables and pita bread.
¼ CUP: 87 cal., 5g fat (1g sat. fat), 0 chol., 131mg sod., 8g carb. (3g sugars, 2g fiber), 2g pro.
DIABETIC EXCHANGES: *1 fat, ½ starch.*

BANANAS FOSTER GELATO

The classic combination of bananas and rum is reinvented as an ice cream dish that's even better with ribbons of caramel topping. It's an outstanding treat for adults!
—Scarlett Elrod, Newnan, GA

PREP: 20 MIN. + FREEZING • **MAKES:** 1 QT.

- 5 large egg yolks
- ⅔ cup packed brown sugar
- ½ tsp. salt
- ¼ tsp. ground cinnamon
- 1¾ cups whole milk
- ¼ cup heavy whipping cream
- 2 Tbsp. dark rum or
   ½ tsp. rum extract
- 1 tsp. vanilla extract
- 2 medium bananas
- 1 tsp. lemon juice
   Sliced bananas and hot caramel
   ice cream topping, optional

1. In a small bowl, beat egg yolks, brown sugar, salt and cinnamon for 4 minutes; set aside.
2. In a small heavy saucepan, heat milk and cream until bubbles form around the sides of the pan. Whisk a small amount of the hot mixture into the egg mixture. Return all to the pan, whisking constantly.
3. Cook and stir over medium heat until mixture reaches at least 160° and coats the back of a spoon. Quickly transfer to a large bowl; place in ice water and stir for 2 minutes. Stir in rum and vanilla. Mash bananas with lemon juice; stir into the rum mixture.
4. Press waxed paper onto the surface of the custard. Refrigerate for several hours or overnight.
5. Fill the cylinder of an ice cream freezer two-thirds full; freeze according to the manufacturer's directions. When the ice cream is frozen, transfer to a freezer container; freeze for 2-4 hours before serving. If desired, top with sliced bananas and caramel topping.
½ **CUP:** *198 cal., 7g fat (4g sat. fat), 129mg chol., 183mg sod., 28g carb. (24g sugars, 1g fiber), 4g pro.*

GINGER-PORK WONTONS

A flavorful, juicy pork filling is jazzed up with a delicious touch of ginger and enclosed in crispy wrappers. These surprisingly simple appetizers are the ultimate finger food and are perfect for parties.
—Sandra Parton, Halifax, NS

PREP: 35 MIN. • **COOK:** 5 MIN./BATCH
MAKES: ABOUT 3 DOZEN

- 2 Tbsp. oyster sauce or
   2 tsp. soy sauce
- 1 Tbsp. dry sherry
- 1 Tbsp. soy sauce
- 1 Tbsp. sesame oil
- 1 tsp. sugar
- 1 lb. ground pork
- ½ medium onion, finely chopped
- 1 celery rib, finely chopped
- 1 medium carrot, finely chopped
- 2 Tbsp. minced fresh gingerroot
- 3 garlic cloves, minced
- 40 wonton wrappers
   Oil for frying
   Plum sauce, optional

1. In a small bowl, mix first 5 ingredients. In a large skillet, cook pork over medium heat until no longer pink, 6-8 minutes; drain. Add the vegetables, ginger and garlic; cook 2-3 minutes longer. Stir in the sauce mixture; cook and stir until the mixture is slightly thickened, 2-3 minutes. Cool slightly.
2. Place about 1 Tbsp. filling in the center of each wonton wrapper. Moisten the wrapper edges with water. Fold 1 corner diagonally over the filling to form a triangle; press edges to seal.
3. For shallow fry: In an electric skillet or deep skillet, heat 1 in. oil to 375°. For deep fry: In an electric skillet or deep fryer, heat oil to 375°. Fry wontons in batches until golden brown, 2-3 minutes, turning once. Drain on paper towels. If desired, serve with plum sauce.
1 WONTON: *70 cal., 4g fat (1g sat. fat), 8mg chol., 104mg sod., 5g carb. (0 sugars, 0 fiber), 3g pro.*

ELF ON
THE SHELF

Whether welcoming the elf's arrival or sending him on his merry way, this new Christmas tradition is the perfect opportunity to host a fun kids holiday party.

WHAT IS ELF ON THE SHELF?

Carol Aebersold and her daughter Chanda Bell published *The Elf on the Shelf: A Christmas Tradition* in 2005, sharing their family's experience with a strange visitor. The idea quickly caught the imaginations of families everywhere as they welcomed their own elves into their homes.

As the story goes, scout elves are sent out from the North Pole to keep an eye on children to make sure they're being nice—or see if they're being naughty! Some elves arrive right on December 1, while others arrive when the Christmas tree goes up, signaling that the house is ready to welcome the elf. Each day, the elf sits motionless, watching. Every night, he disappears on a journey back to the North Pole to report to Santa. Each morning, he returns in a different spot, leading to lots of fun as children find the elf in his new hiding place.

Children choose a name for their elf, and can leave treats and small presents out for him. But they should never touch the elf—it'll drain the little magical creature's energy, preventing him from making the trip back up north. If a child does give in to temptation and cuddle the elf, all can be put right with a sprinkling of cinnamon (filled with magic elf-vitamins!) beside the elf before bedtime.

An elf-themed party to welcome the visitor or to bid farewell before he departs for good on Christmas Eve is a great way to bring children together during the holiday season!

ELF PARTY PUNCH

When friends of mine got married, I absolutely loved the punch they served—but they wouldn't give out the recipe! We spent many Saturdays figuring out just the right combination.
—Annette Lee, Lepanto, AR

PREP: 10 MIN. + CHILLING • **MAKES:** 20 SERVINGS (¾ CUP EACH)

- 8 cups (64 oz.) lemonade
- 1 can (46 oz.) unsweetened pineapple juice
- ¾ cup water or coconut water
- ½ cup sugar
- 2 Tbsp. coconut extract
- Fresh fruit for garnish, optional

In a large pitcher or punch bowl, combine all the ingredients. Refrigerate until serving. Garnish with fresh fruit as desired.
¾ CUP: *109 cal., 0 fat (0 sat. fat), 0 chol., 8mg sod., 26g carb. (23g sugars, 0 fiber), 0 pro.*

ELF CUPCAKES

Rich and buttery vanilla cupcakes have a tender crumb and make a perfect base for these whimsical, low-fuss elves lost in fluffy frosting!
—Taste of Home *Test Kitchen*

PREP: 45 MIN. • **BAKE:** 15 MIN. + COOLING
MAKES: 22 CUPCAKES

⅔ cup butter, softened
1¾ cups sugar
1½ tsp. vanilla extract
2 large eggs, room temperature
2½ cups all-purpose flour
2½ tsp. baking powder
½ tsp. salt
1¼ cups 2% milk
FROSTING
¾ cup butter, softened
¾ cup shortening

1½ tsp. clear vanilla extract
6 cups confectioners' sugar
4 to 6 Tbsp. 2% milk
DECORATIONS
44 miniature candy canes
Pastel miniature marshmallows
Candy cane kisses

1. Preheat oven to 350°. Line 22 muffin cups with paper liners.
2. Cream butter and sugar until light and fluffy. Beat in vanilla and eggs, 1 at a time. In another bowl, whisk together flour, baking powder and salt; add to the creamed mixture alternately with milk, beating well.
3. Fill prepared cups two-thirds full. Bake until a toothpick inserted in the center of a cupcake comes out clean, 15-20 minutes. Cool 10 minutes before removing from pans to wire racks to cool completely.

4. For frosting, beat butter, shortening and vanilla until blended; gradually beat in confectioners' sugar and enough milk to reach spreading consistency. Spread over the cupcakes.
5. To decorate, break off the curved end of candy canes; reserve the straight portion for the elf legs. Cut strawberry or lime marshmallows diagonally in half and press onto the ends of the legs for shoes; insert legs into frosting. Cut orange marshmallows diagonally in half. Insert kisses into frosting for elf heads and the orange marshmallows for ears.
1 CUPCAKE: *422 cal., 19g fat (10g sat. fat), 50mg chol., 218mg sod., 60g carb. (49g sugars, 0 fiber), 3g pro.*

ITALIAN CHOCOLATE SPICE COOKIES

I recently found this old family recipe in my mom's kitchen. I made a few adjustments to streamline the process, and the cookies turned out wonderfully.
—Shawn Barto, Winter Garden, FL

PREP: 30 MIN. • **BAKE:** 10 MIN. + COOLING
MAKES: 5 DOZEN

- ¾ cup shortening
- 1 cup sugar
- 4 large eggs, room temperature
- ½ cup 2% milk
- 1 tsp. vanilla extract
- 4 cups all-purpose flour
- ½ cup baking cocoa
- 2 tsp. ground cinnamon
- 2 tsp. baking soda
- 1 tsp. baking powder
- 1 tsp. ground cloves
- ½ cup chopped walnuts

GLAZE
- 2¼ cups confectioners' sugar
- 2 tsp. light corn syrup
- 3 to 4 Tbsp. 2% milk
  Sprinkles, optional

1. Preheat oven to 350°. In a large bowl, cream shortening and sugar until light and fluffy. Beat in eggs, milk and vanilla. In another bowl, whisk flour, cocoa, cinnamon, baking soda, baking powder and cloves; gradually beat into the creamed mixture. Stir in walnuts.

2. Shape level tablespoonfuls of dough into balls; place 1 in. apart on ungreased baking sheets. Bake until bottoms are light brown, 10-12 minutes. Remove from pans to wire racks to cool completely.

3. For glaze, in a large bowl, mix the confectioners' sugar, corn syrup and enough milk to reach desired consistency. Dip tops of cookies into glaze; if desired, decorate with sprinkles. Let stand until set. Store between pieces of waxed paper in an airtight container.

1 COOKIE: *99 cal., 4g fat (1g sat. fat), 13mg chol., 57mg sod., 15g carb. (8g sugars, 0 fiber), 2g pro.*

CHICKEN PARMESAN PIZZA

This tasty pizza is the perfect combo— quick and easy to make, and a winner with even picky eaters. It's a handy option for a family dinner on a busy night, or at the center of the table at a kids party.
—Karen Wittmeier, Parkland, FL

PREP: 25 MIN. • **BAKE:** 15 MIN.
MAKES: 6 SLICES

- 8 frozen breaded chicken tenders
- 1 loaf (1 lb.) frozen pizza dough, thawed
- ½ cup marinara sauce
- ¼ tsp. garlic powder
- 2 cups (8 oz.) shredded part-skim mozzarella cheese
- ¼ cup shredded Parmesan cheese
- 2 Tbsp. thinly sliced fresh basil
  Additional warmed marinara sauce

1. Bake chicken tenders according to package directions. Remove from oven; increase oven setting to 450°.

2. Meanwhile, grease a 12-in. pizza pan. Roll dough to fit pan. In a small bowl, mix marinara sauce and garlic powder; spread over dough.

3. Cut chicken into 1-in. pieces. Top pizza with chicken and mozzarella cheese. Bake on a lower oven rack 12-15 minutes or until crust is golden brown and cheese is melted. Sprinkle with Parmesan cheese and basil. Serve with additional marinara.

1 SLICE: *440 cal., 17g fat (6g sat. fat), 35mg chol., 774mg sod., 48g carb. (4g sugars, 3g fiber), 23g pro.*

KID-MADE COCOA CUPCAKES

I'm only a kid, and this is the first recipe I've made up. But I spent a year perfecting these cupcakes, asking advice from owners of local bakeries and my baker friends. I make them for every special occasion in my family, and sometimes just for fun. If you want the cupcakes to taste more like hot cocoa, double the amount of hot cocoa mix. This recipe works well with multiple kinds of frosting flavors: mint, maple syrup, marshmallow and buttercream. Decorate them any way you want!
—Maia Hubscher, South Orange, NJ

PREP: 20 MIN. • **BAKE:** 25 MIN. + COOLING
MAKES: 2 DOZEN

- 2 cups all-purpose flour
- 1½ cups sugar
- 2 Tbsp. baking cocoa
- 2 Tbsp. instant hot cocoa mix
- ¼ tsp. baking soda
- 3 large eggs, room temperature
- ⅔ cup whole milk
- ⅓ cup water
- ½ tsp. vanilla extract
- ½ cup butter, softened
- 1 milk chocolate baking bar (4 oz.), melted
  Whipped topping, thawed, optional

1. Preheat oven to 375°. Line 24 muffin cups with paper liners.
2. Combine the first 5 ingredients. In another bowl, mix eggs, milk, water and vanilla. Add the egg mixture to the dry ingredients, beating on medium until smooth. Beat in butter; add melted chocolate and beat just until blended.
3. Fill prepared muffin cups half full. Bake until a toothpick inserted in center comes out clean, 25-30 minutes. Cool in pans 10 minutes before removing to wire racks to cool completely. If desired, top with whipped topping and decorate as desired.
1 CUPCAKE: *162 cal., 6g fat (4g sat. fat), 36mg chol., 64mg sod., 25g carb. (16g sugars, 1g fiber), 3g pro.*

MAKE YOUR OWN ELF COOKIES!

Use your favorite sugar cookie recipe to make these edible cupcake toppers—we'll lead you through decorating them as the famous Elf on the Shelf. The decorating tools and ingredients can be found in craft stores or online.

1. To decorate the cookies, we used royal icing in a pastry bag with a fine tip. First, outline the collar and hat brim, then "color in" the space with icing. For the open spaces, add water to the icing to reach a flooding consistency.

2. Switch to bright red icing, and outline the elf's tunic and hat. Setting the outline first helps keep the colors from running together. Once the outline is done, fill in the space with solid red.

3. Make the elf's face next—again, outlining first and then filling in the area with a solid color. Use different proportions of food coloring to make the face the exact shade you want.

4. Tiny round sprinkles are perfect for the eyes; set them precisely in place using a clean tweezers. After this step, let the cookies sit overnight to allow the icing to set and harden completely.

5. Give your elves spots of color in their cheeks with a cotton swab dipped in edible pink luster dust.

6. Switch the tip on the pastry bag to a leaf-shaped tip to make the ears. Use royal icing in the same shade you used for the face. Use the small round tip to add a single dot of frosting for the nose.

7. We used an edible color marker to draw the mouth on the elf. You can also use the finest tip on your pastry bag to pipe the mouth with royal icing.

8. Use a star-shaped tip on the pastry bag to add the elf's hair. We used store-bought chocolate frosting, but you can tint more royal icing to create whatever hair color you like!

FRENCH-FRY BAKE

When a friend brought this to a gathering at church, I simply had to ask for the recipe—what a fast and fun way to serve potatoes! It's always good to find a recipe that can sneak in a few extra veggies; the kids never find the carrots hidden inside this one.
—Cheryl Newendorp, Pella, IA

PREP: 30 MIN. • **BAKE:** 35 MIN.
MAKES: 12 SERVINGS

- ⅓ cup butter, cubed
- 1 small onion, chopped
- 1 small green pepper, chopped
- ½ cup all-purpose flour
- 3 cups 2% milk
- 1 medium carrot, shredded
- 1 cup shredded cheddar cheese, divided
- ⅓ cup diced pimientos, drained
- ½ tsp. salt
- ⅛ tsp. pepper
- 1 pkg. (32 oz.) frozen french-fried potatoes

1. Preheat oven to 375°. In a Dutch oven, heat butter over medium heat. Add onion and green pepper; cook and stir until tender, 3-4 minutes. Stir in flour until blended; gradually whisk in milk. Bring to a boil, stirring constantly; cook and stir until thickened, 2-3 minutes.
2. Stir in carrot, ½ cup of cheese, the pimientos, salt and pepper until the cheese is melted. Remove from heat. Place frozen potatoes in a greased 13x9-in. baking dish; pour sauce over top. Bake, uncovered, until bubbly, 30 minutes. Sprinkle with the remaining cheese; bake until cheese is melted, 3-5 minutes longer.
1 SERVING: *257 cal., 13g fat (7g sat. fat), 28mg chol., 540mg sod., 24g carb. (5g sugars, 2g fiber), 7g pro.*

ARTS & CRACKERS

A bit of fun with some cookie cutters and a tasty fruit topping transform simple cheese and crackers into a treat kids will love.
—Taste of Home *Test Kitchen*

TAKES: 25 MIN. • **MAKES:** 20 SERVINGS

- 2 slices reduced-fat provolone cheese
- 2 slices reduced-fat cheddar cheese
- 1 large apple, peeled and chopped
- 1 Tbsp. butter
- 2 Tbsp. peach preserves
- ¼ tsp. ground cinnamon
- 20 reduced-fat Triscuits

1. Cut cheese slices with assorted 1-in. cookie cutters; set aside.
2. In a small skillet, saute apple in butter. Add preserves and cinnamon; heat through. Serve with cheese and Triscuits.
1 CRACKER WITH CHEESE AND TOPPING: *42 cal., 2g fat (1g sat. fat), 4mg chol., 54mg sod., 6g carb. (2g sugars, 1g fiber), 2g pro.*
DIABETIC EXCHANGES: *½ starch.*

ABC SALAD TOSS UP

Getting kids to eat their veggies, fruit and protein is as easy as ABC—that's apples, bananas and cheese. This is a slightly sweet salad that appeals to kids' taste buds while still delivering the vitamins Mom demands.
—Christine Maddux, Council Bluffs, IA

TAKES: 25 MIN. • **MAKES:** 16 SERVINGS

- 1 pkg. (12 oz.) broccoli coleslaw mix
- 1 pkg. (8 oz.) ready-to-serve salad greens
- ½ cup mayonnaise
- 1 Tbsp. sugar
- 2 tsp. olive oil
- 8 oz. Colby-Monterey Jack cheese, cut into ½-in. cubes
- 1 medium apple, chopped
- 1 cup seedless red grapes, halved
- ¼ cup raisins
- 1 medium banana, sliced

In a large bowl, combine coleslaw mix and salad greens. Whisk together mayonnaise, sugar and oil; stir in cheese, apple, grapes and raisins. Pour over salad; toss to coat. Top with bananas.
1 CUP: *143 cal., 10g fat (4g sat. fat), 14mg chol., 135mg sod., 10g carb. (6g sugars, 1g fiber), 4g pro.*

CHEESY PEPPERONI BUNS

Like a pizza version of a sloppy joe, this open-faced sandwich is a surefire kid-pleaser!
—Tanya Belt, Newcomerstown, OH

TAKES: 25 MIN. • **MAKES:** 12 SERVINGS

- 1 lb. lean ground beef (90% lean)
- 2 cups pizza sauce or pasta sauce
- 1 pkg. (3½ oz.) sliced pepperoni, chopped
- 4 slices process American cheese, chopped
- 12 mini buns, split
- 2 cups shredded part-skim mozzarella cheese

1. Preheat oven to 350°. In a large skillet, cook beef over medium heat until no longer pink, 5-7 minutes, breaking into crumbles; drain. Stir in pizza sauce, pepperoni and American cheese. Cook and stir until the cheese is melted, 4-5 minutes.
2. Place buns on a baking sheet, cut sides up. Spoon the meat mixture onto buns; top with mozzarella cheese. Bake until the cheese is melted, about 5 minutes. If desired, serve with additional warmed pizza sauce.
2 OPEN-FACED SANDWICHES: *280 cal., 14g fat (6g sat. fat), 46mg chol., 612mg sod., 18g carb. (4g sugars, 1g fiber), 18g pro.*

CHRISTMAS ELF CAKE POPS

Adorable elves that just happen to taste like PB&J can easily be a part of the party decor—until dessert time, when they'll magically disappear!
—Taste of Home *Test Kitchen*

PREP: 1 HOUR • **BAKE:** 35 MIN. + FREEZING
MAKES: 4 DOZEN

- 1   pkg. yellow cake mix (regular size)
- ½   cup seedless strawberry jam
- 48 lollipop sticks
- 1   can (16 oz.) vanilla frosting
- ¼   cup creamy peanut butter
- 1½ cups canned chocolate fudge frosting
      Additional vanilla frosting, red paste food coloring, and dark chocolate and candy cane-flavored kisses

1. Prepare and bake cake according to package directions, using a greased 13x9-in. baking pan. Cool completely on a wire rack.
2. Crumble cake into a large bowl. Add jam and mix well. Shape mixture into 1½-in. balls. Place balls on baking sheets; insert lollipop sticks. Freeze for at least 2 hours or refrigerate for at least 3 hours or until firm and easy to handle.
3. Insert cake pops into a styrofoam block to stand upright. In a microwave, warm vanilla frosting and peanut butter; stir until smooth. Spoon over cake pops.
4. Tint desired amount of additional vanilla frosting red. Using fudge, vanilla and red frostings, pipe hair and faces, using a leaf tip for ears; top each with a chocolate or candy cane-flavored kiss hat. Let stand until set.
1 CAKE POP: *164 cal., 8g fat (2g sat. fat), 13mg chol., 125mg sod., 22g carb. (17g sugars, 0 fiber), 1g pro.*

MAC & CHEESE DINNER

Don't settle for ordinary mac & cheese! This one is my kids' favorite meal, so I always make a huge pot. It's an easy recipe to cut down or double (or triple!). It can also be made into a low-fat recipe if you use nonfat milk, reduced-fat cheeses and lean ham.
—Raymond James, Port Orchard, WA

TAKES: 25 MIN. • **MAKES:** 6 SERVINGS

- 2   cups uncooked elbow macaroni
- 4   medium carrots, thinly sliced
- 1   pkg. (10 oz.) frozen peas
- 1   cup cubed fully cooked ham
- ⅔   cup milk
- ¼   cup cream cheese, softened
- 1   cup (4 oz.) shredded part-skim mozzarella cheese
- 2   Tbsp. grated Parmesan cheese
- 1   tsp. dried basil
- ⅛   tsp. salt
- ⅛   tsp. pepper

1. Cook macaroni in boiling water for 3 minutes. Add carrots and peas; return to a boil. Cook until macaroni is tender, 5-6 minutes longer. Drain; add ham.
2. In a 1-qt. microwave-safe dish, combine the milk and cream cheese. Cover and microwave at 50% power for 3 minutes; stir. Cook until the cream cheese is melted, 2-3 minutes longer. Stir in the mozzarella and Parmesan cheeses, basil, salt and pepper. Pour over the pasta and toss to coat.
1½ CUPS: *284 cal., 10g fat (5g sat. fat), 40mg chol., 609mg sod., 32g carb. (7g sugars, 4g fiber), 18g pro.*

HONEY WALNUT DELIGHTS

Even after being frozen, these no-fail cookies stay moist and taste freshly baked. They are among my best holiday giveaway treats and are so easy to make. If you prefer, you can use other nut varieties, such as pecans or almonds.
—Jessica Clemens, Wimbledon, ND

PREP: 30 MIN. • **BAKE:** 10 MIN./BATCH • **MAKES:** ABOUT 8 DOZEN

- 1 cup butter, softened
- 2¼ cups sugar, divided
- 2 large eggs, room temperature
- ½ cup honey
- 2 Tbsp. lemon juice
- 4 cups all-purpose flour
- 2½ tsp. baking soda
- 1 tsp. ground cinnamon
- ½ tsp. salt
- ½ tsp. ground ginger
- 1 cup finely chopped walnuts, toasted

1. Preheat oven to 350°. In a large bowl, cream butter and 1½ cups sugar until light and fluffy. Beat in eggs, honey and lemon juice. In another bowl, whisk flour, baking soda, cinnamon, salt and ginger; gradually beat into creamed mixture. Stir in walnuts.
2. Shape dough into 1-in. balls; roll in remaining sugar. Place 2 in. apart on ungreased baking sheets. Bake until golden brown, 7-9 minutes. Cool on pans 1 minute. Remove to wire racks to cool completely. Store in an airtight container.
NOTE: To toast nuts, bake in a shallow pan in a 350° oven for 5-10 minutes or cook in a skillet over low heat until lightly browned, stirring occasionally.
1 COOKIE: 66 cal., 3g fat (1g sat. fat), 9mg chol., 60mg sod., 10g carb. (6g sugars, 0 fiber), 1g pro.

PB&J CHEX MIX

As a kid, I loved to add crunchy textures, like chips or popcorn, to my PB&J sandwiches. This mix has all the necessary components of that childhood favorite: sweet grape jelly, rich peanut butter, a little saltiness from peanuts and, finally, that irresistible crunch from the Chex mix.
—Shelley Ward, Isle of Palms, SC

PREP: 10 MIN. • **COOK:** 5 MIN./BATCH + COOLING • **MAKES:** 5 CUPS

- 5 cups Rice Chex
- ¼ cup strawberry jelly
- 2 Tbsp. butter
- 1 Tbsp. light corn syrup
- ½ cup peanut butter chips
- ⅓ cup salted peanuts
  Freeze-dried strawberries, optional

1. Place cereal in a large bowl. In a small bowl, combine jelly, butter and corn syrup. Microwave until smooth; pour over cereal. Toss to coat.
2. Microwave in batches on high for 4 minutes, stirring every minute. Spread onto a parchment-lined baking sheet to cool. Stir in chips, peanuts and, if desired, strawberries. Store in an airtight container.
¾ CUP: 284 cal., 13g fat (5g sat. fat), 10mg chol., 275mg sod., 38g carb. (18g sugars, 2g fiber), 6g pro.

LUNCH-BOX CHICKEN SOUP

A friend gave me this recipe, and I tweaked a few things to make it healthier. It's so delicious and quite easy to make! I use it for family gatherings, church functions, care packages...just about anything. For shortcuts, I sometimes replace the celery and carrots with 2 cups of frozen mixed vegetables. The prepackaged rice saves time, too, so you can have the soup ready and waiting even when the kids are busy with activities.
—Jean Ann Fairchild, Shelby, OH

PREP: 15 MIN. • **COOK:** 30 MIN.
MAKES: 8 SERVINGS (2 QT.)

- 2   Tbsp. olive oil
- 2   cups sliced fresh mushrooms
- 2   medium carrots, chopped
- 2   celery ribs, chopped
- 1   small onion, chopped
- ⅓ cup all-purpose flour
- 1   carton (32 oz.) chicken broth
- 2   cups cubed cooked chicken
- 1   pkg. (8.8 oz.) ready-to-serve roasted chicken-flavored rice
- 2   cups fat-free half-and-half
- ½ tsp. pepper

1. In a Dutch oven, heat oil over medium-high heat. Add vegetables; cook and stir until carrots are crisp-tender.
2. In a bowl, whisk the flour and broth until smooth; stir into the pot. Bring to a boil, stirring constantly; cook and stir until thickened, 5-6 minutes. Add the remaining ingredients; heat through, stirring occasionally (do not boil).
1 CUP: *224 cal., 7g fat (1g sat. fat), 34mg chol., 741mg sod., 23g carb. (6g sugars, 2g fiber), 15g pro.*

MAKE-AHEAD CREAMY FRUIT SALAD

We love fruit salads for holiday dinners. I experimented and came up with this delicious salad—it reminds us of the tropics in the middle of winter! I sometimes add sliced bananas just before serving. Feel free to use your own favorite fruits.
—Joan Hallford, North Richland Hills, TX

PREP: 20 MIN. + CHILLING • **MAKES:** 6 CUPS

- ¾ cup (6 oz.) pina colada yogurt
- ¾ cup (6 oz.) Key lime yogurt
- ½ cup heavy whipping cream, whipped
- 1   Tbsp. Key lime juice
- 2   cups mandarin oranges, drained
- 1   can (15 oz.) peach halves in light syrup, drained and sliced
- 1   cup miniature marshmallows
- 1   cup unsweetened crushed pineapple, drained
- ½ cup sweetened shredded coconut
- ½ cup pitted dark sweet cherries, drained and halved
- ¼ cup chopped pecans, toasted

In a large bowl, combine the yogurts, whipped cream and lime juice. Gently fold in the remaining ingredients. Refrigerate, covered, until serving.
¾ CUP: *250 cal., 11g fat (6g sat. fat), 19mg chol., 56mg sod., 38g carb. (35g sugars, 2g fiber), 4g pro.*

OFFICE PARTY

*Salads, desserts, snacks and main course creations—
share a dish with your co-workers that will take the annual
office holiday party beyond plain old chips and dip.*

MAKE IT A MOCKTAIL!

Hollywood comedies aside, boozy blowouts aren't required (or even recommended!) when celebrating with co-workers. If you're organizing an office party—or providing drinks for a potluck—give the occasion a sophisticated feel everyone will love. The trick is to treat the "mocktails" bar with as much thought as you'd put into regular cocktails. You can play bartender for the event, or everyone can create their own mixes.

A range of drink ingredients is key—different juices and sodas offer guests a chance to mix and match. Club soda is a great way to add effervescence and a subtle mineral flavor to drinks without the extra sugar that comes with regular soda.

Stock the "bar" with fresh ingredients. Muddled fruit (berries or citrus) and herbs (mint, basil, rosemary) will make everything feel a bit fancier—and taste delicious! If your co-workers are the adventurous sort, try zingier ingredients such as slices of fresh ginger, jalapeno or serrano peppers. And of course, save some fresh fruit and herb sprigs for garnish.

A selection of simple syrups is a great way to add sweetness and flavor, and a splash of cider vinegar can stand in for bitters. To make basic syrup, just boil a 1:1 ratio of water and sugar in a saucepan for five minutes, until the sugar dissolves. For flavored syrup, add fruit, fresh herbs or whole spices to the mix. Once it's done boiling, let it cool and then strain the syrup into a decorative bottle. Add pretty label, and guests can choose their own sweetener.

Unless your party is an ultra casual affair, skip the red plastic cups. Party stores offer more options than ever, so you can match the drinkware to the drink—champagne flutes, wine glasses, tumblers, coffee cups or something else entirely. Use traditional bartending tools, like muddlers, shakers and strainers, too. And once you've poured the concoction into that pretty glass, finish it off with a paper straw or a swizzle stick from the party store. Different colors will help everyone keep track of which creation is whose!

SCARLET SIPPER

This sweet, tart and slightly fizzy drink is a favorite for gatherings at our church. The bright color sets a festive tone.
—Amber Goolsby, Geneva, AL

TAKES: 5 MIN. • **MAKES:** 12 SERVINGS

- 4 cups cranberry-apple juice, chilled
- 1 cup orange juice, chilled
- ¼ cup lemon juice, chilled
- 1 liter ginger ale, chilled
  Fresh cranberries and orange and lemon wedges, optional

In a pitcher, combine juices; stir in ginger ale. Serve over ice. If desired, garnish with cranberries and citrus wedges.
¾ CUP: 91 cal., 0 fat (0 sat. fat), 0 chol., 8mg sod., 23g carb. (21g sugars, 0 fiber), 0 pro.

HOT SPICED APPLE JUICE

This delicious spiced apple cocktail is a must for winter parties. It's a winning alternative to an alcoholic punch. Keep it warm in a slow cooker and it'll keep everyone cozy and happy.
—Susan Adams, Victoria, BC

PREP: 10 MIN. • **COOK:** 3 HOURS
MAKES: 22 SERVINGS

 2 bottles (64 oz. each) unsweetened apple juice
 20 cinnamon sticks (3 in.)
 ⅓ cup whole cloves
 2 medium lemons

1. In a 5- or 6-qt. slow cooker, combine apple juice and cinnamon sticks. Place whole cloves on a double thickness of cheesecloth or a coffee filter. Gather corners of cloth to enclose cloves; tie securely with string. Add to slow cooker.
2. Using a citrus zester, remove zest from lemons in long narrow strips. Cut lemons crosswise in half; squeeze out juice. Stir zest and juice into slow cooker.
3. Cook, covered, on low until heated through, 3-4 hours.
¾ CUP: *85 cal., 0 fat (0 sat. fat), 0 chol., 7mg sod., 21g carb. (17g sugars, 1g fiber), 0 pro.*

MEDITERRANEAN BROWN RICE SALAD

My family and friends all love this salad, which they've referred to as "the Greek salad." The recipe makes enough to feed quite a crowd, so it's a perfect bring-along for a big party. No matter what you're looking for—something with the Greek flavors you love, or just a healthy, simple salad—it will not disappoint! If you like, substitute orzo for the rice.
—Sarah Hawkins, Wanatah, IN

PREP: 30 MIN. • **COOK:** 35 MIN. + CHILLING
MAKES: 14 SERVINGS

 1½ cups uncooked long grain brown rice
 3½ cups water
 2 Tbsp. white vinegar
 2 Tbsp. balsamic vinegar
 1 garlic clove, minced
 ¾ tsp. pepper
 ½ tsp. salt

 ½ cup olive oil
 ¼ cup chopped fresh basil
 6 oz. fresh baby spinach (about 8 cups), coarsely chopped
 16 oz. cherry tomatoes, halved
 6 green onions, thinly sliced
 2 cups (8 oz.) crumbled feta cheese

1. In a saucepan, combine brown rice and water; bring to a boil. Reduce heat; simmer, covered, until the rice is tender and the liquid is absorbed, 35-40 minutes.

2. Meanwhile, place vinegars, garlic, pepper and salt in bowl, whisking together. While whisking, gradually add olive oil in a steady stream. Stir in the fresh chopped basil.
3. Place baby spinach in a large bowl; add the cooked rice. Stir in tomatoes, green onions and dressing; toss until the spinach is wilted. Gently stir in the feta. Loosely cover and refrigerate 2 hours or until cold.
¾ CUP: *55 cal., 3g fat (2g sat. fat), 10mg chol., 291mg sod., 3g carb. (1g sugars, 1g fiber), 4g pro.*

SPICY FAJITA MEAT

My husband and I love Tex-Mex food with all the fixings. Cooking the meat in the slow cooker makes prepping the toppings a breeze. We love to serve this at parties, with the filling in the slow cooker to stay warm and the various toppings in bowls so the guests can build their own!
—Rebecca Yankovich, Springfield, VA

PREP: 20 MIN. • **COOK:** 6 HOURS
MAKES: 12 SERVINGS

- 1 boneless beef chuck roast (4 lbs.)
- 1 tsp. salt
- 1 tsp. pepper
- 1 Tbsp. olive oil
- 1 bottle (12 oz.) beer or 1 cup beef broth
- 1 can (28 oz.) pickled jalapeno peppers, undrained
- 1 large onion, chopped
- 1 tsp. garlic powder
- 1 tsp. chili powder
  Corn tortillas (6 in.), crumbled cotija cheese, lime wedges, fresh cilantro leaves, sliced radishes and sour cream, optional

1. Sprinkle roast with salt and pepper. In a large skillet, heat oil over medium-high heat; brown meat. Transfer meat to a 5- or 6-qt. slow cooker. Add beer to skillet, stirring to loosen browned bits from pan; pour over meat. In a large bowl, combine jalapenos, onion, garlic powder and chili powder; pour over meat. Cook, covered, on low until tender, 6-8 hours.
2. Remove roast; shred meat with 2 forks. Strain cooking juices. Reserve vegetables and 2 cups juices; discard the remaining juices. Skim fat from reserved juices. Return shredded beef and the reserved vegetables and cooking juices to slow cooker; heat through. If desired, serve with optional ingredients.
FREEZE OPTION: Freeze cooled meat mixture and juices in freezer containers. To use, partially thaw in refrigerator overnight. Heat through in a saucepan, stirring occasionally and adding a little water if necessary.
½ CUP COOKED MEAT MIXTURE: 307 cal., 21g fat (6g sat. fat), 98mg chol., 829mg sod., 10g carb. (1g sugars, 1g fiber), 31g pro.

CRANBERRY TURKEY SLOPPY JOES

Want a holiday spin on sloppy joes? This combination of turkey and cranberries is a big hit with everyone who tastes it! The flavor has a touch of sweetness, a touch of salt—just right for a holiday get-together. The slow cooker makes it easy to keep warm on a buffet.
—Christine Grimm, Mount Wolf, PA

PREP: 30 MIN. • **COOK:** 5 HOURS
MAKES: 20 SERVINGS

- 4 lbs. lean ground turkey
- 2½ cups ketchup
- 1¾ cups reduced-sodium beef broth
- 1½ cups dried cranberries
- 2 envelopes onion soup mix
- ¼ cup packed brown sugar
- 3 Tbsp. cider vinegar
- 20 hamburger buns, split

In a Dutch oven, cook turkey in batches over medium heat until no longer pink, 6-8 minutes, breaking into crumbles; drain. Transfer to a 5- or 6-qt. slow cooker. Stir in ketchup, broth, cranberries, soup mixes, brown sugar and vinegar. Cook, covered, on low until flavors are blended, 5-6 hours. Serve on buns.
FREEZE OPTION: Freeze cooled meat mixture in freezer containers. To use, partially thaw in refrigerator overnight. Heat through in a saucepan, stirring occasionally and adding a little water if necessary.
1 SANDWICH: 344 cal., 9g fat (2g sat. fat), 63mg chol., 934mg sod., 45g carb. (23g sugars, 2g fiber), 23g pro.

SLOW-COOKER SPINACH BEAN SOUP

This navy bean soup is heartwarming comfort food at its best. It's my signature soup, and I make it for my family and friends. The bright red and green of the spinach and peppers give it a suitably seasonal look.
—Barbara Shay, Pasadena, CA

PREP: 20 MIN. + SOAKING • **COOK:** 7 HOURS
MAKES: 8 SERVINGS (3 QT.)

- 1 lb. dried navy beans
- 2 cartons (32 oz. each) chicken broth
- 2 cups water
- 1 smoked turkey wing (about 7 oz.)
- 1 medium onion, chopped
- 1 jalapeno pepper, seeded and finely chopped
- 1 Tbsp. minced garlic
- 3 bay leaves
- 1 tsp. pepper
- ½ tsp. crushed red pepper flakes
- 10 cups chopped fresh spinach (about 8 oz.)
- 1 large sweet red pepper, chopped
- ½ tsp. kosher salt
   Grated Parmesan cheese, optional

1. Rinse and sort beans; soak according to package directions.

2. In a 5- or 6-qt. slow cooker, combine beans, broth, water, turkey wing, onion, jalapeno, garlic, bay leaves, pepper and pepper flakes. Cook, covered, on low until beans are tender, 7-9 hours.

3. Remove turkey wing and bay leaves; discard. Stir in spinach, red pepper and salt; heat through. If desired, serve with grated Parmesan cheese.

NOTE: Wear disposable gloves when cutting hot peppers; the oils can burn skin. Avoid touching your face.

1½ CUPS: 230 cal., 2g fat (0 sat. fat), 5mg chol., 1171mg sod., 40g carb. (5g sugars, 10g fiber), 15g pro.

BONNIE'S CHILI

This chili is incredibly easy to make, and has a surprising depth of flavor—it tastes like chilis that take all day to create! I can make this for people who like it hot or mild just by changing the salsa. You can make it really spicy if you add hot peppers and hot salsa.
—*Bonnie Altig, North Pole, AK*

PREP: 25 MIN. • **COOK:** 5 HOURS • **MAKES:** 8 SERVINGS (2½ QT.)

 2 lbs. lean ground beef (90% lean)
 2 cans (16 oz. each) kidney beans, rinsed and drained
 2 cans (15 oz. each) tomato sauce
1½ cups salsa
 ½ cup water or reduced-sodium beef broth
4½ tsp. chili powder
 ½ tsp. garlic powder
 ½ tsp. pepper
 ¼ tsp. salt
  Optional toppings: Corn chips, sliced jalapeno peppers and shredded cheddar cheese

In a Dutch oven, cook beef over medium heat until no longer pink, 8-10 minutes, breaking into crumbles; drain. Transfer to a 4- or 5-qt. slow cooker. Stir in remaining ingredients. Cook, covered, on low until heated through, 5-6 hours. If desired, serve with optional toppings.

FREEZE OPTION: Freeze cooled chili in freezer containers. To use, partially thaw in refrigerator overnight. Heat through in a saucepan, stirring occasionally and adding a little water if necessary.

1¼ CUPS: 323 cal., 10g fat (4g sat. fat), 71mg chol., 1027mg sod., 27g carb. (5g sugars, 8g fiber), 31g pro.

AVOCADO BRUSCHETTA

My mother shared this fabulous recipe with me, and I have shared it with my friends. They are always requesting this tasty appetizer— which is not a problem, because you can prepare it in under 15 minutes. The flavor explosion is something else. All this and healthy, too!
—*Stephanie Perenyi, Littleton, CO*

TAKES: 20 MIN. • **MAKES:** 2 DOZEN

 ½ cup olive oil
 ¼ cup lemon juice
 ¼ cup red wine vinegar
 3 garlic cloves, minced
1½ tsp. salt
 1 tsp. crushed red pepper flakes
 1 tsp. dried oregano
 ½ tsp. pepper
 ½ cup chopped fresh cilantro
 ½ cup chopped fresh parsley
 ¼ cup chopped fresh basil
 6 medium ripe avocados, peeled and cubed
 24 slices French bread baguette (½ in. thick)

Preheat broiler. Whisk together first 8 ingredients; stir in herbs. Fold in avocados. Place bread on an ungreased baking sheet. Broil 3-4 in. from heat until golden brown, 1-2 minutes per side. Top with avocado mixture.

1 APPETIZER: 118 cal., 10g fat (1g sat. fat), 0 chol., 199mg sod., 8g carb. (0 sugars, 2g fiber), 2g pro.

RAMEN NOODLE CRANBERRY COLESLAW

The deep red of the cranberries and red cabbage makes this a perfect fit for a Christmas spread. Adults and children love this dish, and I'm often asked to bring it to potlucks and other big dinners. Refrigerate any leftovers—it'll still taste great for a day or two, if you can keep people out of it that long!
—Cornelia Cree, Waynesville, NC

PREP: 25 MIN. + CHILLING • **MAKES:** 24 SERVINGS

- 1 cup peanut or canola oil
- ¾ cup sugar
- ¼ cup cider vinegar
- 1 head Chinese or napa cabbage, thinly sliced
- 1 small head red cabbage, shredded
- 1 small red onion, halved and sliced
- ¾ cup dried cranberries
- 1 cup salted peanuts or sunflower kernels
- 1 pkg. (3 oz.) ramen noodles

1. Whisk together oil, sugar and vinegar until smooth. In a very large bowl, combine the cabbages, red onion and cranberries. Pour 1 cup of the dressing over the coleslaw; toss to coat. Refrigerate, covered, several hours or overnight. Cover and refrigerate the remaining dressing.
2. Drain the coleslaw. Discard seasoning packet from noodles (or save for later use). Break noodles into small pieces; add to coleslaw. Stir in peanuts and remaining dressing; toss to coat.
¾ CUP: *154 cal., 11g fat (2g sat. fat), 0 chol., 39mg sod., 14g carb. (10g sugars, 1g fiber), 2g pro.*

CHICKEN RANGOON EGG ROLLS

This is a recipe that I made into my own—a friend served a layered appetizer paired with crackers, and I made it into a fried egg roll! It makes a great finger-food party appetizer.
—Debbie Carter, Kingsburg, CA

PREP: 20 MIN. • **COOK:** 5 MIN./BATCH • **MAKES:** 1 DOZEN

- 1 pkg. (8 oz.) cream cheese, softened
- 1 Tbsp. 2% milk
- 2 tsp. reduced-sodium soy sauce
- ¾ cup finely chopped cooked chicken
- ½ cup shredded carrot
- 2 green onions, thinly sliced
- 1 garlic clove, minced
- ½ tsp. minced fresh gingerroot
- 12 egg roll wrappers
  Oil for deep-fat frying
  Sweet-and-sour sauce, optional

1. In a small bowl, beat cream cheese, milk and soy sauce; stir in chicken, carrot, onion, garlic and ginger.
2. Place 2 Tbsp. filling in the center of one egg roll wrapper. (Keep the remaining wrappers covered with a damp paper towel until ready to use.) Fold bottom corner over filling. Fold sides toward center over filling. Moisten remaining corner with water; roll up tightly to seal. Repeat.
3. Fry egg rolls, in batches, until golden brown, 2-3 minutes on each side. Drain on paper towels. If desired, serve with sweet-and-sour sauce.
1 EGG ROLL: *241 cal., 15 g fat (5 g sat. fat), 32 mg chol., 284 mg sod., 20 g carb., 1 g fiber, 7 g pro.*

ARTICHOKE & JALAPENO CRAB DIP

This has always been a great potluck dish—I haven't found anyone yet who hasn't loved it. The rich and creamy crab and artichoke flavors get an extra surprising spike from the jalapenos.
—Keely Clary, Spirit Lake, ID

PREP: 15 MIN. • **BAKE:** 30 MIN.
MAKES: 4 CUPS

- 1 pkg. (8 oz.) cream cheese, softened
- 1 cup mayonnaise
- ¾ cup grated Parmesan cheese
- 1 jar (7½ oz.) marinated quartered artichoke hearts, drained and chopped
- 1 can (6 oz.) lump crabmeat, drained
- 1 can (4 oz.) diced jalapeno peppers, drained
  Tortilla chips

1. Preheat oven to 350°. In a small bowl, beat cream cheese, mayonnaise and Parmesan cheese until blended. Stir in artichokes, crab and peppers. Spread into a greased 9-in. pie plate.
2. Bake until heated through, 25-30 minutes. Serve warm with tortilla chips.
¼ CUP: 198 cal., 19 g fat (6 g sat. fat), 33 mg chol., 273 mg sod., 2 g carb., 0 fiber, 5 g pro.

MINT SWIRL FUDGE CAKE

Mint pairs with a silky, mild chocolate flavor for this colorful, beautiful cake that will be the talk of the holiday buffet.
—Heidi Kelly, Norwood, MO

PREP: 15 MIN. • **BAKE:** 40 MIN. + COOLING
MAKES: 12 SERVINGS

- 1 pkg. white cake mix (regular size)
- 1 pkg. (3.4 oz.) instant vanilla pudding mix
- ½ cup + 3 Tbsp. water, divided
- 3 oz. cream cheese, softened
- ¼ cup canola oil
- 3 large eggs, room temperature
- ¼ cup creme de menthe flavoring syrup or creme de menthe
- ½ tsp. peppermint extract
  Green food coloring, optional
- 2 Tbsp. baking cocoa
- 6 oz. unsweetened chocolate, melted

GLAZE
- 1½ cups confectioners' sugar
- 1 oz. semisweet chocolate, melted
- 2 to 3 Tbsp. water
  Crushed spearmint candies, optional

1. Preheat oven to 350°. Grease and flour a 10-in. fluted tube pan; set aside.
2. In a large bowl, combine the cake mix, pudding mix, water, cream cheese, oil and eggs. Beat on low speed for 30 seconds; increase mixer speed to medium and beat for 2 minutes.
3. Remove 1½ cups of the batter to a small bowl; stir in the creme de menthe syrup, peppermint extract and, if desired, food coloring until blended.
4. In another small bowl, whisk 3 Tbsp. water and the cocoa powder until smooth; add to the untinted batter. Add melted chocolate. Spoon half the chocolate batter into prepared pan. Carefully top with green batter; do not swirl. Top with the remaining chocolate batter.
5. Bake until a toothpick inserted in the center comes out clean, 40-50 minutes. Cool in pan 10 minutes before removing to a wire rack to cool completely.
6. In a small bowl, mix confectioners' sugar, chocolate and enough water to reach a drizzling consistency. Spoon glaze over cake; if desired, sprinkle with crushed spearmint candies.
NOTE: To remove cake easily, use solid shortening to grease tube pan.
1 SLICE: 436 cal., 18g fat (8g sat. fat), 54mg chol., 366mg sod., 62g carb. (41g sugars, 3g fiber), 6g pro.

GINGERBREAD MEN S'MORES

A marshmallow and chocolate filling adds an unexpected twist to a holiday classic, making ordinary gingerbread cutouts into sandwich cookies.
—*Maria Regakis, Saugus, MA*

PREP: 45 MIN. + CHILLING • **BAKE:** 10 MIN.
MAKES: 2 DOZEN

- ½ cup butter, softened
- ½ cup packed brown sugar
- 1 large egg, room temperature
- ¼ cup molasses
- 1½ tsp. vanilla extract
- 2½ cups all-purpose flour
- 2½ tsp. ground ginger
- 1½ tsp. ground cinnamon
- ½ tsp. ground nutmeg
- ¼ tsp. ground cloves
- ½ tsp. baking soda
- ¼ tsp. salt
- ½ cup 60% cacao bittersweet chocolate baking chips
- 1 pkg. (8 oz.) cream cheese, softened
- 1 cup marshmallow creme
  Red nonpareils and assorted sprinkles

1. In a large bowl, cream butter and brown sugar until light and fluffy. Beat in egg, molasses and vanilla. In another bowl, whisk flour, spices, baking soda and salt; gradually beat into creamed mixture.
2. Divide dough into 4 portions. Shape each into a disk; wrap each disk in plastic wrap. Refrigerate until firm enough to roll, about 30 minutes.
3. Preheat oven to 350°. On a lightly floured surface, roll each portion of dough to ⅛-in. thickness. Cut with a floured 3-in. gingerbread man-shaped cookie cutter. Place cutouts 1 in. apart on ungreased baking sheets.
4. Bake until edges begin to brown, 8-10 minutes. Let cool on pans 3 minutes; remove to wire racks to cool completely.
5. In a microwave, melt chocolate chips; stir until smooth. Spread over bottoms of half of the cookies; refrigerate until set. Meanwhile, in a large bowl, beat cream cheese and marshmallow creme until smooth. Spread 2 tsp. of the cream cheese mixture over chocolate-spread cookies. Cover with remaining cookies.

6. Refrigerate until set. Decorate as desired with the remaining cream cheese mixture, nonpareils and sprinkles.
1 SANDWICH COOKIE: *178 cal., 9g fat (5g sat. fat), 27mg chol., 121mg sod., 23g carb. (12g sugars, 1g fiber), 2g pro.*

CHOCOLATE CROISSANT PUDDING

This new twist on traditional bread pudding is a decadent and delicious family favorite!
—*Sonya Labbe, West Hollywood, CA*

PREP: 15 MIN. + STANDING
BAKE: 1 HOUR + STANDING
MAKES: 15 SERVINGS

- 6 day-old croissants, split
- 1 cup (6 oz.) semisweet chocolate chips
- 5 large eggs
- 12 large egg yolks
- 5 cups half-and-half cream
- 1½ cups sugar
- 1½ tsp. vanilla extract
- 1 Tbsp. coffee liqueur, optional

1. Preheat oven to 350°. Arrange croissant bottoms in a greased 13x9-in. baking dish. Sprinkle with chocolate chips; replace croissant tops.
2. In a large bowl, whisk eggs, egg yolks, cream, sugar, vanilla and, if desired, coffee liqueur; pour over croissants. Let stand until croissants are softened, 15 minutes.
3. Bake, covered, for 30 minutes. Uncover and bake until puffed and golden and a knife inserted near the center comes out clean, 30-40 minutes longer. Cool in pan on a wire rack for 10 minutes before cutting. Serve warm.
1 PIECE: *400 cal., 21g fat (12g sat. fat), 265mg chol., 178mg sod., 41g carb. (32g sugars, 1g fiber), 9g pro.*

APPLE BRANDY PECAN CAKE

My favorite apple cake is made with a shot of brandy and drizzled with caramel to set off the wonderful flavors. If alcohol is a no-go, use orange juice instead of the apple brandy. If you'd rather go the chocolate route, add mini chocolate chips to the cake and use chocolate ice cream topping for the drizzle.
—Nancy Heishman, Las Vegas, NV

PREP: 20 MIN. • **BAKE:** 1 HOUR + COOLING
MAKES: 20 SERVINGS

- ½ cup butter, softened
- 1 cup packed brown sugar
- 3 large eggs, room temperature
- 2 cups unsweetened applesauce
- 2 Tbsp. apple brandy
- 3 cups all-purpose flour
- 1 tsp. salt
- ½ tsp. baking soda
- 1 tsp. ground cinnamon
- ¾ tsp. ground allspice
- ¼ tsp. ground nutmeg
- 3 medium tart apples, peeled cored and chopped, about 3 cups
- 1 cup finely chopped pecans
  Hot caramel ice cream topping, optional

1. Preheat oven to 350°. Lightly grease a 13x9-in. baking pan; set aside.
2. In a large bowl, beat the butter and sugar until well blended, about 3 minutes. Add 1 egg at a time, beating well after each addition. Beat in applesauce and apple brandy.
3. In another bowl, whisk together flour, salt, baking soda, cinnamon, allspice and nutmeg; gradually add to butter mixture. Fold in apples and pecans.
4. Transfer batter to the prepared pan. Bake until a toothpick inserted in the center comes out clean, 40-50 minutes. Cool completely. If desired, top with caramel topping.
1 PIECE: 223 cal., 10g fat (4g sat. fat), 40mg chol., 201mg sod., 31g carb. (15g sugars, 2g fiber), 4g pro.

COCONUT ORANGE SLICE COOKIES

This is a family recipe that was handed down to me. The coconut and orange combination gives them a distinctive taste unlike any other cookie I've had. They're perfect for Christmas!
—Patricia Ann Stickler, Durand, MI

PREP: 25 MIN. • **BAKE:** 15 MIN./BATCH
MAKES: 2 DOZEN COOKIES

- 1 cup shortening
- 1 cup sugar
- 1 cup packed brown sugar
- 2 large eggs, room temperature
- 1 tsp. vanilla extract
- 2 cups all-purpose flour
- 1 tsp. baking powder
- 1 tsp. baking soda
- ½ tsp. salt
- 2 cups old-fashioned oats
- 2 cups orange candy slices, chopped
- 1 cup sweetened shredded coconut

1. Preheat oven to 350°. In a large bowl, cream shortening and sugars until light and fluffy. Beat in eggs and vanilla. In another bowl, whisk flour, baking powder, baking soda and salt; gradually beat into creamed mixture. Stir in oats, orange candy and coconut.
2. Shape dough into 2-in. balls; place 3 in. apart on parchment-lined baking sheets. Bake until cookies are set and edges begin to brown, 15-18 minutes. Remove from pans to wire racks to cool. Store in an airtight container.
1 COOKIE: 285 cal., 10g fat (3g sat. fat), 16mg chol., 144mg sod., 46g carb. (30g sugars, 1g fiber), 3g pro.

Holiday Helper
Cutting the orange candies on a cutting board sprinkled with granulated sugar will help keep them from sticking together.

DATE-NUT HONEY BARS

The flavor combination here reminds me of baklava—without the hours of work! These bars are perfect for holiday gifts, party platters and bake sales...they never fail to impress.
—*Anna Wood, Cullowhee, NC*

PREP: 45 MIN. • **BAKE:** 30 MIN. + COOLING
MAKES: 2 DOZEN

- ¾ cup butter, softened
- ⅓ cup sugar
- 1¾ cups all-purpose flour
- ½ cup old-fashioned oats
- ¼ tsp. salt

FILLING
- ½ cup honey
- ½ cup apple jelly
- 2 Tbsp. butter
- ½ cup packed brown sugar
- 2 large eggs, lightly beaten
- ½ tsp. vanilla extract
- 2 Tbsp. all-purpose flour
- ½ tsp. baking powder
- ¼ tsp. salt
- ¼ tsp. ground cinnamon
- 1 ¼ cups chopped walnuts
- 1¼ cups chopped dates

1. Preheat oven to 350°. In a large bowl, cream butter and sugar until light and fluffy. In a small bowl, whisk together flour, oats and salt; gradually add to the creamed mixture, mixing well. Press onto bottom and ½ in. up sides of an ungreased 13x9-in. baking pan. Bake until the edges begin to brown, 16-20 minutes. Cool on a wire rack.

2. In a large saucepan, combine honey, apple jelly and butter over medium heat; stir until the jelly and butter are melted. Remove from heat; whisk in brown sugar, eggs and vanilla.

3. In a small bowl, whisk flour, baking powder, salt and cinnamon; whisk into honey mixture. Fold in walnuts and dates. Pour over crust; spread evenly. Bake until golden brown, 24-28 minutes. Cool completely in pan on a wire rack. Cut into bars.

1 BAR: *235 cal., 11g fat (5g sat. fat), 33mg chol., 120mg sod., 33g carb. (22g sugars, 1g fiber), 3g pro.*

PERFECT PIES

During the holiday season, pies are a well-loved and eagerly awaited finish to celebratory meals. This selection of cold-weather pies will make ideal desserts from the harvest through the New Year.

NUTELLA HAND PIES

These pint-size Nutella hand pies made with puff pastry are too good to keep to yourself!
—Taste of Home *Test Kitchen*

TAKES: 30 MIN. • **MAKES:** 9 SERVINGS

- 1 large egg
- 1 Tbsp. water
- 1 sheet frozen puff pastry, thawed
- 3 Tbsp. Nutella
- 1 to 2 tsp. grated orange zest

ICING
- ⅓ cup confectioners' sugar
- ½ tsp. orange juice
- ⅛ tsp. grated orange zest
  Additional Nutella, optional

1. Preheat oven to 400°. In a small bowl, whisk egg with water.
2. Unfold puff pastry; cut into 9 squares. Place 1 tsp. Nutella in center of each; sprinkle with orange zest. Brush edges of pastry with egg mixture. Fold 1 corner over filling to form a triangle; press edges to seal. Transfer to an ungreased baking sheet.
3. Bake until the pastry is golden brown and cooked through, 17-20 minutes. Cool slightly.
4. In a small bowl, mix confectioners' sugar, orange juice and orange zest; drizzle over pies. If desired, warm additional Nutella in a microwave and drizzle over tops.
1 HAND PIE: *190 cal., 10g fat (2g sat. fat), 21mg chol., 100mg sod., 24g carb. (8g sugars, 2g fiber), 3g pro.*

CAN'T-MISS COCONUT CUSTARD PIE

This soft custard pie has a mild coconut flavor. Who wouldn't love a hearty slice topped with a dollop of whipped cream?
—Betty Swain, Bear, DE

PREP: 20 MIN. • **BAKE:** 45 MIN. + COOLING • **MAKES:** 8 SERVINGS

  Pastry for single-crust pie (9 in.)
- 1 cup sweetened shredded coconut, chopped
- 3 large eggs, beaten
- 2½ cups 2% milk
- ⅔ cup sugar
- 3 Tbsp. all-purpose flour
- 1 tsp. vanilla extract
- ½ tsp. salt
- ¼ tsp. ground nutmeg
  Toasted sweetened shredded coconut, optional

1. Preheat oven to 450°. On a lightly floured surface, roll dough to a ⅛-in.-thick circle; transfer to a 9-in. deep-dish pie plate. Trim and flute edge. Line unpricked crust with a double thickness of heavy-duty foil. Bake 10 minutes. Remove foil; bake 5 minutes longer. Sprinkle coconut over crust; set aside. Reduce oven setting to 350°.
2. In a large bowl, combine the eggs, milk, sugar, flour, vanilla and salt. Pour over coconut; sprinkle with nutmeg.
3. Bake, uncovered, 45-50 minutes or until a knife inserted in the center comes out clean. Cool on a wire rack 1 hour. If desired, top with toasted coconut to serve. Refrigerate any leftovers.
1 PIECE: *322 cal., 15g fat (8g sat. fat), 90mg chol., 345mg sod., 42g carb. (26g sugars, 1g fiber), 7g pro.*

GINGERSNAP CRUMB PEAR PIE

This recipe was one my grandmother used for making crumble pies from fresh fruit. She simply substituted oats, gingersnaps or vanilla wafers depending on the fruit. Pear was always my favorite—and I added ginger and caramel to give it a new twist.
—Fay Moreland, Wichita Falls, TX

PREP: 35 MIN. + CHILLING
BAKE: 1 HOUR + COOLING
MAKES: 8 SERVINGS

Pastry for single-crust pie (9 in.)
TOPPING
- 1 cup crushed gingersnap cookies (about 16 cookies)
- ¼ cup all-purpose flour
- ¼ cup packed brown sugar
  Pinch salt
- ½ cup cold butter, cubed

FILLING
- ⅔ cup sugar
- ⅓ cup all-purpose flour
- ½ tsp. ground ginger
- ¼ tsp. salt
- 2½ lbs. ripe pears (about 4 medium), peeled and thinly sliced
- 1 Tbsp. lemon juice
- 1 tsp. vanilla extract
  Hot caramel ice cream topping, optional

1. On a lightly floured surface, roll dough to a ⅛-in.-thick circle; transfer to a 9-in. pie plate. Trim and flute edge. Refrigerate for 30 minutes. Preheat oven to 400°.
2. Line unpricked crust with a double thickness of foil. Fill with pie weights, dried beans or uncooked rice. Bake for 15-20 minutes or until the edges are light golden brown. Remove foil and weights; bake 3-6 minutes longer or until the bottom is golden brown. Cool on a wire rack. Reduce oven setting to 350°.

3. For the topping, in a food processor, combine the crushed cookies, flour, brown sugar and salt. Add butter; pulse until crumbly.
4. For filling, in a large bowl, mix sugar, flour, ginger and salt. Add pears, lemon juice and vanilla; toss gently to combine. Transfer to the crust; cover with topping.
5. Place pie on a baking sheet; bake for 60-70 minutes or until the topping is lightly browned and pears are tender. Cover pie loosely with foil during the last 15 minutes if needed to prevent overbrowning. Cool on a wire rack for at least 1 hour before serving. If desired, drizzle with caramel topping.
NOTE: Let pie weights cool before storing. Beans and rice may be reused for pie weights, but not for cooking.
1 PIECE: *530 cal., 25g fat (15g sat. fat), 61mg chol., 394mg sod., 76g carb. (39g sugars, 5g fiber), 4g pro.*

GINGER-STREUSEL PUMPKIN PIE

I love to bake and have spent a lot of time making goodies for my family and friends. The streusel topping gives this pie a special touch your family will love.
—Sonia Parvu, Sherrill, NY

PREP: 25 MIN. • **BAKE:** 55 MIN. + COOLING
MAKES: 8 SERVINGS

- 1 sheet refrigerated pie crust
- 3 large eggs
- 1 can (15 oz.) solid-pack pumpkin
- 1½ cups heavy whipping cream
- ½ cup sugar
- ¼ cup packed brown sugar
- 1½ tsp. ground cinnamon
- ½ tsp. salt
- ¼ tsp. ground allspice
- ¼ tsp. ground nutmeg
- ¼ tsp. ground cloves

STREUSEL
- 1 cup all-purpose flour
- ½ cup packed brown sugar
- ½ cup cold butter, cubed
- ½ cup chopped walnuts
- ⅓ cup finely chopped crystallized ginger

1. Preheat oven to 350°. On a lightly floured surface, unroll crust. Transfer to a 9-in. pie plate and trim to ½ in. beyond edge of plate; flute edge.
2. In a large bowl, whisk eggs, pumpkin, cream, sugars, cinnamon, salt, allspice, nutmeg and cloves. Pour into crust. Bake for 40 minutes.
3. In a small bowl, combine flour and brown sugar; cut in butter until crumbly. Stir in walnuts and ginger. Gently sprinkle over the filling.
4. Bake 15-25 minutes longer or until a knife inserted in the center comes out clean. Cool on a wire rack. Refrigerate any leftovers.
1 PIECE: 684 cal., 42g fat (21g sat. fat), 176mg chol., 388mg sod., 73g carb. (39g sugars, 3g fiber), 9g pro.

BUTTERSCOTCH PIE

This creamy pudding-like pie is crowned with golden peaks of meringue. It's an old-fashioned, decadent classic. Be sure to give it plenty of time to set—it's worth the wait!
—Cary Letsche, Brandenton, FL

PREP: 30 MIN. • **BAKE:** 15 MIN. + CHILLING
MAKES: 8 SERVINGS

- 6 Tbsp. butter
- 6 Tbsp. all-purpose flour
- 1½ cup packed brown sugar
- 2 cups milk
- ¼ tsp. salt
- 3 large egg yolks, beaten
- 1 tsp. vanilla extract
- 1 pastry shell (9 in.), baked

MERINGUE
- 3 large egg whites
- ¼ tsp. cream of tartar
- ½ cup sugar

1. Preheat oven to 350°. In a saucepan, melt the butter. Remove from the heat; add flour and stir until smooth. Stir in brown sugar. Return to heat; stir in milk and salt until blended. Cook and stir over medium-high heat until thickened and bubbly. Reduce heat; cook and stir for 2 minutes longer. Remove from the heat. Stir about 1 cup hot filling into the egg yolks; return all to pan, stirring constantly. Bring to a gentle boil; cook and stir for 2 minutes longer. Remove from heat. Gently stir in vanilla. Pour into the crust.
2. For meringue, beat egg whites and cream of tartar in a small bowl on medium speed until soft peaks form. Gradually beat in sugar, about 1 Tbsp. at a time, on high until stiff glossy peaks form and the sugar is dissolved. Spread meringue evenly over the hot filling, sealing the edges to the crust.
3. Bake 12-15 minutes or until meringue is golden brown. Cool on a wire rack for 1 hour. Refrigerate for at least 3 hours before serving. Refrigerate leftovers.
1 PIECE: 487 cal., 20g fat (10g sat. fat), 116mg chol., 330mg sod., 73g carb. (56g sugars, 0 fiber), 6g pro.

SALTED DARK CHOCOLATE TART

When I was littlex, my grandpa kept a bag of caramels in his truck and a few in his pocket. Whether we were camping or going to a movie, he shared them with me. Now I try to put caramel in as many of my desserts as possible, including this sweet and salty tart.
—Leah Tackitt, Austin, TX

PREP: 30 MIN. • **COOK:** 15 MIN. + CHILLING
MAKES: 16 SERVINGS

1½ cups Oreo cookie crumbs
⅓ cup butter, melted
CARAMEL
¾ cup sugar
3 Tbsp. water
⅓ cup heavy whipping cream
2 Tbsp. butter, cubed
Dash salt
FILLING
4 cups dark chocolate chips
1¼ cups heavy whipping cream
1 tsp. vanilla extract
½ tsp. large-crystal sea salt

1. In a small bowl, combine cookie crumbs and butter; press onto the bottom and up the sides of a greased 9-in. fluted tart pan with removable bottom. Cover and refrigerate for 30 minutes.
2. For caramel, combine sugar and water in a small saucepan over medium heat. Cook, shaking pan occasionally, until the sugar is melted and the mixture is almost clear (do not boil).
3. Increase heat to medium high; bring to a boil, without stirring. Cover and boil for 2 minutes, tightly holding the lid of the pan down. Uncover; shake pan. Cook for 1-2x minutes longer, or until the mixture is amber, shaking pan several times.
4. Remove from the heat; stir in cream (mixture will bubble) until smooth. Stir in butter (mixture will bubble) and salt until blended. Pour into crust; refrigerate for 15 minutes.
5. Place chocolate in a large bowl. In a small saucepan, bring cream just to a boil. Pour over chocolate; whisk until smooth. Stir in vanilla. Let stand for 20 minutes.
6. Pour chocolate mixture over caramel. Sprinkle with sea salt. Refrigerate at least 3 hours. Remove from the refrigerator about 45 minutes before serving.

1 PIECE: *552 cal., 37g fat (21g sat. fat), 46mg chol., 200mg sod., 56g carb. (43g sugars, 1g fiber), 5g pro.*

HARVEST SWEET POTATO PIE

Years ago, we baked pies a few days before holiday gatherings and placed them in a tall pie safe on our back porch. My father called this sweet potato pie recipe "royal pie," because he thought it was fit for a king. It's a treasured hand-me-down family recipe.
—Fae Fisher, Callao, VA

PREP: 15 MIN. • **BAKE:** 45 MIN.
MAKES: 16 SERVINGS (2 PIES)

4 large eggs
1 can (12 oz.) evaporated milk
1¼ cups sugar
¾ cup butter, melted
2 tsp. ground cinnamon
2 tsp. pumpkin pie spice
1 tsp. vanilla extract
1 tsp. lemon extract
½ tsp. ground nutmeg
½ tsp. salt
4 cups mashed cooked sweet potatoes
2 pastry shells (9 in.), unbaked
Whipped cream, optional

Preheat oven to 425°. In a bowl, combine the first 10 ingredients; mix well. Beat in sweet potatoes. Pour into crusts. Bake for 15 minutes. Reduce heat to 350°; bake for 30-35 minutes longer or until a knife inserted in the center comes out clean. Cool completely. Serve with whipped cream if desired. Store in the refrigerator.
1 PIECE: *343 cal., 14g fat (9g sat. fat), 83mg chol., 289mg sod., 48g carb. (23g sugars, 3g fiber), 6g pro.*

BRAIDED PIE CRUST

This lovely braided crust works to dress up any any single-crust pie. Start by making enough pastry for a double-crust pie. Line a 9-in. pie plate with the bottom pastry and trim it even with the edge of the pie plate.

Roll the second pastry into a 10x8-in. rectangle. With a sharp knife, cut twelve ¼-in.-wide strips (1); gently braid 3 strips at a time (2).

Brush the edge of crust with water (3); place the braid on edge and press lightly to secure. Repeat with remaining strips, attaching additional braids until entire edge is covered (4). Cover with foil while baking to protect from overbrowning.

APRICOT-ALMOND TARTLETS

These delicate, buttery tarts melt in your mouth. With their jeweled apricot tops, they make an eye-catching presentation on a holiday cookie tray.
—Julie Dunsworth, Oviedo, FL

PREP: 25 MIN. • **BAKE:** 20 MIN. + COOLING • **MAKES:** 2 DOZEN

- 1 cup all-purpose flour
- 3 Tbsp. confectioners' sugar
- ⅓ cup cold butter
- 1 large egg yolk
- 1 to 2 Tbsp. water

FILLING
- ½ cup almond paste
- ¼ cup butter, softened
- 1 large egg white
- ¼ tsp. almond extract
- ½ cup apricot preserves

1. Preheat oven to 350°. In a large bowl, combine flour and confectioners' sugar; cut in butter until mixture resembles coarse crumbs. Add egg yolk and water; stir until dough forms a ball. Roll into twenty-four 1-in. balls. Press onto the bottoms and up the sides of greased miniature muffin cups.
2. In a small bowl, beat almond paste and butter until blended; beat in egg white and almond extract. Spoon into shells, about 2 tsp. in each.
3. Bake until golden brown, 20-25 minutes. Cool for 5 minutes before removing from pans to wire racks. Top with apricot preserves.
1 TARTLET: *103 cal., 6g fat (3g sat. fat), 20mg chol., 37mg sod., 12g carb. (5g sugars, 0 fiber), 1g pro.*
DIABETIC EXCHANGES: *1 starch, 1 fat.*

SILKY CHOCOLATE PIE

*Chocolate makes the world go round!
We have a family that loves chocolate pies,
and this version with a splash of brandy
is smooth as silk and oh, so special.*
—Kathy Hewitt, Cranston, RI

PREP: 25 MIN. • **COOK:** 15 MIN. + CHILLING
MAKES: 8 SERVINGS

Pastry for single-crust pie (9 in.)
⅓ cup sugar
¼ cup cornstarch
2½ cups half-and-half cream
4 large egg yolks
6 oz. semisweet chocolate,
   finely chopped
3 Tbsp. Cognac or brandy
1 tsp. vanilla extract
TOPPING
1 cup heavy whipping cream
1 Tbsp. Cognac or brandy
1 tsp. confectioners' sugar
   Baking cocoa

1. Preheat the oven to 400°. On a lightly floured surface, roll the dough to a ⅛-in.-thick circle; transfer to a 9-in. pie plate. Trim crust to ½ in. beyond the rim of the plate; flute edge. Line unpricked crust with a double thickness of foil. Fill with pie weights, dried beans or uncooked rice.
2. Bake for 20 minutes. Remove foil and weights; bake 10-12 minutes longer or until golden brown. Cool on a wire rack.
3. In a heavy saucepan, mix sugar and cornstarch. Whisk in cream. Cook and stir over medium heat until thickened and bubbly. Remove from the heat. In a small bowl, whisk a small amount of hot mixture into egg yolks; return all to the pan, whisking constantly. Cook and stir over low heat 1 minute longer. Remove from the heat; stir in the chocolate, Cognac and vanilla until chocolate is melted.
4. Transfer to a clean bowl; press waxed paper onto surface of filling. Cool filling to room temperature. Spoon into crust. Refrigerate, covered, until cold, about 4 hours.
5. For topping, in a small bowl, beat cream until it begins to thicken. Add Cognac and confectioners' sugar; beat until soft peaks form. Spread topping over pie. Dust lightly with cocoa.

NOTE: Let pie weights cool before storing. Beans and rice may be reused for pie weights, but not for cooking.
1 PIECE: 579 cal., 39g fat (24g sat. fat), 211mg chol., 171mg sod., 44g carb. (23g sugars, 2g fiber), 8g pro.

PUMPKIN CHEESECAKE PIE

If you're looking for a classic winter dessert, try this pumpkiny cheesecake pie. It's a winner at potlucks and on the holiday table. The gingersnap crust forms a spicy-sweet foundation.
—Sharon Crockett, La Palma, CA

PREP: 30 MIN. • **BAKE:** 35 MIN. + CHILLING
MAKES: 10 SERVINGS

1½ cups crushed gingersnap cookies
1 Tbsp. sugar
¼ cup butter, melted
FILLING
2 pkg. (8 oz. each) cream cheese,
   softened
¾ cup sugar
2 large eggs, lightly beaten
1 can (15 oz.) solid-pack pumpkin
1 tsp. ground cinnamon
¼ tsp. ground ginger
¼ tsp. ground nutmeg
⅛ tsp. salt

TOPPING
1 cup sour cream
¼ cup sugar
1 tsp. vanilla extract
   Ground cinnamon, optional

1. Preheat oven to 350°. In a small bowl, combine gingersnap crumbs and sugar. Stir in butter. Press onto the bottom and up the sides of a greased 9-in. deep-dish pie plate. Bake for 8-10 minutes or until lightly browned.
2. In a large bowl, beat the cream cheese and sugar until smooth. Add the eggs; beat on low speed just until combined. Stir in the pumpkin, cinnamon, ginger, nutmeg and salt.
3. Pour filling into the crust. Bake for 30-35 minutes or until the center is almost set.
4. In a small bowl, combine the sour cream, sugar and vanilla. Spread over the pie. Bake for 5-7 minutes longer or until set. Cool on a wire rack. Cover and refrigerate for at least 4 hours. Sprinkle with cinnamon if desired.
1 PIECE: 374 cal., 20g fat (11g sat. fat), 96mg chol., 316mg sod., 44g carb. (31g sugars, 2g fiber), 6g pro.

EGGNOG PIE

Even better than holiday eggnog in a glass is eggnog on a plate! This creamy pie delivers all that rich, wonderful flavor. It's pretty, too, with a sprinkling of nutmeg on top.
—Florence Shaw, East Wenatchee, WA

PREP: 30 MIN. + CHILLING
MAKES: 8 SERVINGS

- 1 Tbsp. unflavored gelatin
- ¼ cup cold water
- ⅓ cup sugar
- 2 Tbsp. cornstarch
- ¼ tsp. salt
- 2 cups eggnog
- 1 tsp. vanilla extract
- 1 tsp. rum extract
- 1 cup heavy whipping cream, whipped
- 1 pastry shell (9 in.), baked
  Ground nutmeg, optional

1. In a small bowl, sprinkle gelatin over water; let stand 1 minute. In a saucepan, combine the sugar, cornstarch and salt. Stir in eggnog until smooth. Bring to a boil; cook and stir for 2 minutes or until thickened. Stir in gelatin until dissolved. Remove from heat; let cool to room temperature.

2. Stir in extracts; fold in whipped cream. Pour into crust. Refrigerate until firm. If desired, dust pie with nutmeg.
1 PIECE: *324 cal., 21g fat (12g sat. fat), 76mg chol., 218mg sod., 29g carb. (15g sugars, 0 fiber), 6g pro.*

FLORIDA CITRUS MERINGUE PIE

I love my citrus trees and look forward to wheelbarrows full of fruit every year. The fruit is ripe during the holiday season, so many of my friends are the recipients of edible goodies. I tried this pie in a little bakery in St. Augustine and adapted it to make at home. Thanks to orange and lemon, this lovely pie packs a bold sweet-tart flavor!
—Barbara Carlucci, Orange Park, FL

PREP: 30 MIN. • **BAKE:** 15 MIN. + CHILLING
MAKES: 8 SERVINGS

  Pastry for single-crust pie (9 in.)
- 1 cup sugar
- 5 Tbsp. cornstarch
- ½ tsp. salt
- 1 cup water
- 1 cup orange juice
- 4 large egg yolks
- ½ cup lemon juice
- 2 Tbsp. butter
- 1 tsp. grated lemon zest
- 1 tsp. grated orange zest

MERINGUE
- 4 large egg whites
- 1 tsp. vanilla extract
- ¼ tsp. cream of tartar
- ½ cup sugar

1. Preheat the oven to 450°. On a lightly floured surface, roll dough to a ⅛-in.-thick circle; transfer to a 9-in. pie plate. Trim to ½ in. beyond rim of plate; flute edge. Line unpricked crust with a double thickness of foil. Fill with pie weights, dried beans or uncooked rice.
2. Bake for 8-10 minutes or until the bottom is lightly browned. Remove foil and weights; bake 5-8 minutes longer or until golden brown. Cool on a wire rack. Reduce oven setting to 350°.
3. Meanwhile, in a large saucepan, mix sugar, cornstarch and salt. Whisk in water and orange juice. Cook and stir over medium-high heat until thickened and bubbly. Reduce heat to low; cook and stir 2 minutes longer (mixture will be thick). Remove from heat.
4. In a small bowl, whisk a small amount of hot mixture into egg yolks; return all to pan, whisking constantly. Bring to a gentle boil; cook and stir 2 minutes. Remove from heat. Gently stir in lemon juice, butter, and lemon and orange zests.
5. For meringue, in a large bowl, beat the egg whites with vanilla and cream of tartar on medium speed until foamy. Gradually add sugar, 1 Tbsp. at a time, beating on high after each addition until sugar is dissolved. Continue beating until soft glossy peaks form.
6. Transfer hot filling to crust. Spread meringue over filling, sealing to edge of crust; swirl top with the back of a spoon.
7. Bake 13-16 minutes or until meringue is golden brown. Cool on a wire rack 1 hour. Chill 3 hours before serving. Refrigerate any leftovers.
NOTE: Let pie weights cool before storing. Beans and rice may be reused for pie weights, but not for cooking.
1 PIECE: *415 cal., 17g fat (10g sat. fat), 140mg chol., 318mg sod., 62g carb. (41g sugars, 1g fiber), 6g pro.*

FRUITCAKE PIE

This recipe came from a friend who knows how much we love fruitcake. The pie has similar flavors, but it's easier to make than a large batch of fruitcake. I serve it with whipped cream or ice cream.
—Doris Heath, Franklin, NC

PREP: 20 MIN. • **BAKE:** 35 MIN. + COOLING • **MAKES:** 8 SERVINGS

Pastry for single-crust pie (9 in.)
- 1 cup pecan halves, divided
- ¾ cup red candied cherries, divided
- ½ cup chopped dates
- ¼ cup chopped candied pineapple
- 6 Tbsp. butter, softened
- ½ cup packed brown sugar
- 3 large eggs, lightly beaten
- ½ cup light corn syrup
- ¼ tsp. each ground cloves, ginger and nutmeg

1. On a lightly floured surface, roll dough to a ⅛-in.-thick circle; transfer to a 9-in. pie plate. Trim and flute edge; set aside. Chop ½ cup pecans; set remaining pecan halves aside. Chop ½ cup cherries; halve remaining cherries and set aside. Combine dates, pineapple and chopped pecans and cherries; sprinkle over crust.
2. In a small bowl, cream butter and brown sugar until light and fluffy. Beat in the eggs, corn syrup, cloves, ginger and nutmeg. Pour over the fruit mixture. Top with the reserved pecan and cherry halves.
3. Bake at 350° for 35-40 minutes or until set. Cool on a wire rack. Refrigerate leftovers.
1 PIECE: *519 cal., 27g fat (10g sat. fat), 107mg chol., 219mg sod., 68g carb. (40g sugars, 2g fiber), 5g pro.*

WALNUT TOFFEE TART

I usually serve this scrumptious tart on Christmas and New Year's Day. It really showcases walnuts and is so impressive to serve.
—Patricia Green, Yuba City, CA

PREP: 30 MIN. • **BAKE:** 20 MIN. • **MAKES:** 10 SERVINGS

- 2 cups all-purpose flour
- 3 Tbsp. sugar
- ¾ cup cold butter
- 2 large egg yolks, lightly beaten
- ¼ cup cold milk

FILLING
- 1½ cups sugar
- 1½ cups heavy whipping cream
- ½ tsp. ground cinnamon
- ¼ tsp. salt
- 2 cups coarsely chopped walnuts

1. Preheat oven to 375°. Combine flour and sugar. Cut in butter until mixture resembles coarse crumbs. Combine egg yolks and milk; stir into flour mixture until blended. With lightly floured hands, press dough onto the bottom and 1 in. up the sides of a 12-in. tart pan with removable bottom. Line unpricked crust with a double thickness of heavy-duty foil. Fill with pie weights. Place pan on a baking sheet. Bake until the edges are lightly browned, 12-15 minutes.
2. Meanwhile, in a saucepan, combine the sugar, cream, cinnamon and salt. Bring to a boil over medium heat, stirring constantly. Remove from the heat; stir in walnuts. Remove foil from crust; pour filling into crust. Bake until golden brown, 20-25 minutes. Cool on a wire rack. Store in the refrigerator.
NOTE: Let pie weights cool before storing. Beans and rice may be reused for pie weights, but not for cooking.
1 PIECE: *529 cal., 36g fat (16g sat. fat), 96mg chol., 153mg sod., 48g carb. (30g sugars, 2g fiber), 7g pro.*

BLOOD ORANGE & GOAT CHEESE GALETTE

I made this galette for my mother-in-law's birthday, and it was a sensational hit. The gorgeous hue of the oranges transforms a rustic pie into a dessert.
—Tia Laws, Enterprise, OR

PREP: 1 HOUR + FREEZING
BAKE: 1 HOUR + COOLING
MAKES: 8 SERVINGS (⅔ CUP SAUCE)

- 1 cup all-purpose flour
- 2 Tbsp. sugar
- ½ tsp. salt
- ⅓ cup cold butter, cubed
- ¼ cup quick-cooking oats
- 4 to 6 Tbsp. ice water

FILLING
- 10 medium blood oranges
- ¾ cup crumbled goat cheese
- 3 oz. cream cheese, softened
- ⅓ cup sour cream
- ¼ cup honey
- 2 large egg yolks, divided use
- ¼ tsp. salt
- 3 Tbsp. coarse sugar, divided
- 1 Tbsp. butter
- 1 Tbsp. water

SAUCE
- ¼ cup butter, cubed
- ½ cup packed brown sugar
- 2 Tbsp. half-and-half cream
- 2 Tbsp. honey
- ½ tsp. ground cinnamon

1. In a large bowl, mix flour, sugar and salt; cut in butter until crumbly. Stir in oats. Gradually add ice water, tossing with a fork until dough holds together when pressed. Shape into a disk. Cover and refrigerate for 1 hour or overnight.

2. On a lightly floured surface, roll dough to a 13-in. circle. Transfer to a parchment-lined 14-in. pizza pan. Refrigerate, covered, while preparing the oranges and the filling.

3. Cut a thin slice from the top and bottom of the oranges; stand oranges upright on a cutting board. With a knife, cut the peel and the outer membrane from oranges. Cut along the membrane of each segment to remove fruit from 8 oranges. Thinly slice the remaining 2 oranges; remove seeds. Place orange segments and slices between layers of paper towels to remove excess moisture; let stand while preparing the filling.

4. In a small bowl, beat goat cheese, cream cheese, sour cream, honey, 1 egg yolk and salt until smooth. Spread over pastry to within 2 in. of edge. Arrange the orange segments over cheese mixture. Sprinkle with 2 Tbsp. coarse sugar; dot with butter.

5. Fold crust edge over filling, pleating as you go and leaving an opening in the center. Whisk remaining egg yolk and water; brush over folded crust. Arrange orange slices over crust to within 1 in. of edge. Sprinkle with remaining coarse sugar. Freeze, covered, overnight.

6. Preheat oven to 375°. Bake frozen galette until the crust is golden and the filling is bubbly, 60-70 minutes. Transfer to a wire rack to cool.

7. For sauce, in a small saucepan, melt butter over medium heat. Add brown sugar, cream, honey and cinnamon; bring to a boil. Boil 1 minute, stirring constantly to dissolve sugar. Serve with galette.

1 PIECE: *488 cal., 25g fat (15g sat. fat), 79mg chol., 434mg sod., 63g carb. (46g sugars, 4g fiber), 6g pro.*

MERINGUE CRANBERRY PIE

PICTURED ON P. 176

The airy meringue hides the crimson beauty of the cranberries, at least until slicing time!
—*Marie Rizzio, Interlochen, MI*

PREP: 40 MIN. • **BAKE:** 20 MIN. + CHILLING
MAKES: 8 SERVINGS

	Pastry for single-crust pie (9 in.)
4	cups fresh or frozen cranberries, thawed
2	cups sugar
¾	cup water
4	large egg yolks
2	Tbsp. all-purpose flour
¼	tsp. salt
2	Tbsp. butter
½	tsp. almond extract

MERINGUE

4	large egg whites
¼	tsp. cream of tartar
1	tsp. vanilla extract
½	cup sugar

1. Preheat oven to 450°. On a lightly floured surface, roll dough to a ⅛-in.-thick circle. Transfer to a 9-in. deep-dish pie plate; flute edge. Line unpricked crust with a double thickness of heavy-duty foil. Bake for 8 minutes. Remove foil; bake 5 minutes longer. Cool on a wire rack.
2. In a large saucepan, combine the cranberries, sugar and water. Cook, stirring occasionally, over medium heat until berries pop, about 15 minutes. In a small bowl, combine egg yolks, flour and salt. Remove cranberry mixture from the heat; stir a small amount into egg mixture. Return all to the pan, stirring constantly. Bring to a gentle boil; cook and stir for 2 minutes. Remove from heat. Stir in butter and extract. Pour into crust.
3. For meringue, in a large bowl, beat the egg whites, cream of tartar and vanilla on medium speed until soft peaks form. Gradually beat in sugar, 1 Tbsp. at a time, on high until stiff peaks form. Spread over hot filling, sealing edges to crust.
4. Bake at 350° until golden brown, 18-22 minutes. Cool on a wire rack 1 hour; refrigerate for 1-2 hours before serving.
1 PIECE: *509 cal., 17g fat (10g sat. fat), 130mg chol., 285mg sod., 86g carb. (66g sugars, 2g fiber), 6g pro.*

PERSIMMON SQUASH PIE

I created this for our local persimmon festival, using homegrown butternut squash. Make sure the persimmons are ripe! I often add extra toffee bits for garnish.
—*Betty Milligan, Bedford, IN*

PREP: 25 MIN. • **BAKE:** 40 MIN. + COOLING
MAKES: 8 SERVINGS

	Pastry for single-crust pie (9 in.)
¼	cup buttermilk
½	cup mashed cooked butternut squash
½	cup mashed ripe persimmon pulp
¾	cup sugar
¼	cup packed brown sugar
3	Tbsp. all-purpose flour
½	tsp. ground cinnamon
¼	tsp. baking powder
¼	tsp. baking soda
¼	tsp. salt
2	large eggs
¼	cup heavy whipping cream
¼	cup butter, melted
1	tsp. vanilla extract

CARAMEL TOPPING

30	caramels
2	Tbsp. 2% milk
⅓	cup chopped pecans
⅓	cup English toffee bits or almond brickle chips

1. Preheat oven to 450°. On a lightly floured surface, roll dough to a ⅛-in.-thick circle. Transfer to a 9-in. pie plate; flute edge. Line unpricked crust with a double thickness of heavy-duty foil. Bake for 5-6 minutes or until lightly browned; cool on a wire rack. Reduce heat to 350°.
2. In a blender, combine the buttermilk, squash and persimmon pulp; cover and process until smooth. In a large bowl, combine the sugars, flour, cinnamon, baking powder, baking soda and salt.
3. Combine eggs, cream, butter, vanilla and the squash mixture; stir into the dry ingredients just until moistened.
4. Pour into crust. Bake for 40-45 minutes or until a knife inserted in the center comes out clean.
5. In a small saucepan, combine caramels and milk. Cook and stir over medium heat until melted and smooth. Pour over hot pie. Sprinkle with pecans and toffee bits. Cool completely on a wire rack. Store in the refrigerator.
1 PIECE: *578 cal., 27g fat (13g sat. fat), 90mg chol., 465mg sod., 82g carb. (60g sugars, 2g fiber), 6g pro.*

Pies in Disguise

When is a pie not a pie? When it's ice cream! Or a cocktail. Each of these delicious and creative recipes is inspired by a popular holiday pie.

PUMPKIN PIE ICE CREAM WITH SALTED CARAMEL SAUCE

Pumpkin pie is the perfect southern comfort food that everyone has on the table at the holidays. This ice cream has just the right balance of spices, and no matter when you make it, you'll find yourself surrounded in the warmth and love that pumpkin pie has to offer.
—Angie Stewart, Memphis, TN

PREP: 30 MIN. + CHILLING
PROCESS: 20 MIN. + FREEZING
MAKES: 1½ QT. ICE CREAM AND 1¼ CUPS SAUCE

- 3 large egg yolks
- ¾ cup packed brown sugar
- 2 cups heavy whipping cream
- 1½ cups half-and-half cream
- 1 cup canned pumpkin
- 2 tsp. pumpkin pie spice
- 1 tsp. vanilla extract
- ½ tsp. salt

SALTED CARAMEL SAUCE

- 1 cup sugar
- 1 cup heavy whipping cream
- 3 Tbsp. butter, cubed
- 1½ tsp. salt
- 1 tsp. almond extract

1. In a large heavy saucepan, whisk egg yolks and brown sugar until blended; stir in heavy cream. Cook over low heat, stirring constantly, until the mixture is just thick enough to coat a metal spoon and a thermometer reads at least 160°. Do not allow to boil. Remove from the heat immediately.

2. Quickly transfer to a large bowl; place bowl in a pan of ice water. Stir gently and occasionally for 2 minutes. Stir in half-and-half, pumpkin, pumpkin pie spice, vanilla and salt. Press plastic wrap onto surface of custard. Refrigerate several hours or overnight.

3. Fill cylinder of ice cream maker no more than two-thirds full; freeze according to manufacturer's directions. (Refrigerate any remaining mixture until ready to freeze.) Transfer ice cream to freezer containers, allowing headspace for expansion. Freeze until firm, 2-4 hours.

4. For caramel sauce, spread the sugar in a large, heavy saucepan; cook, without stirring, over medium-low heat until sugar begins to melt. Gently drag melted sugar to center of pan so it melts evenly. Cook, without stirring, until melted sugar turns a medium-dark amber color, 5-10 minutes. Immediately remove pan from heat, then slowly stir in cream, butter, salt and almond extract. Serve with ice cream. Refrigerate leftover sauce; keep leftover ice cream frozen.

½ **CUP ICE CREAM WITH ABOUT 4 TSP. SAUCE:** *410 cal., 29g fat (18g sat. fat), 137mg chol., 455mg sod., 35g carb. (34g sugars, 1g fiber), 4g pro.*

PECAN PIE COBBLER

I couldn't find a recipe, so I took it upon myself and devised this amazing dessert that combines the ease of a cobbler and the rich taste of pecan pie. It tastes even better with ice cream or whipped topping.
—Willa Kelley, Edmond, OK

PREP: 20 MIN. • **BAKE:** 30 MIN. + COOLING
MAKES: 12 SERVINGS

- ½ cup butter, cubed
- 1 cup plus 2 Tbsp. all-purpose flour
- ¾ cup sugar
- 3 tsp. baking powder
- ¼ tsp. salt
- ⅔ cup 2% milk
- 1 tsp. vanilla extract
- 1½ cups coarsely chopped pecans
- 1 cup packed brown sugar
- ¾ cup brickle toffee bits
- 1½ cups boiling water
  Vanilla ice cream, optional

1. Preheat oven to 350°. Place butter in a 13x9-in. baking pan; heat pan in oven for 3-5 minutes or until the butter is melted. Meanwhile, combine flour, sugar, baking powder and salt. Stir in milk and vanilla until combined.

2. Remove baking pan from oven; add batter. Sprinkle with pecans, brown sugar and toffee bits. Slowly pour boiling water over top (do not stir). Bake, uncovered, until golden brown, 30-35 minutes. Cool on wire rack for 30 minutes (cobbler will thicken upon cooling). Serve warm, with ice cream if desired.

1 **SERVING:** *411 cal., 23g fat (8g sat. fat), 26mg chol., 327mg sod., 51g carb. (41g sugars, 2g fiber), 3g pro.*

CHOCOLATE MINCEMEAT BARS

What would the holidays be without mincemeat for dessert?
Even people who say they don't care for the taste will love
these tender chocolate bars.
—Darlene Berndt, South Bend, IN

PREP: 15 MIN. • **BAKE:** 20 MIN. • **MAKES:** 3 DOZEN

- ½   cup shortening
- 1   cup sugar
- 3   large eggs
- 2   cups all-purpose flour
- 2   tsp. baking soda
- 1¾ cups mincemeat
- 2   cups (12 oz.) semisweet chocolate chips
-     Confectioners' sugar

1. Preheat oven to 375°. In a large bowl, cream shortening and
sugar until light and fluffy. Add eggs, 1 at a time, beating well
after each addition. Combine flour and baking soda; gradually
add to the creamed mixture and mix well. Beat in mincemeat.
Stir in chocolate chips.

2. Spread into a greased 15x10x1-in. baking pan. Bake until dark
golden brown, 15-20 minutes. Cool on a wire rack. Dust with
confectioners' sugar.

1 BAR: *142 cal., 6g fat (2g sat. fat), 18mg chol., 80mg sod.,*
21g carb. (15g sugars, 1g fiber), 2g pro.

SPARKLING APPLE PIE ON THE ROCKS

This is the perfect cold-weather cocktail. Apple cider mixed
with a cinnamon caramel apple simple syrup and topped with
bubbly—it's the best holiday drink ever!
—Becky Hardin, St. Peters, MO

PREP: 30 MIN. + COOLING • **MAKES:** 8 SERVINGS

- 3   cups apple cider or juice, divided
- 1   cup caramel ice cream topping, plus additional for dipping
- 2   cinnamon sticks (3 in.)
- 1   tsp. ground cinnamon
-     Gold sprinkles
- 1   bottle (750 ml) brut champagne
-     Apple slices and additional cinnamon sticks (3 in.),
      optional

1. In a small saucepan, bring 1 cup cider, 1 cup caramel topping,
cinnamon sticks and cinnamon to a boil. Reduce heat; simmer
until liquid is reduced to 1 cup, about 15 minutes. Cool slightly;
discard cinnamon sticks.

2. Place sprinkles and additional caramel topping in separate
shallow bowls. Hold each glass upside down and dip rim in
caramel topping, then dip in sprinkles.

3. To serve, fill glasses with ice. Add 2 Tbsp. cooled cinnamon
syrup to each; top with remaining cider and the champagne.
If desired, garnish cocktail with apple slices and additional
cinnamon sticks.

⅔ CUP: *198 cal., 0 fat (0 sat. fat), 0 chol., 149mg sod., 36g carb.*
(33g sugars, 0 fiber), 1g pro.

OLD-WORLD COOKIES

Make your holiday cookie spread something special with the most traditional creations—delicacies that immigrants from Europe and Scandinavia brought with them to North America.

ITALIAN SESAME COOKIES

These European cookies aren't overly sweet and have a wonderful crunch from sesame seeds. They're the ideal accompaniment to a freshly brewed cup of coffee or tea.
—Sarah Knoblock, Hyde Park, IN

PREP: 35 MIN. • **BAKE:** 10 MIN./BATCH
MAKES: 8 DOZEN

- ½ cup butter, softened
- 1 cup sugar
- 3 large eggs, room temperature
- 1 tsp. vanilla extract
- 3 cups all-purpose flour
- 3 tsp. baking powder
- ½ tsp. salt
- 1¾ cups sesame seeds
- ¾ cup 2% milk

1. Preheat oven to 350°. In a large bowl, cream butter and sugar until light and fluffy. Add 1 egg at a time, beating well after each addition. Add vanilla. Combine flour, baking powder and salt; gradually add to the creamed mixture and mix well.

2. Turn dough onto a lightly floured surface, knead 10-12 times or until smooth. Divide into 8 portions. Shape each portion into a 24-in. log. Cut logs into 2-in. pieces.

3. Place sesame seeds and milk in separate shallow bowls. Brush each piece of dough with milk, then roll in sesame seeds. Place 2 in. apart on greased baking sheets. Bake until cookies are set and the bottoms are lightly browned, 7-9 minutes. Cool on pans for 2 minutes before removing to wire racks to cool completely.

1 COOKIE: *45 cal., 2g fat (1g sat. fat), 9mg chol., 35mg sod., 6g carb. (2g sugars, 0 fiber), 1g pro.*
DIABETIC EXCHANGES: *½ starch.*

NEAPOLITAN COOKIES

My sister shared her recipe for these tricolor treats several years ago. The crisp cookies are fun to eat one section at a time or with all three in one bite.
—Jan Mallo, White Pigeon, MI

PREP: 20 MIN. + CHILLING
BAKE: 10 MIN./BATCH
MAKES: ABOUT 11 DOZEN

- 1 cup butter, softened
- 1½ cups sugar
- 1 large egg, room temperature
- 1 tsp. vanilla extract
- 2½ cups all-purpose flour
- 1½ tsp. baking powder
- ½ tsp. salt
- ½ tsp. almond extract
- 6 drops red food coloring
- ½ cup chopped walnuts
- 1 oz. unsweetened chocolate, melted

1. Line a 9x5-in. loaf pan with waxed paper, letting the ends of the paper extend up the sides of the pan. In a large bowl, cream butter and sugar until light and fluffy. Beat in the egg and vanilla. In another bowl, whisk flour, baking powder and salt; gradually beat into the creamed mixture.

2. Divide dough into 3 portions. Mix almond extract and food coloring into 1 portion; spread evenly into prepared pan. Mix walnuts into the second portion; spread evenly over the first layer. Mix melted chocolate into the remaining portion; spread over top. Refrigerate, covered, overnight.

3. Preheat oven to 350°. Lifting with waxed paper, remove dough from pan. Cut dough lengthwise in half; cut each half crosswise into ⅛-in. slices.

4. Place slices 1 in. apart on ungreased baking sheets. Bake for 10-12 minutes or until the edges are firm. Remove from pans to wire racks to cool.

1 COOKIE: *35 cal., 2g fat (1g sat. fat), 5mg chol., 25mg sod., 4g carb. (2g sugars, 0 fiber), 0 pro.*

5 TIPS FOR MAKING THE PERFECT COOKIE DISPLAY

CHOOSE YOUR DISH
Too large a tray and the presentation will look underwhelming. Too small a tray will lead to an unwieldy pile of cookies. Ideally, the cookies should be in either a single or double layer—you want all the varieties to show. If space allows, use several plates so guests won't have to crowd around a single dish. And think beyond the tray. Arranging cookies on cake stands or in decorative boxes will lend height and visual interest to your display.

INCLUDE A VARIETY
You may have heard the saying that people eat with their eyes first, so you want your cookie tray to be enticing—and variety is key. Choose about five to seven different kinds of cookies to keep things interesting, but not overwhelming. Include a few nostalgic childhood favorites.

GROUP LIKE TYPES TOGETHER
To keep your cookies at their best, organize similar types together. Strongly flavored cookies, such as mint or molasses cookies, can transfer their flavor to milder cookies, such as sugar cookies. Soft cookies can transfer moisture to crisper cookies, affecting the texture of both. And powdered sugar gets everywhere! Consider using Christmas candies or cupcake liners to make a decorative border.

USE GEOMETRY TO YOUR ADVANTAGE
Round cookies work welll in concentric (think snail shell) arrangements. Put a single cookie in the center of the tray, then arrange the rest in circles around the central cookie. Square or rectangular cookies are ideal for horizontal or vertical line arrangements. Layer one cookie slightly on top of the next to create texture in your display.

LABEL "SAFE" COOKIES
If you know in advance that some guests have food allergies, prepare separate platters that are safe for them to eat. Add labels to identify any gluten-free, nut-free, dairy-free or other allergen-free treats. Have a list of ingredients on hand for each type of cookie in case guests ask what's in them.

GRANDMA'S POLISH COOKIES
This traditional khruchiki recipe has been handed down through my mother's side from my great-grandmother. As a child, it was my job to loop the end of each cookie through its hole.
—Sherine Elise Gilmour, Brooklyn, NY

PREP: 45 MIN. • **COOK:** 5 MIN./BATCH • **MAKES:** 40 COOKIES

- 4 cups all-purpose flour
- 1 tsp. salt
- 1 cup cold butter
- 4 large egg yolks
- 1 cup evaporated milk
- 2 tsp. vanilla extract
  - Oil for deep-fat frying
  - Confectioners' sugar

1. In a large bowl, combine flour and salt. Cut in butter until mixture resembles coarse crumbs. In another bowl, beat egg yolks until foamy; add milk and vanilla. Stir into crumb mixture until dough is stiff enough to knead.

2. Turn onto a lightly floured surface; knead 8-10 times. Divide dough into 4 pieces. Roll each portion into a ¼-in.-thick rectangle; cut into 4x1½-in. strips. Cut a 2-in. lengthwise slit down the middle of each strip; pull one of the ends through the slit like a bow.

3. In an electric skillet or deep-fat fryer, heat oil to 375°. Fry dough strips, a few at a time, until golden brown on both sides. Drain on paper towels. Dust with confectioners' sugar.

1 COOKIE: *122 cal., 8g fat (4g sat. fat), 35mg chol., 98mg sod., 10g carb. (1g sugars, 0 fiber), 2g pro.*
DIABETIC EXCHANGES: *2 fat, ½ starch.*

RUSSIAN TEA CAKES

I present my favorite holiday cookies in a special way. I pile these fresh-baked tea cakes on pretty plates that I buy throughout the year, then wrap them with colored cellophane to give to friends.
—Valerie Hudson, Mason City, IA

PREP: 15 MIN. + CHILLING • **BAKE:** 20 MIN.
MAKES: ABOUT 3½ DOZEN

- 1 cup butter, softened
- ½ cup confectioners' sugar
- 1 tsp. vanilla extract
- 2¼ cups all-purpose flour
- ¼ tsp. salt
- ¾ cup finely chopped nuts
  Additional confectioners' sugar

1. In a large bowl, cream butter and sugar until light and fluffy. Beat in vanilla. Combine dry ingredients; gradually add to creamed mixture. Stir in nuts. Cover dough and refrigerate for 1-2 hours.

2. Preheat oven to 350°. Roll dough into 1-in. balls. Place 2 in. apart on ungreased baking sheets. Bake for 12-13 minutes. Roll in confectioners' sugar while still warm. Cool on wire racks.

1 COOKIE: *83 cal., 6g fat (3g sat. fat), 12mg chol., 49mg sod., 7g carb. (1g sugars, 0 fiber), 1g pro.*

PIZZELLE

This recipe was adapted from one used by my Italian-born mother and grandmother. They used old irons on a gas stove, but now we have the convenience of electric pizzelle irons. The cookies are so delectable and beautiful, they're worth it!
—Elizabeth Schwartz, Trevorton, PA

PREP: 10 MIN. • **COOK:** 5 MIN./BATCH • **MAKES:** 7 DOZEN

- 18 large eggs
- 3½ cups sugar
- 1¼ cups canola oil
- 1 Tbsp. anise oil
- 6½ cups all-purpose flour

In a large bowl, beat the eggs, sugar and oils until smooth. Gradually add flour and mix well. Bake in a preheated pizzelle iron according to manufacturer's directions until golden brown. Remove to wire racks to cool. Store in an airtight container.

1 PIZZELLE: *113 cal., 5g fat (1g sat. fat), 45mg chol., 15mg sod., 16g carb. (9g sugars, 0 fiber), 2g pro.*
DIABETIC EXCHANGES: *1 starch, 1 fat.*

HAZELNUT MADELEINE COOKIES

These soft, cakelike cookies have a delicate hazelnut flavor—perfect for making great memories! They're baked in the distinctive shell-shaped madeleine pan, available in kitchen specialty stores.
—Taste of Home *Test Kitchen*

PREP: 30 MIN. • **BAKE:** 20 MIN.
MAKES: 2 DOZEN

- ½ cup whole hazelnuts, toasted
- 1 Tbsp. confectioners' sugar
- 1 Tbsp. plus ½ cup butter, divided
- 2 Tbsp. plus 1 cup all-purpose flour, divided
- 2 eggs, room temperature, separated
- ⅔ cup sugar
- ¼ tsp. vanilla extract
- 1 tsp. baking powder
- ⅛ tsp. salt
  Additional confectioners' sugar, optional

1. Preheat oven to 325°. In a food processor, combine the hazelnuts and confectioners' sugar; cover and process until nuts are finely chopped. Set aside. Melt 1 Tbsp. butter. Brush 2 Madeleine pans with butter. Dust with 2 Tbsp. flour; tap pans to remove excess flour and set aside. Place the remaining butter in a saucepan. Melt over low heat until a light amber color, 4-5 minutes; set aside to cool.

2. In a large bowl, beat egg yolks and sugar until thick and a pale lemon color. Stir in the melted butter and vanilla. Combine the baking powder, salt and the remaining flour; stir into the butter mixture just until combined. In a small bowl, beat egg whites on high speed until stiff peaks form; fold into the batter. Gently fold in the reserved nut mixture.

3. With a tablespoon, fill the prepared pans two-thirds full. Bake for 18-20 minutes or until golden brown. Cool for 2 minutes before inverting pans onto wire racks to remove cookies. Cool completely. Lightly dust with additional confectioners' sugar if desired.

1 COOKIE: *103 cal., 6g fat (3g sat. fat), 29mg chol., 78mg sod., 11g carb. (6g sugars, 0 fiber), 1g pro.*
DIABETIC EXCHANGES: *1 starch, 1 fat.*

NORWEGIAN CHOCOLATE CHIP COOKIES

My best friend, Amber, taught me how to make these cookies. They are a great mashup of a sugar cookie and chocolate chip cookie. A pizza cutter is the best tool for cutting into slices after baking.
—Bonnie Brien, Pacific Grove, CA

PREP: 25 MIN. • **BAKE:** 15 MIN./BATCH
MAKES: 5 DOZEN

- 1 cup butter, softened
- 1⅓ cups plus 3 Tbsp. sugar, divided
- 2 large eggs, room temperature
- 1 tsp. vanilla extract
- 3 cups all-purpose flour
- 1 tsp. baking powder
- 1 cup miniature semisweet chocolate chips
- ¾ tsp. ground cinnamon

1. Preheat oven to 350°. In a large bowl, cream butter and 1⅓ cups sugar until light and fluffy. Beat in eggs and vanilla. In another bowl, whisk flour and baking powder; gradually beat into the creamed mixture. Stir in chocolate chips.

2. Divide dough into 4 portions. On a lightly floured surface, roll each portion into a 15-in. rope. Place 2 ropes 4 in. apart on a parchment-lined 15x10x1-in. baking pan; with a fork, flatten each rope to ¼-in. thickness. Mix cinnamon and remaining sugar; sprinkle about 2 tsp. of the mixture over each rectangle. Repeat with the remaining ropes.

3. Bake for 15-17 minutes or until edges are light brown. Cool on pans 2 minutes; cut each rectangle into 1-in. slices. Remove slices to wire racks to cool.

1 COOKIE: *59 cal., 1g fat (1g sat. fat), 6mg chol., 11mg sod., 12g carb. (7g sugars, 0 fiber), 1g pro.*

LINZER COOKIES

These cookies have an old-world elegance that delights. They take a little extra effort, but the results are so sweet! They really help to make the holidays feel special. You can match the shape of the cutout to the outer shape of the cookie, or use a contrasting cutter a star or a tree. Raspberry jam is traditional, but you can use a different flavor if you prefer.
—Jane Pearcy, Verona, WI

PREP: 30 MIN. + CHILLING
BAKE: 10 MIN./BATCH + COOLING
MAKES: 3 DOZEN

- 1¼ cups butter, softened
- 1   cup sugar
- 2   large eggs, room temperature
- 3   cups all-purpose flour
- 1   Tbsp. baking cocoa
- ½   tsp. salt
- ¼   tsp. ground cinnamon
- ¼   tsp. ground nutmeg
- ⅛   tsp. ground cloves
- 2   cups ground almonds
- 6   Tbsp. seedless raspberry jam
- 3   Tbsp. confectioners' sugar

1. In a large bowl, cream butter and sugar until light and fluffy. Add 1 egg at a time, beating well after each addition. Combine flour, cocoa, salt and spices; gradually add to creamed mixture and mix well. Stir in almonds. Refrigerate for 1 hour or until easy to handle.

2. Preheat oven to 350°. On a lightly floured surface, roll out dough to ⅛-in. thickness. Cut with a floured 2½-in. round cookie cutter. Cut out a 1½-in. shape from the center of half the cookies.

3. Place on ungreased baking sheets. Bake 10-12 minutes or until edges are golden brown. Remove to wire racks to cool.

4. Spread the bottom of each solid cookie with ½ tsp. jam. Sprinkle the cutout cookies with confectioners' sugar; carefully place over jam.

1 COOKIE: 161 cal., 9g fat (4g sat. fat), 28mg chol., 82mg sod., 17g carb. (9g sugars, 1g fiber), 3g pro.
DIABETIC EXCHANGES: *1½ fat, 1 starch.*

SWEDISH ALMOND RUSKS

Not too sweet, these nutty, crunchy cookies go well with a cup of hot coffee...and travel well in care packages, too!
—Judy Videen, Moorehead, MN

PREP: 20 MIN. • **BAKE:** 40 MIN.
MAKES: 6 DOZEN

- 1   cup butter, softened
- 1¾ cups sugar
- 2   large eggs, room temperature
- 2   tsp. almond extract
- 5   cups all-purpose flour
- 1   tsp. ground cardamom
- 1   tsp. baking soda
- 1   cup sour cream
- 1   cup finely chopped almonds

1. Preheat oven to 350°. In a bowl, cream butter and sugar. Add 1 egg at a time, beating well after each addition. Stir in extract. Sift together flour, cardamom and soda; add alternately with sour cream to creamed mixture. Fold in almonds.

2. Divide the dough into 6 parts; shape each into a roll. Place 3 rolls on each of 2 greased baking sheets. Bake for about 30 minutes or until light brown. Remove rolls to a cutting board.

3. Using a sharp knife, slice rolls diagonally into ½-in.-thick slices. Place on sheets; return to oven and bake until light brown. Cool; store in tightly covered containers.

1 COOKIE: 92 cal., 4g fat (2g sat. fat), 13mg chol., 41mg sod., 12g carb. (5g sugars, 0 fiber), 2g pro.

KOURAMBIETHES

My daughter-in-law gave me this recipe. Her grandmother was born in Greece and bakes these cookies for special occasions, including Christmas.
—Carol Dale, Greenville, TX

PREP: 40 MIN.
BAKE: 15 MIN./BATCH + COOLING
MAKES: 5 DOZEN

- 1   cup blanched almonds
- 2   cups butter, softened
- 2½   cups confectioners' sugar, divided
- 1   large egg yolk, room temperature
- 3   Tbsp. whiskey or orange juice
- 2   tsp. vanilla extract
- 5   cups all-purpose flour
- 1   tsp. baking powder
       Additional confectioners' sugar

1. Preheat oven to 350°. Place almonds in an ungreased 9-in. square baking pan. Bake until lightly browned, 5-10 minutes, stirring several times. When cool, process in a food processor until finely chopped; set aside.
2. In a large bowl, cream butter and ¾ cup confectioners' sugar until light and fluffy. Add the egg yolk, whiskey or juice and vanilla; mix well. Combine the flour, baking powder and reserved almonds; gradually beat into creamed mixture.
3. Shape tablespoonfuls of dough into 3-in. logs. Place 1 in. apart on ungreased baking sheets; shape into crescents. Bake until set and bottoms are lightly browned, 14-18 minutes.
4. Carefully roll warm cookies in the remaining confectioners' sugar. Cool on wire racks. Once cool, sprinkle with additional confectioners' sugar.
1 COOKIE: *128 cal., 7g fat (4g sat. fat), 19mg chol., 51mg sod., 13g carb. (5g sugars, 1g fiber), 2g pro.*
DIABETIC EXCHANGES: *1½ fat, 1 starch.*

HAZELNUT-ALMOND ZIMTSTERNE

These nutty, nicely spiced cutouts dusted with sugar are a German tradition. Serve them with cups of tea or coffee for dunking.
—Pat Habiger, Spearville, KS

PREP: 35 MIN. + CHILLING • **BAKE:** 10 MIN./BATCH + COOLING
MAKES: ABOUT 6½ DOZEN

- 1½ cups unblanched almonds
- ¾ cup hazelnuts
- 2 large egg whites, room temperature
- 1 cup sugar
- 2 Tbsp. all-purpose flour
- 1 tsp. ground cinnamon
- ¼ tsp. ground nutmeg
  Confectioners' sugar, optional

1. Toast almonds and hazelnuts; cool completely. Place nuts in a food processor; cover and process until finely ground.
2. In large bowl, beat egg whites on medium speed until soft peaks form. Gradually beat in sugar, 1 Tbsp. at a time, on high until stiff glossy peaks form and sugar is dissolved. Combine the nut mixture, flour, cinnamon and nutmeg; fold into egg whites. Cover and refrigerate for 1 hour.
3. Preheat oven to 325°. On a lightly floured surface, roll dough to ¼-in. thickness. Cut with a floured 2-in. star-shaped cookie cutter. Place 1 in. apart on parchment-lined baking sheets.
4. Bake until edges are lightly browned, 9-11 minutes. Remove to wire racks to cool. If desired, sprinkle with confectioners' sugar.
1 COOKIE: 36 cal., 2g fat (0 sat. fat), 0 chol., 2mg sod., 3g carb. (3g sugars, 0 fiber), 1g pro.

SANDBAKKELSE

Translated from Norwegian, the name of these cookies is "sand tarts." They're most attractive if baked in authentic sandbakkelse molds, which can be purchased in a Scandinavian import shop or from specialty kitchen stores. Most any decorative cookie mold will do, though, and the interesting shapes will make these tarts the focus of your cookie tray!
—Karen Hoylo, Duluth, MN

PREP: 15 MIN. + CHILLING • **BAKE:** 10 MIN.
MAKES: ABOUT 8 DOZEN

- 1 cup plus 2 Tbsp. butter, softened
- 1 cup sugar
- 1 large egg, room temperature
- 1 tsp. almond extract
- ½ tsp. vanilla extract
- 3 cups all-purpose flour

1. In a bowl, cream butter and sugar. Add egg and extracts. Blend in flour. Cover and chill for 1-2 hours or overnight.
2. Preheat oven to 375°. Using ungreased sandbakkelse molds, press 1 Tbsp. dough into each mold. Bake until cookies appear set and just begin to brown around the edges, 10-12 minutes. Cool for 2-3 minutes in molds. When cool to the touch, remove from molds. To remove more easily, gently tap the mold with a knife and carefully squeeze it.
2 COOKIES: 80 cal., 4g fat (2g sat. fat), 15mg chol., 40mg sod., 10g carb. (4g sugars, 0 fiber), 1g pro.

FINNISH PINWHEELS

When my sister was hosting an exchange student from Finland, she served my pinwheel cookies to her guest. The young lady instantly recognized them. I felt good knowing they're still being made in our ancestors' country!
—Ilona Barron, Ontonagon, MI

PREP: 1 HOUR • **BAKE:** 15 MIN./BATCH
MAKES: ABOUT 7 DOZEN

FILLING
- ¼ lb. pitted dried plums, chopped
- ¼ lb. pitted dates, chopped
- ½ cup boiling water
- 1 Tbsp. sugar
- 1½ tsp. butter

PASTRY
- 3 cups all-purpose flour
- 1 cup sugar
- 2 tsp. baking powder
- ½ tsp. salt
- 1 cup cold butter
- 1 large egg, room temperature, beaten
- 3 Tbsp. heavy whipping cream
- 1 tsp. vanilla extract
   Confectioners' sugar

1. Preheat oven to 325°. In a saucepan, combine dried plums, dates, water and sugar. Cook over low heat, stirring constantly, until thickened. Remove from the heat and stir in butter. Cool.
2. Meanwhile, in a bowl, sift together the flour, sugar, baking powder and salt. Cut in butter as for a pie crust. Blend in egg, cream and vanilla. Form into 2 balls.
3. Place 1 ball at a time on a floured surface and roll to ⅛-in. thickness. Cut into 2-in. squares. Place on ungreased baking sheets. Make 1-in. slits in corners. Place ½ tsp. filling in the center of each square. Bring every other corner up into center to form a pinwheel; press lightly.
4. Bake until the points are light golden brown, about 12 minutes. Cool on wire racks. Dust with confectioners' sugar.
1 PINWHEEL: *56 cal., 3g fat (2g sat. fat), 9mg chol., 45mg sod., 8g carb. (4g sugars, 0 fiber), 1g pro.*

NORWEGIAN COOKIES

This recipe was passed down to me from my mother-in-law. These soft sugar cookies are a favorite with our four children.
—Karen Skowronek, Minot, ND

PREP: 20 MIN. + CHILLING • **BAKE:** 10 MIN.
MAKES: ABOUT 5½ DOZEN

- 1 cup butter, softened
- 1 cup sugar
- 1 large egg, room temperature
- ½ tsp. vanilla extract
- ½ tsp. almond extract
- 2 cups all-purpose flour
- ½ cup finely chopped walnuts
   Red and/or green colored sugar

1. In a bowl, cream butter and sugar. Add egg and extracts; beat until light and fluffy. Add flour and nuts; beat just until moistened. Cover and chill 1 hour or until firm enough to handle.
2. Preheat oven to 350°. Shape dough into 1-in. balls; place 2 in. apart on parchment-lined baking sheets. Flatten to ¼-in. thickness with a glass dipped in colored sugar. Sprinkle with additional sugar if desired. Bake for 10-12 minutes or until cookies are set.
1 COOKIE: *68 cal., 4g fat (2g sat. fat), 12mg chol., 28mg sod., 7g carb. (4g sugars, 0 fiber), 1g pro.*

AUSTRIAN WALNUT COOKIES

Known as palatschinkens in Austria, these rich cookies melt in your mouth. The delicate, tender pastry surrounds a walnut filling that's just sweet enough. The recipe comes from a co-worker who was known for her wonderful baked goods.
—Donna Gaston, Coplay, PA

PREP: 35 MIN. + CHILLING
BAKE: 10 MIN. + COOLING
MAKES: ABOUT 2 DOZEN

- 1 cup butter, softened
- 8 large egg yolks, room temperature
- 2¾ cups all-purpose flour

FILLING

- 3 large egg whites, room temperature
- 1 cup confectioners' sugar
- 1 cup ground walnuts
  Additional confectioners' sugar

1. In a large bowl, beat butter until creamy. Beat in egg yolks, 2 at a time. Gradually beat in flour.

2. Divide dough into 3 portions. Shape each portion into a disk; wrap each disk in plastic. Refrigerate overnight.

3. Preheat oven to 350°. In a small bowl, using clean beaters, beat egg whites on medium speed until foamy. Gradually add confectioners' sugar, 2 Tbsp. at a time, beating on high after each addition until sugar is dissolved. Continue beating until stiff glossy peaks form. Fold in walnuts.

4. On a lightly floured surface, roll each portion of dough to ⅛-in. thickness. Cut with a floured 3-in. round cookie cutter. Spread each cookie with 1 tsp. walnut mixture to within ¼ in. of edges. Fold dough almost in half over filling, allowing filling to show. Place 1 in. apart on ungreased baking sheets.

5. Bake 8-10 minutes or until light brown. Remove from pans to wire racks to cool completely.

6. Dust the cookies with additional confectioner's sugar. Store in airtight containers in the refrigerator.

1 COOKIE: *182 cal., 12g fat (6g sat. fat), 82mg chol., 71mg sod., 17g carb. (5g sugars, 1g fiber), 3g pro.*

WHIPPED CREAM KRUMKAKE

Our town's rich Norwegian heritage is evident at holidays and during our annual Nordic Fest, when krumkake is king! There are demonstrations of krumkake-making in store windows, and this delicious pastry is served at family dinners and bake sales.
—Imelda Nesteby, Decorah, IA

PREP: 20 MIN. + CHILLING • **BAKE:** 20 MIN.
MAKES: ABOUT 3 DOZEN

- 3 large eggs, room temperature
- 1 cup sugar
- ½ cup sweet butter, melted
- ½ cup heavy whipping cream, whipped
- ½ tsp. nutmeg
- 1½ cups all-purpose flour
  Sweet butter for krumkake plates
  Sweetened whipped cream

1. Beat eggs in bowl until very light. Add sugar gradually, beating to blend. Slowly add melted butter, then whipped cream and nutmeg. Mix in flour. (Dough will be consistency of cookie dough.) Chill dough thoroughly.

2. Preheat krumkake plates over medium heat for about 10 minutes or until a drop of water dances when dropped on plates. Brush plates with sweet butter; place a tablespoonful of dough in the center of the lower plate; close iron and press handles together. If excess dough comes out sides, remove with table knife.

3. Bake for about 30 seconds; flip iron and bake for about 30 seconds on other side. Remove krumkake and immediately roll over cone-shaped form. Place seam side down on parchment to cool; remove form.

4. Fill cooled cones with whipped cream if desired. Serve immediately.

1 KRUMKAKE: *161 cal., 8g fat (5g sat. fat), 58mg chol., 14mg sod., 19g carb. (11g sugars, 0 fiber), 2g pro.*

PFEFFERNUESSE

These mild spice cookies, perfect for dunking, come from an old family recipe. The dough sits overnight to let the spices blend. The extraordinary flavors make these a holiday classic.
—*Betty Hawkshaw, Alexandria, VA*

PREP: 20 MIN. + CHILLING • **BAKE:** 10 MIN. • **MAKES:** 8 DOZEN

  1   **cup butter, softened**
  1   **cup sugar**
  2   **large eggs, room temperature**
 ½   **cup light corn syrup**
 ½   **cup molasses**
 ⅓   **cup water**
6⅔ **cups all-purpose flour**
 ¼   **cup crushed aniseed**
  1   **tsp. baking soda**
  1   **tsp. ground cinnamon**
 ½   **tsp. ground nutmeg**
 ¼   **tsp. ground cloves**
 ¼   **tsp. ground allspice**
      Confectioners' sugar

1. In a bowl, cream the butter and sugar. Add 1 egg at a time, beating well after each addition. In a bowl, combine corn syrup, molasses and water; set aside. Combine the flour, aniseed, baking soda and spices; add to the creamed mixture alternately with the molasses mixture. Cover and refrigerate overnight.
2. Preheat oven to 400°. Roll into 1-in. balls. Place 2 in. apart on greased baking sheets. Bake 11 minutes or until golden brown. Roll warm cookies in confectioners' sugar. Cool on wire racks.
2 COOKIES: *137 cal., 4g fat (2g sat. fat), 19mg chol., 73mg sod., 23g carb. (8g sugars, 1g fiber), 2g pro.*

CHOCOLATE AMARETTI

These classic almond paste cookies are like ones you'd find in an Italian bakery. My husband and children are always excited when I include them in my holiday baking lineup.
—*Kathy Long, Whitefish Bay, WI*

PREP: 15 MIN. • **BAKE:** 20 MIN./BATCH • **MAKES:** 2 DOZEN

1¼ **cups almond paste**
 ¾   **cup sugar**
  2   **large egg whites, room temperature**
 ½   **cup confectioners' sugar**
 ¼   **cup baking cocoa**

1. Preheat oven to 350°. Crumble almond paste into a food processor; add sugar and pulse until evenly combined. Add egg whites and process until incorporated. Transfer mixture to a bowl. Sift together confectioners' sugar and cocoa; gradually add to almond mixture and mix well.
2. Drop dough by tablespoonfuls 2 in. apart onto parchment-lined baking sheets. Bake until tops are cracked, 17-20 minutes. Cool for 1 minute before removing from pans to wire racks. Store in an airtight container.
1 COOKIE: *92 cal., 3g fat (0 sat. fat), 0 chol., 6mg sod., 15g carb. (13g sugars, 1g fiber), 2g pro.*

TORCETTI

Our Sicilian grandmother often had my sister and me roll out the dough for these tasty torcetti. They're melt-in-your-mouth delicious without being overly sweet. We still make them for our family celebrations.
—Joy Quici, Upland, CA

PREP: 30 MIN. + RISING
BAKE: 15 MIN./BATCH + COOLING
MAKES: 6 DOZEN

- 5 cups all-purpose flour
- 1 cup cold butter, cubed
- 1 cup shortening
- 1 pkg. (¼ oz.) active dry yeast
- ½ cup warm milk (110° to 115°)
- 2 large eggs, room temperature
- 1 Tbsp. sugar
- 1½ tsp. vanilla extract
- 2 cups confectioners' sugar
  Additional confectioners' sugar

1. Place flour in a large bowl; cut in butter and shortening until mixture resembles coarse crumbs. Set aside.
2. In a large bowl, dissolve yeast in warm milk. Add eggs, sugar, vanilla and 2 cups of the crumb mixture; beat until well blended. Gradually beat in the remaining crumb mixture.
3. Turn dough onto a floured surface; knead for 3-4 minutes. Place in a greased bowl, turning once to grease top. Cover and let rise in a warm place until doubled, about 1 hour.
4. Preheat oven to 375°. Punch dough down; divide into 6 portions. Shape each portion into twelve 6-in. ropes about ¼ in. thick; roll in confectioners' sugar. Shape each rope into a loop. Holding both ends of loop, twist together 3 times.
5. Place 2 in. apart on greased baking sheets. Bake 12-14 minutes or until golden brown. Roll warm cookies in additional confectioners' sugar. Cool on wire racks.
1 COOKIE: *102 cal., 5g fat (2g sat. fat), 13mg chol., 21mg sod., 12g carb. (5g sugars, 0 fiber), 1g pro.*
DIABETIC EXCHANGES: *1 starch, 1 fat.*

SWEDISH SPRITZ

A touch of almond extract gives these spritz wonderful flavor. For Christmas, you could tint half the dough with red food coloring and the other half with green—or dress them up however you like with colorful frosting and sprinkles.
—Irmgard Sinn, Sherwood Park, AB

PREP: 20 MIN.
BAKE: 10 MIN./BATCH + COOLING
MAKES: 4 DOZEN

- 1 cup butter, softened
- ⅔ cup sugar
- 1 large egg, room temperature
- ½ tsp. almond extract
- ½ tsp. vanilla extract
- 2¼ cups all-purpose flour
- 1 tsp. baking powder
  Prepared frosting, assorted sprinkles and decorating sugars

1. Preheat oven to 350°. In a large bowl, cream butter and sugar until light and fluffy. Beat in egg and the extracts. Combine the flour and baking powder; gradually add to the creamed mixture.
2. Using a cookie press fitted with the disk of your choice, press dough 1 in. apart onto ungreased baking sheets. Bake until edges are firm and lightly browned, 12-13 minutes. Remove to wire racks to cool. Frost and decorate as desired.
2 COOKIES: *108 cal., 6g fat (4g sat. fat), 23mg chol., 77mg sod., 12g carb. (4g sugars, 0 fiber), 1g pro.*

CHRISTMAS
CANDIES

Hard candy, caramels, truffles and more...Christmas is the perfect time to make candy! Present these confections as gifts, or have fun making them together.

ALMOND CRUNCH

Once you start eating this taste-tempting treat, you may not be able to stop! Matzo crackers are topped with buttery caramel, chocolate and slivered almonds, and then baked to perfection.
—Sharalyn Zander, Jacksonville, AL

PREP: 20 MIN. • **BAKE:** 15 MIN. + CHILLING • **MAKES:** 1 LB.

  4 to 6 unsalted matzo crackers
  1 cup butter, cubed
  1 cup packed brown sugar
  ¾ cup semisweet chocolate chips
  1 tsp. shortening
  1 cup slivered almonds, toasted

1. Preheat oven to 350°. Line a 15x10x1-in. baking pan with a layer of foil and then a layer of parchment. Arrange the crackers in the pan; set aside.
2. In a large heavy saucepan over medium heat, melt butter. Stir in brown sugar. Bring to a boil; cook and stir for 3-4 minutes or until sugar is dissolved. Spread evenly over crackers.
3. Bake 15-17 minutes (cover loosely with foil if top browns too quickly). Cool on a wire rack for 5 minutes. Melt chocolate and shortening; stir until smooth. Stir in almonds; spread over top. Cool for 1 hour.
4. Break into pieces. Cover and refrigerate for at least 2 hours or until set. Store in an airtight container.
2 OZ. CANDY: *517 cal., 36g fat (18g sat. fat), 61mg chol., 329mg sod., 50g carb. (36g sugars, 3g fiber), 5g pro.*

CHRISTMAS HARD CANDY

When you make a batch of this beautiful jewel-toned candy, the whole house fills with the wonderful scent of mint or cinnamon. My mom always makes this candy, and people request it every year. She puts it in clear jars with a holiday calico fabric on the lid. Now I've started making it, too.
—Jane Holman, Moultrie, GA

PREP: 5 MIN. • **COOK:** 1 HOUR + COOLING • **MAKES:** ABOUT 2 LBS.

 3½ cups sugar
  1 cup light corn syrup
  1 cup water
  ¼ to ½ tsp. cinnamon or peppermint oil
  1 tsp. red or green food coloring

1. Grease a baking sheet with butter or cooking spray; set aside. In a large heavy saucepan, combine sugar, corn syrup and water. Cook on medium-high heat until a candy thermometer reads 300° (hard-crack stage), stirring occasionally. Remove from the heat; stir in oil and food coloring. Keep your face away from mixture, as the smell of the oil is very strong.
2. Immediately pour onto prepared baking sheet. Cool; break into pieces. Store in airtight containers.
1 PIECE: *114 cal., 0 fat (0 sat. fat), 0 chol., 13mg sod., 30g carb. (26g sugars, 0 fiber), 0 pro.*

6 TIPS FOR MAKING HOMEMADE CANDY

If you've never made candy before, you may think it's hard to do. But while there are pitfalls to candy-making, you can avoid them by taking a few simple precautions. Don't let potential candymaking mistakes stand in your way of delicious holiday treats! And what better time to make candy than at Christmas?

1. SWIRL THE SUGAR
Ever bite into fudge and notice it's crystallized? There's a reason for that: The sugar was stirred the same way a cook would stir anything else. To avoid this undesirable sandy, grainy texture, "stir" the sugar by swirling the pot with a turn of the wrist, lifting the pot off the burner.

2. USE A CANDY THERMOMETER
A difference of just a few degrees can turn caramels from soft and chewy to a trip to the dentist, and hard candy to a burned mess that might just cost you a saucepan. So if you're serious about making candy, invest in a candy thermometer. Note these important candy stages:
- **Soft-ball (235-240°):** Syrup added to cold water forms a "soft ball" that is fudge-like, flexible and can flatten easily.
- **Firm-ball (245-250°):** This is the perfect stage for molding into balls or other shapes, applying some pressure.
- **Soft-crack (270-290°):** The mixture begins to become pliable.
- **Hard-crack (300-310°):** Candy becomes brittle, almost ready for eating.

3. TEST THE THERMOMETER
Testing your candy thermometer before each use is as simple as boiling water! Bring a pot of water to a boil and measure its temperature; the thermometer should read 212°. If it reads high or low, adjust the recipe temperature up or down as needed.

4. COAT THE PAN
Candy can easily stick to the bottom of your pan, so always butter your pan or coat it with a spritz of cooking spray. You can also use coconut oil, which imparts a sweet flavor.

5. WAIT TO SLICE
Once your kitchen smells like chocolate or caramel, it can be tempting to cut right into the goodies. But doing so can cause harm. Let the candy cool for at least eight hours or overnight before cutting unless the specific recipe indicates otherwise.

6. STORE IT PROPERLY
If your candied citrus has gone soft or your caramels have dried out, it's likely because the candy wasn't stored properly. Be sure to use an airtight container to keep air out (and freshness in).

CRANBERRY BUTTER CRUNCH BARK

One Christmas I dreamed this recipe up when making buttercrunch toffee. It is an addictive treat that disappears fast.
—*Heather Ferris, Vanderhoof, BC*

PREP: 20 MIN. • **COOK:** 1 HOUR + CHILLING
MAKES: 4 LBS.

1½ tsp. plus 1 cup butter, divided
1 cup sugar
3 Tbsp. water
8 cups chopped white candy coating (about 3 lbs.), divided
3 cups dried cranberries, divided

1. Grease a 15x10x1-in. pan with ½ tsp. butter; set aside. In a heavy saucepan over medium-low heat, bring 1 cup butter, the sugar and water to a boil, stirring constantly. Cook over medium heat until a candy thermometer reads 290° (soft-crack stage). Pour into the prepared pan (do not scrape the sides of the saucepan). Refrigerate for 1 hour or until hard.
2. Break toffee into pieces. Place in a food processor; cover and process until coarsely chopped. Divide in half; set aside
3. Butter two 15x10x1-in. pans with the remaining butter. In a microwave, melt 4 cups white candy coating. Stir in 1½ cups dried cranberries and half the reserved toffee pieces.
4. Pour onto 1 prepared pan; spread to edges of pan. Repeat with the remaining white candy coating, dried cranberries and toffee pieces. Refrigerate until firm. Break into pieces.
2 OZ. CANDY: 336 cal., 18g fat (15g sat. fat), 16mg chol., 42mg sod., 46g carb. (43g sugars, 1g fiber), 0 pro.

HOMEMADE HOLIDAY MARSHMALLOWS

This recipe was my grandpa's favorite. Every Christmastime, he would be busy making marshmallows for his family and friends.
—*Diana Byron, New London, OH*

PREP: 55 MIN. + STANDING
MAKES: ABOUT 9½ DOZEN

2 tsp. butter
3 envelopes unflavored gelatin
1 cup cold water, divided
2 cups sugar
1 cup light corn syrup
⅛ tsp. salt
1 tsp. clear vanilla extract
    Optional toppings: Melted chocolate, hot fudge and/or caramel ice cream topping
    Optional garnishes: Baking cocoa, confectioners' sugar, crushed assorted candies, chopped nuts, colored sugars and/or sprinkles

1. Line a 13x9-in. pan with foil and grease the foil with butter; set aside.
2. In a large metal bowl, sprinkle gelatin over ½ cup water; set aside. In a large heavy saucepan, combine the sugar, corn syrup, salt and remaining water. Bring to a boil, stirring occasionally. Cook, without stirring, until a candy thermometer reads 240° (soft-ball stage).
3. Remove from heat and gradually add to the gelatin. Beat on high speed until the mixture is thick and the volume is doubled, about 15 minutes. Beat in vanilla. Spread into prepared pan. Cover and let stand at room temperature for 6 hours or overnight.
4. Using foil, lift marshmallows out of pan. With a knife or pizza cutter coated with cooking spray, cut into 1-in. squares. Dip or drizzle marshmallows with toppings if desired; coat with garnishes as desired. Store in an airtight container in a cool, dry place.
1 MARSHMALLOW: 22 cal., 0 fat (0 sat. fat), 0 chol., 5mg sod., 6g carb. (4g sugars, 0 fiber), 0 pro.

COCONUT JOYS

If you like coconut, you'll love these no-bake, no-fuss sweets. They're cute as can be and make a great snack to keep in the fridge during the holiday season.
—Flo Burtnett, Gage, OK

PREP: 20 MIN. + CHILLING • **MAKES:** 1½ DOZEN

- 1½ cups sweetened shredded coconut
- 1 cup confectioners' sugar
- ¼ cup butter, melted
- 1 oz. milk chocolate, melted
- 2 Tbsp. chopped pecans

1. In a large bowl, combine the coconut, confectioners' sugar and butter. Form into 1-in. balls.
2. Using the end of a wooden spoon handle, make an indentation in the center of each ball. Fill with chocolate. Sprinkle with pecans. Place on a waxed paper-lined baking sheet. Chill until the chocolate is firm. Store in the refrigerator.
1 CANDY: *101 cal., 6g fat (4g sat. fat), 7mg chol., 38mg sod., 11g carb. (10g sugars, 0 fiber), 0 pro.*
DIABETIC EXCHANGES: *1 starch, 1 fat.*

TRUFFLE CHERRIES

My family and I are a bunch of chocolate lovers, especially during the holidays. Double chocolate gems like these don't stand a chance of lasting long at our house!
—Anne Drouin, Dunnville, ON

PREP: 20 MIN. + CHILLING • **MAKES:** ABOUT 2 DOZEN

- ⅓ cup heavy whipping cream
- 2 Tbsp. butter
- 2 Tbsp. sugar
- 4 oz. semisweet chocolate, chopped
- 1 jar (8 oz.) maraschino cherries with stems, well drained

COATING
- 6 oz. semisweet chocolate, chopped
- 2 Tbsp. shortening

1. In a small saucepan, bring the cream, butter and sugar to a boil, stirring constantly. Remove from the heat; stir in chocolate until melted. Cover and refrigerate for at least 4 hours or until easy to handle.
2. Pat cherries with paper towels until very dry. Shape a teaspoonful of the chocolate mixture around each cherry, forming a ball. Cover and refrigerate for 2-3 hours or until firm.
3. In a microwave, melt chocolate and shortening; stir until smooth. Dip cherries until coated; allow excess chocolate to drip off. Place on waxed paper to set.
1 CHERRY: *57 cal., 4g fat (2g sat. fat), 7mg chol., 11mg sod., 6g carb. (6g sugars, 0 fiber), 0 pro.*

NUTTY STICKY BUN CANDIES

Save room on your holiday treat trays for these sweet and salty spirals. Oh, and put a few aside for yourself, too. They'll be in high demand!
—Josh Carter, Birmingham, AL

PREP: 20 MIN. • **COOK:** 15 MIN. + COOLING
MAKES: ABOUT 6 DOZEN (2¼ LBS.)

2 tsp. plus ½ cup softened butter, divided
3¾ cups confectioners' sugar
½ cup nonfat dry milk powder
½ cup sugar
½ cup light corn syrup
1 tsp. vanilla extract

FILLING

¼ cup sugar
1 tsp. ground cinnamon
2¼ cups deluxe mixed nuts, divided
1 Tbsp. light corn syrup

1. Butter an 8-in. square pan with 2 tsp. butter; set aside. Combine confectioners' sugar and milk powder. In a large heavy saucepan, combine ½ cup granulated sugar, ½ cup corn syrup and remaining butter; cook and stir until sugar is dissolved and mixture comes to a boil. Stir in the confectioners' sugar mixture, about a third at a time, until blended.
2. Remove from heat; stir in vanilla. Continue stirring until mixture mounds slightly when dropped from a spoon and a thermometer reads 150°. Spread into the prepared pan. Cool for 15 minutes.
3. For filling, combine ¼ cup granulated sugar and the cinnamon. Place ¾ cup nuts in a food processor; cover and pulse until coarsely ground.
4. Cut cooled candy into quarters. Roll each into a 9x5-in. rectangle. Sprinkle each rectangle with a fourth of the sugar mixture and a fourth of the ground nuts to within ½ in. of edges. Roll up tightly jelly-roll style, starting with a long side.
5. Chop remaining nuts. Brush each roll with corn syrup; roll in nuts. Using a serrated knife, cut each roll into ½-in. slices. Store at room temperature in an airtight container.
1 CANDY: *71 cal., 3g fat (1g sat. fat), 4mg chol., 28mg sod., 11g carb. (10g sugars, 0 fiber), 1g pro.*

BUTTERSCOTCH-RUM RAISIN TREATS

I love making rum raisin rice pudding around the holidays—and those classic flavors inspired this confection. Crispy rice cereal adds crunch, but nuts, toasted coconut or candied pineapple could do the job, too.
—Crystal Schlueter, Babbitt, MN

TAKES: 20 MIN. • **MAKES:** ABOUT 4½ DOZEN

1 pkg. (10 to 11 oz.) butterscotch chips
1 pkg. (10 to 12 oz.) white baking chips
½ tsp. rum extract
3 cups Rice Krispies
1 cup raisins

1. Line 56 mini muffin cups with paper liners; set aside. In a large bowl, combine butterscotch and white chips. Microwave, uncovered, on high for 30 seconds; stir. Microwave in additional 30-second intervals, stirring until smooth.
2. Stir in extract, Rice Krispies and raisins. Drop mixture by rounded tablespoonfuls into the prepared mini muffin cups. Chill until set.
FREEZE OPTION: Freeze treats in freezer containers, separating layers with waxed paper. Thaw before serving.
1 TREAT: *76 cal., 4g fat (3g sat. fat), 1mg chol., 21mg sod., 11g carb. (9g sugars, 0 fiber), 0 pro.*

Holiday Helper
It's important to stir the mixture while it cools so it sets up properly. When it reaches 150°, you're done and ready to let it cool on its own.

CASHEW BRITTLE

I like this quick and easy recipe because it doesn't require a candy thermometer. It also makes a great gift.
—Rhonda Glenn, Prince Frederick, MD

PREP: 10 MIN. • **COOK:** 10 MIN. + CHILLING
MAKES: ¾ LB.

- 2 tsp. butter, divided
- 1 cup sugar
- ½ cup light corn syrup
- 1 to 1½ cups salted cashew halves
- 1 tsp. baking soda
- 1 tsp. vanilla extract

1. Grease a baking sheet with 1 tsp. butter; set aside. In a microwave-safe bowl, mix the sugar and corn syrup; microwave, uncovered, on high 3 minutes. Stir to dissolve sugar; microwave another 2 minutes. Stir in cashews and remaining butter; microwave on high for 40 seconds. Stir; continue microwaving in 20-second intervals until mixture turns a light amber color, 1-2 minutes. (The mixture will be very hot.)

2. Quickly stir in baking soda and vanilla until light and foamy. Immediately pour onto prepared pan, spreading with a metal spatula; cool slightly. Refrigerate until set, 15-20 minutes.

3. Break brittle into pieces. Store candy between layers of waxed paper in an airtight container.

1 OZ. BRITTLE: *184 cal., 6g fat (2g sat. fat), 2mg chol., 170mg sod., 32g carb. (29g sugars, 0 fiber), 2g pro.*

CHOCOLATE-COVERED POMEGRANATE SEEDS

I dunk pomegranate seeds in chocolate to get these easy little treats my friends and family love. If you like, you can sprinkle the confection with toasted coconut or ground almonds after spooning them onto the waxed paper.
—Jim Javorsky, Havre de Grace, MD

PREP: 10 MIN. + CHILLING
MAKES: 2 DOZEN (ABOUT 1 LB.)

- 1 pkg. (12 oz.) dark chocolate chips
- 1 cup pomegranate seeds, patted dry (one large pomegranate)

1. In a microwave, melt dark chocolate chips and stir until smooth. Stir in the pomegranate seeds.

2. Drop by tablespoonfuls onto waxed paper-lined baking sheets. Refrigerate until firm, about 1 hour. Store between layers of waxed paper in an airtight container in the refrigerator.

1 PIECE: *70 cal., 4g fat (3g sat. fat), 0 chol., 5mg sod., 10g carb. (9g sugars, 1g fiber), 1g pro.*

Holiday Helper
To help prevent scorching when melting chocolate, remove it from the heat before the last of the chocolate melts. Keep stirring; the residual heat will melt all of the remaining chocolate.

MULLED WINE JELLY CANDIES

These candies make a lovely hostess gift! In the summer, I make a white wine variation using a sweet moscato and 1 teaspoon of lemon juice. Omit the orange ingredients, spices and the simmering step; just combine the wine and lemon juice and proceed.
—Jennifer Mack, Pensacola, FL

PREP: 10 MIN. • **COOK:** 25 MIN. + STANDING
MAKES: 3 DOZEN (1¾ LBS.)

- 1 cup dry red wine
- 4 orange peel strips (3x1 in. each)
- 1 Tbsp. orange juice
- 1 cinnamon stick (3 in.)
- 3 whole cloves
- ½ cup powdered fruit pectin
- ¾ tsp. baking soda
- 1⅓ cups sugar
- 1⅓ cups light corn syrup

COATING
- ¼ cup sugar

1. In a small saucepan, combine wine, orange peel, juice, cinnamon stick and cloves; bring just to a simmer (do not boil) over medium-low heat. Reduce heat; simmer gently, uncovered, 10 minutes to allow flavors to blend. Let stand 1 hour.
2. Line a 9x5-in. loaf pan with foil; coat foil with cooking spray. Strain wine mixture, discarding orange peel and spices. Return mulled wine to saucepan; stir in pectin and baking soda. Heat over medium-high heat.
3. In a large saucepan, combine sugar and corn syrup; bring to a full rolling boil over high heat, stirring constantly. Stir in the wine mixture. Continue to boil 1 minute, stirring constantly. Remove from heat; skim off foam, if necessary. Immediately pour into the prepared pan. Let stand until set, about 5 hours or overnight.
4. For coating, sprinkle 2 Tbsp. sugar over a 14x12-in. sheet of parchment. Invert candy onto sugar. With a knife dipped in warm water, cut candy into 1-in. squares; coat with the remaining sugar.
5. Transfer candies to a wire rack. Let stand, uncovered, at room temperature overnight. Store in airtight containers up to 1 week.
1 PIECE: 77 cal., 0 fat (0 sat. fat), 0 chol., 35mg sod., 19g carb. (19g sugars, 0 fiber), 0 pro.

CHOCOLATE TRUFFLES

You may be tempted to save these divinely smooth, creamy chocolates for a special occasion—and they really are perfect for Christmas. But with just a few ingredients, they're easy enough to make anytime.
—Darlene Wiese-Appleby, Creston, OH

PREP: 20 MIN. + CHILLING
MAKES: 4 DOZEN

- 3 cups (18 oz.) semisweet chocolate chips
- 1 can (14 oz.) sweetened condensed milk
- 1 Tbsp. vanilla extract

Optional coatings: Chocolate sprinkles, Dutch-processed cocoa, espresso powder and cacao nibs

In a microwave, melt the chocolate chips and milk; stir until smooth. Stir in vanilla. Refrigerate, covered, for 2 hours or until firm enough to roll. Shape into 1-in. balls. Roll in coatings as desired.
1 TRUFFLE: 77 cal., 4g fat (2g sat. fat), 3mg chol., 12mg sod., 11g carb. (10g sugars, 1g fiber), 1g pro.

MACADAMIA & COCONUT CARAMELS

I collect cookbooks from all over the world, and I use them to create new and different dishes. These smooth caramels have a scrumptious macadamia-coconut flavor.
—Sharon Delaney-Chronis,
South Milwaukee, WI

PREP: 25 MIN. • **COOK:** 25 MIN. + CHILLING
MAKES: 64 PIECES (1½ LBS.)

- 1 tsp. plus ½ cup butter, divided
- 1 cup packed light brown sugar
- ½ cup light corn syrup
- ¼ tsp. cream of tartar
- ¾ cup sweetened condensed milk
- ½ cup sweetened shredded coconut
- ½ cup chopped macadamia nuts
- ½ tsp. vanilla extract

1. Line an 8-in. square baking dish with foil and grease the foil with 1 tsp. butter; set aside. In a large heavy saucepan, combine the brown sugar, corn syrup, cream of tartar and the remaining butter; bring to a boil over medium heat, stirring constantly. Remove from heat; gradually stir in milk. Cook and stir mixture over medium-low heat until a candy thermometer reads 245° (firm-ball stage).
2. Remove from heat; stir in the remaining ingredients. Pour into the prepared dish. Refrigerate until set, at least 2 hours.
3. Using foil, lift candy out of dish. Gently peel off the foil; cut caramel into 1-in. squares. Wrap individual caramels in waxed paper; twist ends. Store in an airtight container.
1 PIECE: *56 cal., 3g fat (1g sat. fat), 5mg chol., 23mg sod., 8g carb. (6g sugars, 0 fiber), 0 pro.*

PEPPERMINT SWIRL FUDGE

Indulge your sweet tooth with these rich swirled squares. For Christmasy color, I add crushed peppermint candies and red food coloring.
—Suzette Jury, Keene, CA

PREP: 15 MIN. + CHILLING
MAKES: 81 PIECES (ABOUT 1½ LBS.)

- 1 tsp. butter
- 1 pkg. (10 to 12 oz.) white baking chips
- 1 can (16 oz.) vanilla frosting
- ½ tsp. peppermint extract
- 8 drops red food coloring
- 2 Tbsp. crushed peppermint candies

1. Line a 9-in. square pan with foil and grease the foil with butter; set aside. In a small saucepan, melt the chips; stir until smooth. Remove from the heat. Stir in frosting and extract.
2. Spread mixture into prepared pan. Randomly place drops of food coloring over the fudge; cut through with a knife to swirl. Sprinkle with candies. Refrigerate for 1 hour or until set.
3. Using foil, lift the fudge out of the pan. Gently peel off the foil; cut fudge into 1-in. squares. Store in an airtight container.
1 PIECE: *45 cal., 3g fat (1g sat. fat), 1mg chol., 17mg sod., 6g carb. (5g sugars, 0 fiber), 0 pro.*
DIABETIC EXCHANGES: *1 starch.*

NOTE: If toffee separates during cooking, add ½ cup hot water and stir vigorously. Bring mixture back up to 300° and proceed as recipe directs.

1 PIECE: *397 cal., 30g fat (15g sat. fat), 52mg chol., 197mg sod., 32g carb. (26g sugars, 1g fiber), 4g pro.*

COCONUT MARSHMALLOW SQUARES

One of my favorite childhood memories involves eating these melt-in-your-mouth candies. My mother always rolled them in coconut or ground nuts to keep the marshmallows from sticking together.
—Heather Warner, Salt Lake City, UT

PREP: 15 MIN. • **BAKE:** 25 MIN.
MAKES: 3 DOZEN (ABOUT 1½ LBS.)

- 2 envelopes unflavored gelatin
- 1¼ cups cold water, divided
- 2 cups sugar
- 2 large egg whites, lightly beaten
- 1 tsp. vanilla extract
- 2½ cups sweetened shredded coconut, chopped
- 2 to 3 drops food coloring of your choice, optional

1. Grease a 9-in. square pan; set aside. In a large bowl of a heavy-duty mixer, sprinkle gelatin over ½ cup cold water; set aside. In a heavy saucepan, combine sugar and the remaining water. Cook and stir over low heat until sugar is dissolved. Increase the heat to medium and cook, stirring occasionally, until a candy thermometer reads 235° (soft-ball stage).

2. Remove from the heat; slowly pour over the gelatin, beating constantly. Immediately add egg whites. Use the candy thermometer to make sure mixture is at least 160°. Continue to beat 15-20 minutes longer. Beat in vanilla. Pour into prepared pan. Cool for 3 hours or until firm enough to cut into squares.

3. Place the coconut in a shallow bowl. Add food coloring, if desired. Roll the marshmallow squares in coconut. Store in an airtight container in the refrigerator.

1 PIECE: *78 cal., 2g fat (2g sat. fat), 0 chol., 21mg sod., 14g carb. (14g sugars, 0 fiber), 1g pro.*

THREE-CHIP ENGLISH TOFFEE

With its melt-in-your-mouth texture and scrumptiously rich flavor, this is the ultimate toffee! Drizzled on top are three different kinds of melted chips, plus a sprinkling of walnuts. Packaged in colorful tins, these pretty pieces make great gifts.
—Lana Petfield, Richmond, VA

PREP: 15 MIN. + CHILLING • **COOK:** 30 MIN.
MAKES: 20 PIECES (ABOUT 2½ LBS.)

- ½ tsp. plus 2 cups butter, divided
- 2 cups sugar
- 1 cup slivered almonds
- 1 cup milk chocolate chips
- 1 cup chopped walnuts
- ½ cup semisweet chocolate chips
- ½ cup white baking chips
- 1½ tsp. shortening

1. Butter a 15x10x1-in. pan with ½ tsp. butter; set aside. In a heavy saucepan over medium-low heat, bring sugar and the remaining butter to a boil, stirring constantly. Cover and cook 2-3 minutes.

2. Uncover; add almonds. Cook and stir mixture with a clean spoon until a candy thermometer reads 300° (hard-crack stage) and the mixture is golden brown.

3. Pour into prepared pan (do not scrape the sides of saucepan). The surface will be buttery. Cool for 1-2 minutes. Sprinkle with milk chocolate chips. Let stand for 1-2 minutes; spread chocolate over the top. Sprinkle with walnuts; press down gently with the back of a spoon. Chill for 10 minutes.

4. In a microwave, melt semisweet chips; stir until smooth. Drizzle over the walnuts. Refrigerate for 10 minutes. Melt vanilla chips and shortening; stir until smooth. Drizzle over top. Cover and refrigerate for 1-2 hours. Break into pieces.

PEPPERMINT LOLLIPOPS

These lollipops can be made with any shape cookie cutter. Gingerbread men, snowmen, Christmas trees and reindeer—the options are endless, so let your creative juices flow!
—Taste of Home *Test Kitchen*

PREP: 5 MIN. • **COOK:** 30 MIN. + STANDING
MAKES: 10 LOLLIPOPS

1½ cups sugar
¾ cup water
⅔ cup light corn syrup
½ tsp. cream of tartar
½ tsp. peppermint oil
10 lollipop sticks
   Crushed peppermint candies

1. Butter 10 assorted metal cookie cutters and place them on a parchment-lined baking sheet; set aside. In a large heavy saucepan, combine the sugar, water, corn syrup and cream of tartar. Cook and stir over medium heat until sugar is dissolved. Bring to a boil. Cook, without stirring, until a candy thermometer reads 300° (hard-crack stage).
2. Remove from heat. Stir in oil, keeping face your away from mixture (the scent of the peppermint oil is very strong).
3. Immediately pour sugar mixture into prepared cookie cutters. Remove cutters just before lollipops are set; firmly press a stick into each. Sprinkle peppermint candies over tops.

1 LOLLIPOP: *179 cal., 0 fat (0 sat. fat), 0 chol., 27mg sod., 47g carb. (40g sugars, 0 fiber), 0 pro.*

SHOWSTOPPING DESSERTS

An amazing holiday meal should end with a dessert that's at least as attention-getting as what's gone before it. These gorgeous next-level delights will earn raves from everyone at the table.

6 SECRETS TO MAKING MERINGUE

Meringue may look as if it's made of marshmallow fluff, but it's actually a sweet foam made mainly from egg whites. For foolproof meringue, follow these tips:

TIP 1: USE OLDER EGGS
Older eggs produce fluffier and higher meringues than fresh ones. To test the age of eggs, gently place an uncracked egg in a glass of water. If it floats, it's too old to use for anything. If it lies on its side on the bottom of the glass, it's very fresh. If it stands up on its end, it's ideal for meringue.

TIP 2: BRING EGG WHITES TO ROOM TEMPERATURE
Separate the eggs while they're still cold. Let the whites stand at room temperature for 30 minutes before beating. This'll help you whip the eggs to lofty heights.

TIP 3: USE A CLEAN BOWL
Place whites in a small, clean metal or glass bowl. Even a drop of fat from the egg yolk or oil—or the grease sometimes found on plastic bowls—will prevent egg whites from foaming, so be sure to use clean beaters, too.

TIP 4: STABILIZE IT
For the strongest and most stable meringue, add ⅛ tsp. of cream of tartar for every egg white before beating. If you don't have any cream of tartar, use ½ tsp. lemon juice for every egg white. (A copper-lined bowl will produce the same effect.)

TIP 5: TAKE YOUR TIME
Don't rush adding the sugar. The more slowly you add the sugar, the better it'll dissolve. Try pouring in 1 Tbsp. at a time for a silky-smooth texture.

TIP 6: CHECK THE WEATHER
It's best to make meringues on a dry day. On humid or rainy days, they can absorb moisture and become limp or sticky.

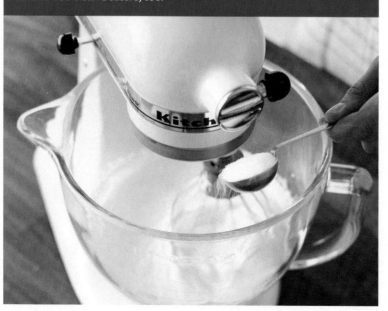

HUMMINGBIRD CAKE

This impressive cake is my dad's favorite, so I always make it for his birthday. The beautiful, old-fashioned layered delight makes a memorable celebration dessert.
—Nancy Zimmerman, Cape May Court House, NJ

PREP: 40 MIN. • **BAKE:** 25 MIN. + COOLING
MAKES: 14 SERVINGS

- 2 cups mashed ripe bananas
- 1½ cups canola oil
- 3 large eggs, room temperature
- 1 can (8 oz.) unsweetened crushed pineapple, undrained
- 1½ tsp. vanilla extract
- 3 cups all-purpose flour
- 2 cups sugar
- 1 tsp. salt
- 1 tsp. baking soda
- 1 tsp. ground cinnamon
- 1 cup chopped walnuts

PINEAPPLE FROSTING
- ¼ cup shortening
- 2 Tbsp. butter, softened
- 1 tsp. grated lemon zest
- ¼ tsp. salt
- 6 cups confectioners' sugar
- ½ cup unsweetened pineapple juice
- 2 tsp. half-and-half cream
    Chopped walnuts

1. Preheat oven to 350°. Grease and flour three 9-in. round baking pans; set aside. In a large bowl, beat bananas, oil, eggs, pineapple and vanilla until well blended. In another bowl, combine flour, sugar, salt, baking soda and cinnamon; gradually beat into the banana mixture until blended. Stir in walnuts.

2. Pour into prepared baking pans. Bake until a toothpick inserted in the center comes out clean, 25-30 minutes. Cool for 10 minutes before removing from pans to wire racks to cool completely.

3. In a large bowl, beat shortening, butter, lemon zest and salt until fluffy. Add the confectioners' sugar alternately with pineapple juice. Beat in cream. Spread between layers and over top and sides of cake. Sprinkle with chopped walnuts.

1 SLICE: *777 cal., 35g fat (6g sat. fat), 50mg chol., 333mg sod., 113g carb. (85g sugars, 2g fiber), 7g pro.*

SPUMONI BAKED ALASKA

For a dazzling yet refreshing end to a rich holiday meal, try this freezer finale. Its cool, intriguing interior and Christmasy color scheme are bound to garner oohs and aahs.
—Taste of Home *Test Kitchen*

PREP: 50 MIN. + FREEZING • **BAKE:** 5 MIN.
MAKES: 12 SERVINGS

- ½ cup butter, cubed
- 2 oz. unsweetened chocolate, chopped
- 1 cup sugar
- 1 tsp. vanilla extract
- 2 large eggs, room temperature
- ¾ cup all-purpose flour
- ½ tsp. baking powder
- ½ tsp. salt
- 1 cup chopped hazelnuts
- 2 qt. vanilla ice cream, softened, divided
- ½ cup chopped pistachios
- ½ tsp. almond extract
- 6 drops green food coloring, optional
- ⅓ cup chopped maraschino cherries
- 1 Tbsp. maraschino cherry juice
- 1 Tbsp. rum

MERINGUE
- 8 large egg whites
- 1 cup sugar
- 1 tsp. cream of tartar

1. Grease an 8-in. round baking pan; set aside. Preheat the oven to 350°. In a microwave-safe bowl, melt butter and chocolate; stir until smooth. Stir in sugar and vanilla. Add the eggs, 1 at a time, beating well after each addition. Combine flour, baking powder and salt; gradually stir into the chocolate mixture. Stir in the hazelnuts.

2. Spread into the prepared pan. Bake for 35-40 minutes or until a toothpick inserted in the center comes out with moist crumbs (do not overbake). Cool 10 minutes before removing from pan to a wire rack to cool completely.

3. Meanwhile, line an 8-in. round bowl (1½ qt.) with foil. In a smaller bowl, place 1 qt. ice cream; add pistachios, almond extract and, if desired, food coloring. Quickly spread ice cream over the bottom and up the sides of foil-lined bowl, leaving the center hollow; cover and freeze for 30 minutes.

4. In a small bowl, combine cherries, cherry juice, rum and the remaining 1 qt. ice cream. Pack ice cream into the center of the bowl; cover and freeze.

5. In a large heavy saucepan, combine egg whites, sugar and cream of tartar. With a hand mixer, beat on low speed for 1 minute. Continue beating over low heat until the egg mixture reaches 160°, about 8 minutes. Transfer to a bowl; beat until stiff glossy peaks form and the sugar is dissolved.

6. Place brownie on an ungreased foil-lined baking sheet; top with the inverted ice cream mold. Remove foil. Immediately spread meringue over the ice cream, sealing it to the edges of the brownie. Freeze until ready to serve, up to 24 hours.

7. Preheat oven to 400°. Bake for 2-5 minutes or until the meringue is lightly browned. Transfer to a serving plate; serve immediately.

1 PIECE: *554 cal., 29g fat (13g sat. fat), 94mg chol., 314mg sod., 68g carb. (52g sugars, 3g fiber), 11g pro.*

MINTED CHOCOLATE TORTE

Our family has enjoyed this remarkable cake for years. We love seeing it being carried out on special occasions!
—Barbara Humiston, Tampa, FL

PREP: 30 MIN. • **BAKE:** 30 MIN. + COOLING
MAKES: 16 SERVINGS

½ cup shortening
1⅓ cups sugar, divided
2¼ cups cake flour
3 tsp. baking powder
½ tsp. salt
1 cup whole milk
1½ tsp. vanilla extract
2 oz. semisweet chocolate, finely chopped
3 large egg whites, room temperature

FILLING/TOPPING

6 oz. semisweet chocolate, chopped
¼ cup butter
1¼ cups confectioners' sugar
3 Tbsp. hot water
1 tsp. vanilla extract
Dash salt

FROSTING

2 cups whipped topping
½ tsp. vanilla extract
⅛ tsp. peppermint extract
1 to 2 drops food coloring, optional
Mint Andes candies, chopped

1. Grease and flour two 9-in. round baking pans; set aside. Preheat oven to 350°. In a large bowl, cream shortening and 1 cup sugar until light and fluffy. Combine flour, baking powder and salt; add to creamed mixture alternately with milk; beat well after each addition. Stir in vanilla and the finely chopped chocolate.

2. In a small bowl, beat egg whites on medium until soft peaks form. Gradually beat in remaining sugar, 1 Tbsp. at a time, on high until stiff peaks form. Fold into the batter.

3. Pour into prepared pans. Bake 30-35 minutes or until a toothpick inserted in center comes out clean. Cool 10 minutes before removing from pans to wire racks.

4. In a small saucepan, melt the chocolate and butter over low heat; stir until smooth. Remove from the heat; transfer to a large bowl. Beat in the confectioners' sugar, hot water, vanilla and salt until smooth.

5. Cut each cake into 2 horizontal layers. Place a bottom layer on a serving plate; top with ⅓ cup filling. Repeat layers 3 times. In a large bowl, gently combine the whipped topping, extracts and, if desired, food coloring. Frost the sides of the cake. Sprinkle top with candies. Store in the refrigerator.

1 SLICE: *308 cal., 12g fat (6g sat. fat), 10mg chol., 205mg sod., 46g carb. (29g sugars, 1g fiber), 3g pro.*

CARAMEL FUDGE CHEESECAKE

I combined several recipes to satisfy both chocolate lovers and cheesecake fans in my family. With a brownie crust, crunchy pecans and a gooey layer of caramel, this gem of a dessert is hard to resist.
—Brenda Ruse, Truro, NS

PREP: 30 MIN. • **BAKE:** 35 MIN. + CHILLING
MAKES: 12 SERVINGS

1 pkg. fudge brownie mix (8-in. square pan size)
1 pkg. (14 oz.) caramels
¼ cup evaporated milk
1¼ cups coarsely chopped pecans
2 pkg. (8 oz. each) cream cheese, softened
½ cup sugar
2 large eggs, room temperature, lightly beaten
2 oz. unsweetened chocolate, melted and cooled

1. Prepare brownie batter according to package directions. Spread into a greased 9-in. springform pan. Place on a baking sheet. Bake at 350° for 20 minutes. Place pan on a wire rack for 10 minutes (leave oven on).

2. Meanwhile, in a microwave-safe bowl, melt caramels with milk. Pour over brownie crust; sprinkle with pecans.

3. In a large bowl, beat cream cheese and sugar until light and fluffy. Add eggs; beat on low speed just until combined. Stir in melted chocolate. Pour over pecans. Return pan to baking sheet.

4. Bake until the center is almost set, 35-40 minutes. Cool on a wire rack for 10 minutes. Run a knife around the edge of the pan to loosen; cool 1 hour longer. Refrigerate overnight, covering when completely cool. Remove the sides of the pan.

1 SLICE: *635 cal., 38g fat (13g sat. fat), 90mg chol., 369mg sod., 69g carb. (51g sugars, 3g fiber), 10g pro.*

TOFFEE ANGEL FOOD CAKE

Toffee bits and whipped cream make angel food even more indulgent. For best results, refrigerate the cake for at least an hour.
—Collette Gaugler, Fogelsville, PA

PREP: 45 MIN. • **BAKE:** 50 MIN. + COOLING
MAKES: 16 SERVINGS

- 11 large egg whites
- 1 cup cake flour
- 1 cup confectioners' sugar
- 1 tsp. cream of tartar
- 1 tsp. vanilla extract
  Pinch salt
- 1¼ cups superfine sugar

WHIPPED CREAM
- 2 cups heavy whipping cream
- ½ cup hot caramel ice cream topping, room temperature
- 1 tsp. vanilla extract
- 4 Heath candy bars (1½ oz. each), chopped
  Chocolate curls, optional

1. Place egg whites in a large bowl; let stand at room temperature 30 minutes.
2. Meanwhile, place oven rack in lowest position and remove upper rack if needed. Preheat oven to 325°. Sift cake flour and confectioners' sugar together twice.
3. Add cream of tartar, vanilla and salt to egg whites; beat on medium speed until soft peaks form. Gradually add superfine sugar, 1 Tbsp. at a time, beating on high after each addition until sugar is dissolved. Continue beating until soft glossy peaks form. Gradually fold in the flour mixture, about ½ cup at a time.
4. Gently transfer to an ungreased 10-in. tube pan. Cut through batter with a knife to remove air pockets. Bake on lowest rack until the top crust is golden brown and the cracks feel dry, 50-60 minutes. Immediately invert pan; cool completely in pan, about 1½ hours.
5. Run a knife around sides and center tube of pan. Remove cake to a serving plate. Using a long serrated knife, cut cake horizontally into 3 layers. In a large bowl, beat cream until it begins to thicken. Gradually add caramel topping and vanilla; beat until soft peaks form.
6. Place 1 cake layer on a serving plate; spread with 1 cup of the whipped cream mixture. Sprinkle with a third of the chopped candies. Repeat layers. Top with the remaining cake layer. Frost top and sides of cake with remaining whipped cream mixture; sprinkle with remaining candy. If desired, sprinkle chocolate curls over top and around the bottom of cake.
1 SLICE: *315 cal., 14g fat (9g sat. fat), 36mg chol., 117mg sod., 44g carb. (36g sugars, 0 fiber), 5g pro.*

HOT COCOA SOUFFLE

A friend and I went to a church cooking demo years ago, and one of the recipes we prepared was this luscious souffle. It's decadent and delicious.
—Joan Hallford, North Richland Hills, TX

PREP: 20 MIN. • **BAKE:** 40 MIN.
MAKES: 6 SERVINGS

- 5 large eggs
- 4 tsp. plus ¾ cup sugar, divided
- ½ cup baking cocoa
- 6 Tbsp. all-purpose flour
- ¼ tsp. salt
- 1½ cups fat-free milk
- 2 Tbsp. butter
- 1½ tsp. vanilla extract
  Confectioners' sugar, optional

1. Separate eggs; let stand at room temperature for 30 minutes. Coat a 2-qt. souffle dish with cooking spray and lightly sprinkle with 4 tsp. sugar; set aside.
2. Preheat the oven to 350°. In a small saucepan, combine the cocoa, flour, salt and the remaining sugar. Gradually whisk in milk. Bring to a boil, stirring constantly. Cook and stir for 1-2 minutes longer or until thickened. Stir in butter. Transfer to a large bowl.
3. Stir a small amount of the hot mixture into the egg yolks; return all to the bowl, stirring constantly. Add the vanilla; let cool slightly.
4. In another large bowl, beat egg whites with clean beaters until stiff peaks form. With a spatula, stir a fourth of the egg whites into the chocolate mixture until no white streaks remain. Fold in the remaining egg whites until combined.
5. Transfer to prepared dish. Bake for 40-45 minutes or until the top is puffed and the center appears set. If desired, dust with confectioners' sugar. Serve immediately.
1 SERVING: *272 cal., 9g fat (4g sat. fat), 188mg chol., 209mg sod., 41g carb. (31g sugars, 2g fiber), 9g pro.*

RASPBERRY FUDGE TORTE

People are surprised to hear that this impressive torte starts with a simple cake mix—they're sure I bought it at a bakery!
—Julie Hein, York, PA

PREP: 30 MIN. + CHILLING
BAKE: 25 MIN. • **MAKES:** 12 SERVINGS

1 pkg. devil's food cake mix (regular size)
1 cup sour cream
¾ cup water
3 large eggs, room temperature
⅓ cup canola oil
1 tsp. vanilla extract
1 cup miniature semisweet chocolate chips

GANACHE
1 cup (6 oz.) semisweet chocolate chips
½ cup heavy whipping cream
1 Tbsp. butter

RASPBERRY CREAM
1 pkg. (10 oz.) frozen sweetened raspberries, thawed
3 Tbsp. sugar
4 tsp. cornstarch
½ cup heavy whipping cream, whipped
   Fresh raspberries, mint and confectioners' sugar, optional

1. Grease and flour three 9-in. round baking pans; set aside. Preheat oven to 350°. In a large bowl, combine cake mix, sour cream, water, eggs, oil and vanilla; beat on low for 30 seconds. Beat on medium for 2 minutes. Fold in miniature chocolate chips.

2. Pour batter into prepared pans. Bake for 25-30 minutes or until a toothpick inserted in the center comes out clean. Cool for 10 minutes before removing from pans to wire racks to cool completely.

3. For ganache, place chocolate chips in a small bowl. In a small saucepan, bring cream just to a boil. Pour over chocolate; whisk until smooth. Whisk in butter. Chill until the mixture reaches spreading consistency, stirring occasionally.

4. For raspberry cream, mash and strain raspberries, reserving juice; discard seeds. In a small saucepan, combine sugar and cornstarch; stir in the raspberry juice. Bring to a boil, cook and stir over low heat for 1-2 minutes or until thickened. Place in a bowl; chill for 30 minutes. Fold in the whipped cream.

5. Place 1 cake layer on a serving plate; spread with half of the ganache. Top with the second cake layer and the raspberry cream. Top with the remaining cake layer; spread with remaining ganache. Store in the refrigerator. If desired, top with raspberries, mint and confectioners' sugar to serve.

1 SLICE: *544 cal., 31g fat (15g sat. fat), 95mg chol., 377mg sod., 62g carb. (43g sugars, 4g fiber), 6g pro.*

MALTED CHOCOLATE & STOUT LAYER CAKE

If you want a dessert that will take the cake at your celebration, look no further! The rich chocolate cake is incredibly moist and has a nice malt flavor that's perfectly complemented by the Irish cream frosting.
—Jennifer Wayland, Morris Plains, NJ

PREP: 45 MIN. + CHILLING
BAKE: 35 MIN. + COOLING
MAKES: 16 SERVINGS

2 cups stout beer
1¾ cups butter, cubed
3 oz. bittersweet chocolate, chopped
1 cup malted milk powder
1 cup baking cocoa
1½ cups sour cream
4 large eggs, room temperature
3½ cups sugar
3 cups cake flour
1 Tbsp. baking soda
1 tsp. salt

FROSTING
1 cup sugar
½ cup Irish cream liqueur
6 large egg yolks, beaten
1½ tsp. vanilla extract
1½ cups butter, softened
½ cup malted milk powder
Chopped malted milk balls, optional

1. Grease and flour three 9-in. round baking pans; set aside. Preheat oven to 350°.

2. In a large saucepan, combine beer, butter and chocolate. Cook and stir over medium-low heat until the butter and chocolate are melted. Remove from heat; whisk in milk powder and cocoa. Transfer to a large bowl. Let stand for 15 minutes.

3. Add the sour cream and eggs to the chocolate mixture; beat until well blended. Combine sugar, flour, baking soda and salt; gradually beat into the chocolate mixture until blended. Pour batter into prepared pans.

4. Bake until a toothpick inserted in the center comes out clean, 32-36 minutes. Cool 10 minutes before removing from pans to wire racks to cool completely.

5. In a large heavy saucepan, bring sugar and liqueur to a gentle boil over medium heat; cook until sugar is dissolved. Remove from heat. Add a small amount of hot mixture to egg yolks; return all to pan, stirring constantly. Cook until mixture thickens, about 2 minutes longer, stirring constantly. Remove from heat; stir in vanilla. Cool to room temperature.

6. In a large bowl with a whisk attachment, cream butter until fluffy, about 5 minutes. Gradually beat in the sugar mixture. Add milk powder; beat until fluffy, about 5 minutes. If necessary, refrigerate until frosting reaches spreading consistency.

7. Place bottom cake layer on a serving plate; spread with ⅔ cup frosting. Repeat layers. Top with the remaining cake layer. Spread the remaining frosting over top and sides of cake. Refrigerate for at least 1 hour before serving. If desired, top with chopped malted milk balls.

1 SLICE: *821 cal., 48g fat (29g sat. fat), 220mg chol., 760mg sod., 90g carb. (64g sugars, 2g fiber), 7g pro.*

CHOCOLATE PEAR HAZELNUT TART

As an exchange student in France, I was horribly homesick. Then my host family's grandmother arrived and asked if I'd like to help her bake a tart from scratch. I figured it would beat crying into my pillows! As soon as we started creating this nutty tart, a bond formed that needed no words. Weighing ingredients, roasting nuts, kneading dough—the art of baking transcends language!
—Lexi McKeown, Los Angeles, CA

PREP: 45 MIN. + CHILLING
BAKE: 30 MIN. + COOLING
MAKES: 12 SERVINGS

1¼ cups all-purpose flour
⅓ cup ground hazelnuts
¼ cup packed brown sugar
   Dash salt
½ cup cold butter, cubed
3 to 5 Tbsp. ice water

FILLING
3 large eggs, separated
⅓ cup butter, softened
⅓ cup packed brown sugar
2 Tbsp. amaretto or ½ tsp. almond extract
1 cup ground hazelnuts
2 Tbsp. baking cocoa
6 canned pear halves, drained, sliced and patted dry
2 Tbsp. honey, warmed
   Confectioners' sugar

1. In a small bowl, mix flour, hazelnuts, brown sugar and salt; cut in butter until crumbly. Gradually add ice water, tossing with a fork until dough holds together when pressed. Shape into a disk. Wrap; refrigerate for 30 minutes or overnight.

2. Place egg whites in a large bowl; let stand at room temperature 30 minutes. Preheat oven to 400°. On a lightly floured surface, roll dough to a ⅛-in.-thick circle; transfer to a 9-in. fluted tart pan with a removable bottom. Trim crust even with the pan's edge. Prick the bottom of the crust with a fork. Refrigerate the crust while preparing the filling.

3. In a large bowl, cream butter and brown sugar until blended. Beat in egg yolks and amaretto. Beat in hazelnuts and cocoa.

4. With clean beaters, beat egg whites on medium speed until stiff peaks form. Fold a third of the egg whites into the hazelnut mixture, then fold in the remaining whites. Spread mixture onto bottom of the crust. Arrange pears over top.

5. Bake on a lower oven rack until the crust is golden brown, 30-35 minutes. Brush the pears with warm honey. Cool on a wire rack. If desired, dust with confectioners' sugar before serving.

1 SLICE: *302 cal., 19g fat (9g sat. fat), 86mg chol., 125mg sod., 29g carb. (15g sugars, 2g fiber), 5g pro.*

S'MORES CREME BRULEE

A big bite into a scrumptious s'more brings back sweet campfire memories. This fancy take on the classic treat will be adored by young and old alike.
—Rose Denning, Overland Park, KS

PREP: 30 MIN. • **BAKE:** 25 MIN. + CHILLING
MAKES: 6 SERVINGS

- 1 cup 2% milk
- 3 large eggs
- ⅔ cup sugar
- ⅓ cup baking cocoa
- 2 Tbsp. coffee liqueur or strong brewed coffee
- ⅔ cup graham cracker crumbs
- 2 Tbsp. butter, melted
- ⅓ cup sugar or coarse sugar
- 2 cups miniature marshmallows
- 1 milk chocolate candy bar (1.55 oz.), broken into 12 pieces

1. Preheat the oven to 325°. In a small saucepan, heat milk until bubbles form around the sides of pan; remove from heat. In a large bowl, whisk eggs, sugar, cocoa and liqueur until blended but not foamy. Slowly whisk in the hot milk.
2. Place six 4-oz. broiler-safe ramekins in a baking pan large enough to hold them without touching. Pour the egg mixture into the ramekins. Place pan on oven rack; add very hot water to pan to within ½ in. of top of ramekins. Bake 20-25 minutes or until a knife inserted in the center comes out clean; centers will still be soft. Remove ramekins from water bath immediately to a wire rack; cool 10 minutes. Refrigerate until cold.
3. In a small bowl, mix cracker crumbs and butter; set aside. Caramelize the topping with either a kitchen torch (step 4) or broiler (step 5).
4. To use a kitchen torch, sprinkle custards evenly with sugar. Hold torch flame 2 in. above custard surface and rotate it slowly until the sugar is evenly caramelized. Sprinkle custards with crumb mixture; top with marshmallows. Heat marshmallows with torch until browned. Top with chocolate pieces. Serve immediately or refrigerate for up to 1 hour.
5. To use a broiler, place ramekins on a baking sheet; let stand at room temperature 15 minutes. Preheat broiler.

Sprinkle custards evenly with sugar. Broil 3-4 in. from heat 3-5 minutes or until sugar is caramelized. Sprinkle custards with the crumb mixture; top with the marshmallows. Broil 30-45 seconds or until marshmallows are browned. Top with chocolate pieces. Serve immediately or refrigerate up to 1 hour.
1 SERVING: *419 cal., 11g fat (5g sat. fat), 108mg chol., 163mg sod., 74g carb. (59g sugars, 2g fiber), 7g pro.*

CHOCOLATE COOKIE CHEESECAKE

I used to think cheesecakes sounded intimidating, but since I started making them I can't stop! This simple version will make your family feel fussed over.
—Rose Yoder, Middlebury, IN

PREP: 15 MIN. • **BAKE:** 1 HOUR + CHILLING
MAKES: 12 SERVINGS

- 1½ cups crushed cream-filled chocolate sandwich cookies (about 20 cookies)
- 2 Tbsp. butter, melted
- 3 pkg. (8 oz. each) cream cheese, softened
- 1 cup sugar
- 1 cup sour cream
- ¼ cup all-purpose flour
- 2 tsp. vanilla extract
- ¼ tsp. salt
- 3 large eggs, room temperature, lightly beaten
- 15 coarsely chopped cream-filled chocolate sandwich cookies (about 2¼ cups), divided

1. Preheat oven to 325°. In a bowl, combine crushed cookies and butter. Press onto the bottom and 1 in. up the sides of a greased 9-in. springform pan; set aside.
2. In a large bowl, beat cream cheese and sugar until smooth. Beat in sour cream, flour, vanilla and salt. Add eggs; beat on low speed just until combined. Fold in ¾ cup chopped cookies. Pour into crust. Top with the remaining chopped cookies.
3. Place on a baking sheet. Bake for 60-65 minutes or until center is almost set. Cool on a wire rack for 10 minutes. Carefully run a knife around the edge of pan to loosen; cool 1 hour longer. Refrigerate overnight. Remove sides of pan.
1 SLICE: *505 cal., 33g fat (18g sat. fat), 134mg chol., 425mg sod., 44g carb. (30g sugars, 1g fiber), 8g pro.*

6. Cool pudding on a wire rack 10 minutes. Loosen sides from the pan with a knife; remove rim from pan. Cool at least 1 hour before serving. If desired, top with orange zest and serve with whipped cream.

NOTE: If made ahead, pudding can be warmed in a 350° oven for 10 minutes before orange zest and whipped cream are added.

1 SLICE: 402 cal., 10g fat (6g sat. fat), 71mg chol., 143mg sod., 75g carb. (57g sugars, 3g fiber), 4g pro.

FROZEN MOCHA TORTE

For an easy make-ahead dessert that's elegant and delectable, try this recipe. The perfect blend of mocha and chocolate is in each cool, refreshing slice.
—Aelita Kivirist, Glenview, IL

PREP: 20 MIN. + FREEZING
MAKES: 12 SERVINGS

- 1 cup chocolate wafer crumbs
- ¼ cup sugar
- ¼ cup butter, melted
- 1 pkg. (8 oz.) cream cheese, softened
- 1 can (14 oz.) sweetened condensed milk
- ⅔ cup chocolate syrup
- 2 Tbsp. instant coffee granules
- 1 Tbsp. hot water
- 1 cup heavy whipping cream, whipped Chocolate-covered coffee beans, optional

1. In a small bowl, combine wafer crumbs, sugar and butter. Press onto the bottom and 1 in. up the sides of a greased 9-in. springform pan; set aside.

2. In a large bowl, beat the cream cheese, milk and chocolate syrup until smooth. Dissolve coffee granules in hot water; add to the cream cheese mixture. Fold in whipped cream. Pour over crust. Cover and freeze for 8 hours or overnight.

3. Remove from the freezer 10-15 minutes before serving. Carefully run a knife around the edge of the pan to loosen. Remove the sides of pan. Garnish with coffee beans if desired.

1 SLICE: 414 cal., 23g fat (14g sat. fat), 74mg chol., 222mg sod., 47g carb. (39g sugars, 1g fiber), 6g pro.

BAKED CRANBERRY PUDDING

This bright vintage dessert makes us happy—which makes it perfect for Christmas. It's especially good served warm with whipped cream.
—Lucy Meyring, Walden, CO

PREP: 20 MIN. • **BAKE:** 55 MIN. + COOLING
MAKES: 10 SERVINGS

- 2 large eggs, separated
- 1 cup packed brown sugar
- ½ cup heavy whipping cream
- ¼ cup butter, melted
- 2 tsp. vanilla extract
- 1½ cups all-purpose flour
- 3 Tbsp. grated orange zest
- 1 tsp. baking powder
- 1 tsp. ground cinnamon
- ½ tsp. ground nutmeg
- ½ tsp. cream of tartar, divided
- ⅛ tsp. salt
- 3 cups coarsely chopped cranberries

TOPPING
- 1½ cups sugar
- ½ cup orange juice
- 2½ cups whole cranberries
  Orange zest strips and whipped cream, optional

1. Place the egg whites in a large bowl; let stand at room temperature for 30 minutes.

2. Preheat oven to 350°. In a large bowl, beat brown sugar, cream, melted butter, vanilla and egg yolks until well blended. In another bowl, whisk flour, orange zest, baking powder, cinnamon, nutmeg, ¼ tsp. cream of tartar and the salt. Add chopped cranberries; toss to coat. Gradually add to the sugar mixture, mixing well. (Batter will be stiff.)

3. Add the remaining cream of tartar to egg whites; with clean beaters, beat on medium until soft peaks form. Fold into batter. Transfer to a greased 9-in. springform pan. Bake until a toothpick comes out clean, 45-50 minutes.

4. Meanwhile, combine sugar and orange juice in a small saucepan. Bring to a boil, stirring frequently; cook until sugar is dissolved, 2-3 minutes. Add cranberries; return to a boil. Reduce heat; simmer, uncovered, until berries pop, stirring occasionally, 6-8 minutes. Remove from heat; cover and keep warm.

5. When pudding tests done, place the springform pan in a 15x10x1-in. baking pan. Spoon the cranberry mixture over top. Bake 10 minutes longer.

CREME DE MENTHE CREAM PUFF TREE

A tower of creme de menthe-flavored puffs makes a spectacular centerpiece for your dessert table. Guests will have this sumptuous pyramid deconstructed in no time at all!
—Agnes Ward, Stratford, ON

PREP: 1½ HOURS + CHILLING
BAKE: 25 MIN. + COOLING
MAKES: ABOUT 60 MINI CREAM PUFFS

1¼ cups water
⅔ cup butter, cubed
1¼ cups all-purpose flour
5 large eggs, room temperature

FILLING
2 cups heavy whipping cream
⅓ cup green creme de menthe

GLAZE
⅓ cup butter, cubed
2 oz. unsweetened chocolate, chopped
2 cups confectioners' sugar

1½ tsp. vanilla extract
3 to 6 Tbsp. hot water
Additional confectioners' sugar, optional

1. Preheat the oven to 400°. In a large saucepan, bring water and butter to a boil. Add flour all at once and stir until a smooth ball forms. Remove from the heat; let stand for 5 minutes. Add eggs, 1 at a time, beating well after each addition. Continue beating until mixture is smooth and shiny. Drop by rounded teaspoonfuls 2 in. apart onto greased baking sheets.
2. Bake for 20-25 minutes or until golden brown. Remove to wire racks. Cut a small slit in the side of each puff to allow steam to escape. Cool puffs.
3. For filling, in a large bowl, beat cream until soft peaks form. Fold in creme de menthe. Use a pastry bag to pipe about 1 Tbsp. filling into each puff. Refrigerate for up to 2 hours.
4. For glaze, in a small saucepan, combine butter and chocolate. Cook and stir over low heat until melted. Remove from heat. Using a whisk, stir in the confectioners' sugar, vanilla and enough water to reach desired consistency for dipping. Stir until smooth and no lumps appear.
5. To assemble tree: Separate puffs according to size and shape, choosing the flattest ones for the bottom layer and the smallest, roundest ones for the top. Dip the bottoms of the 21 flattest puffs into the glaze. Place puffs on a 10-in. round serving platter, arranging in concentric circles to form a solid circle.
6. For the second layer, dip the bottoms of 15 puffs into the glaze, then position the puffs on the base layer. Continue building the tree, using about 11 puffs in the third layer, about 6 puffs in the fourth layer, about 4 puffs in the fifth layer and 1 puff on top.
7. Drizzle the remaining glaze over tree, thinning with hot water if necessary.
8. Loosely cover tree with plastic wrap and refrigerate for up to 2 hours. If desired, dust with confectioners' sugar just before serving.

1 MINI CREAM PUFF: 96 cal., 7g fat (4g sat. fat), 37mg chol., 31mg sod., 7g carb. (4g sugars, 0 fiber), 1g pro.

BUTTERSCOTCH CAKE

I always get lots of compliments and recipe requests whenever I make this eye-catching cake. The filling is similar to German chocolate cake.

—Judy Lamon, Louisville, TN

PREP: 35 MIN. • **BAKE:** 25 MIN. + COOLING
MAKES: 12 SERVINGS

⅔ cup butterscotch chips
¼ cup water
½ cup shortening
¾ cup sugar
¾ cup packed brown sugar
3 large eggs, room temperature
2¼ cups all-purpose flour
¾ tsp. baking soda
½ tsp. baking powder
½ tsp. salt
1 cup buttermilk

FILLING/TOPPING
½ cup sugar
1 Tbsp. cornstarch
½ cup evaporated milk
⅓ cup water
1 large egg yolk, lightly beaten
⅓ cup butterscotch chips
2 Tbsp. butter
1 cup pecans, chopped
1 cup sweetened shredded coconut
2 to 3 cups buttercream frosting

1. Preheat oven to 375°. Line 2 greased 9-in. round baking pans with waxed paper; set aside. In a microwave set at 70% power, melt butterscotch chips with ¼ cup water for 1 minute; stir. Microwave at additional 10- to 20-second intervals, stirring until smooth. Cool to room temperature.

2. In a large bowl, cream shortening and sugars until light and fluffy. Add eggs, 1 at a time, beating well after each addition. Beat in butterscotch mixture. Combine the flour, baking soda, baking powder and salt; add to creamed mixture alternately with buttermilk just until combined.

3. Pour into prepared pans. Bake 25-30 minutes or until a toothpick inserted in the center comes out clean. Cool for 10 minutes before removing from pans to wire racks to cool completely.

4. In a large saucepan, combine sugar and cornstarch. Stir in evaporated milk and water until smooth. Cook and stir over medium heat until thickened and bubbly. Reduce heat; cook and stir 2 minutes longer. Remove from the heat. Stir a small amount of the hot filling into the egg yolk; return all to the pan, stirring constantly. Bring to a gentle boil; cook and stir 2 minutes longer.

5. Remove from heat. Gently stir in the chips and butter. Stir in the pecans and coconut. Cool to room temperature without stirring.

6. Place 1 cake layer on a serving plate; spread with half of the filling. Top with the second layer and the remaining filling. Frost sides of the cake with buttercream frosting. Store in the refrigerator.

1 SLICE: *765 cal., 36g fat (15g sat. fat), 81mg chol., 422mg sod., 103g carb. (79g sugars, 2g fiber), 7g pro.*

RICH CHOCOLATE PEANUT BUTTER CAKE

The combination of mocha and peanut butter will satisfy every sweet tooth at your table. The garnish is a little extra work, but what are special occasions for?
—Tammy Bollman, Minatare, NE

PREP: 35 MIN. + CHILLING
BAKE: 25 MIN. + COOLING
MAKES: 12 SERVINGS

- 2 cups sugar
- 1 cup 2% milk
- 1 cup strong brewed coffee
- 1 cup canola oil
- 2 large eggs, room temperature
- 1 tsp. vanilla extract
- 2 cups all-purpose flour
- ¾ cup baking cocoa
- 1 Tbsp. instant coffee granules
- 2 tsp. baking soda
- 1 tsp. salt

FILLING
- 1 cup butter, softened
- ¾ cup creamy peanut butter
- 1½ cups confectioners' sugar

FROSTING
- ½ cup creamy peanut butter
- 6 oz. bittersweet chocolate, chopped
- 1 cup butter, softened
- 2 cups marshmallow creme
- ⅓ cup confectioners' sugar
- ¾ tsp. vanilla extract
- 2 cups dark chocolate chips, optional
- 1 cup peanut butter chips, optional
- 1 tsp. shortening, optional

1. Grease and flour two 9-in. round baking pans; set aside. Preheat oven to 350°. In a large bowl, beat the sugar, milk, coffee, oil, eggs and vanilla until well blended. Combine the flour, cocoa, instant coffee granules, baking soda and salt; gradually beat into the sugar mixture until blended.
2. Transfer to the prepared pans. Bake for 25-30 minutes or until a toothpick inserted in the center comes out clean.
3. Cool for 10 minutes before removing cake from pans to wire racks to cool completely.
4. For filling, in a large bowl, beat butter and peanut butter until blended. Add confectioners' sugar; beat until smooth.

5. For frosting, melt peanut butter and chocolate in a microwave; stir until smooth. Cool. In a large bowl, beat butter and chocolate mixture until fluffy. Add marshmallow creme, confectioners' sugar and vanilla; beat until smooth. If needed, refrigerate until spreading consistency.
6. Place 1 cake layer on a serving plate; spread with filling. Top with the remaining cake layer. Spread frosting over the top and sides of cake. Refrigerate for at least 1 hour before serving.
7. For optional garnish, place chocolate chips in a small microwave-safe bowl; microwave 1-2 minutes or until melted, stirring every 20 seconds. Repeat with peanut butter chips and shortening. Line a 15x10x1 pan with waxed paper; spread the melted chocolate into a ¼-in. layer. Drizzle the melted peanut butter mixture over the melted chocolate; swirl with the tip of a spoon. Tap pan on counter to smooth. Refrigerate until set; break into pieces and arrange as desired on top of cake.
1 SLICE: *883 cal., 60g fat (23g sat. fat), 100mg chol., 670mg sod., 83g carb. (60g sugars, 4g fiber), 11g pro.*

A Trio of Trifles

Served up in a straight-walled glass bowl to reveal tempting layers, a trifle is a magnificent holiday treat. For a grown-up edge, douse the cake with a liqueur before layering on the fillings.

HONEY GINGERBREAD TRIFLE

My husband's grandma made the most amazing honey gingerbread. It's wonderful all on its own, but when you add it to a trifle, your guests are sure to ask for the recipe.
—Tami Kuehl, Loup City, NE

PREP: 25 MIN. + CHILLING
BAKE: 25 MIN. + COOLING
MAKES: 12 SERVINGS

- 1 cup sour cream
- 1 cup honey
- 1 large egg, room temperature
- ¼ cup canola oil
- 2½ cups all-purpose flour
- ½ tsp. salt
- 1 tsp. baking soda
- 1 tsp. baking powder
- 2 tsp. ground ginger
- ½ tsp. ground cinnamon

PUDDING LAYER
- 2 cups 2% milk
- 1 pkg. (3.3 oz.) instant white chocolate pudding mix

PUMPKIN MOUSSE LAYER
- 1 cup 2% milk
- 1 pkg. (3.4 oz.) instant pumpkin spice pudding mix
- 1 carton (8 oz.) frozen whipped topping, thawed

1. Grease a 9-in. square baking pan; set aside. Preheat oven to 350°. Beat the sour cream, honey, egg and oil until well blended. In another bowl, whisk together the next 6 ingredients; gradually beat into the sour cream mixture. Transfer to the prepared pan. Bake until a toothpick comes out clean, 25-30 minutes. Cool in pan 5 minutes. Remove to a wire rack to cool completely.

2. For the pudding layer, whisk milk and white chocolate pudding mix 2 minutes. Let stand until soft-set, about 5 minutes. Refrigerate. For the mousse layer, whisk milk and pumpkin spice pudding mix in another bowl for 2 minutes. Fold in the whipped topping. Refrigerate.

3. To assemble, cut cake into 1-in. cubes. In a 3-qt. trifle bowl or other glass serving dish, layer a third of the cake cubes, the white chocolate pudding and the pumpkin mousse. Repeat layers twice. Refrigerate, covered, 4 hours or overnight.

1 CUP: *413 cal., 14g fat (7g sat. fat), 25mg chol., 514mg sod., 64g carb. (44g sugars, 1g fiber), 6g pro.*

WINTER WISHES TRIFLE

I created this light and fluffy trifle for a dear friend who was looking for a stunning dessert for a holiday gathering. This recipe certainly hit the mark!
—Susan Stetzel, Gainesville, NY

PREP: 20 MIN. + CHILLING
MAKES: 12 SERVINGS

- 1   prepared angel food cake (8 to 10 oz.)
- 4   oz. white baking chocolate
- 4   cups heavy whipping cream, divided
- ½   tsp. peppermint extract
- 12 peppermint candies, crushed

1. Place mixer beaters in a large metal bowl; refrigerate 30 minutes. Cut or tear cake into bite-sized pieces; set aside.
2. Break white chocolate into smaller pieces; microwave at 70% power, stirring after 45 seconds. Microwave until melted, about 30 seconds more. Stir until smooth. Let stand 5 minutes; stir ¼ cup heavy cream into white chocolate until smooth.
3. In the chilled bowl, beat the remaining heavy cream until soft peaks form. Gently fold two-thirds of the whipped cream into the white chocolate. Stir extract into the remaining whipped cream.
4. In a trifle bowl, layer cake and white chocolate mixture, repeating layers. Top with peppermint-flavored whipped cream. Refrigerate, covered, until serving. Sprinkle with crushed candies.
1 SERVING: *392 cal., 32g fat (20g sat. fat), 90mg chol., 173mg sod., 25g carb. (12g sugars, 0 fiber), 4g pro.*

CANADIAN CRANBERRY TRIFLE

Rich pound cake, hand-whipped custard and tart cranberries give you so much to celebrate. In the summer, I make this with blueberries and homemade blueberry wine.
—Raymonde Bourgeois, Swastika, ON

PREP: 30 MIN. + COOLING
COOK: 25 MIN. + CHILLING
MAKES: 12 SERVINGS

- 2   cups fresh cranberries
- 1   can (14 oz.) whole-berry cranberry sauce
- 1   cup sugar
- 1   cup water
- ½   cup sweet white wine
- ¼   tsp. coconut extract

CUSTARD
- 1   cup sugar
- 2   Tbsp. cornstarch
- ¼   tsp. salt
- 3   cups 2% milk
- 6   large egg yolks, beaten
- ¼   tsp. coconut extract

CAKE
- 1   frozen pound cake (16 oz.), thawed
- 3   Tbsp. sweet white wine, optional
- ½   cup slivered almonds, toasted
     Whipped cream
     Additional fresh cranberries and toasted slivered almonds

1. In a large saucepan, combine the cranberries, cranberry sauce, sugar and water. Bring to a boil, stirring to dissolve sugar. Reduce heat to medium; cook, uncovered, until thickened, 10-15 minutes. Add wine and extract. Remove from heat; cool completely.
2. For custard, mix sugar, cornstarch and salt in another large saucepan; gradually whisk in milk until smooth. Cook and stir over medium heat until thickened and bubbly. Reduce heat to low; cook and stir 2-3 minutes longer. Remove from heat.
3. In a small bowl, whisk a small amount of the hot mixture into the egg yolks. Return all to pan, whisking constantly. Bring to a gentle boil; cook and stir 2 minutes. Stir in the coconut extract. Cool 30 minutes. Refrigerate, covered, for 1 hour.
4. To assemble trifle, cut cake into 1-in. cubes. In a 3-qt. trifle bowl or other glass serving dish, place half of the cake cubes; sprinkle with wine if desired. Layer with half the almonds, cranberry mixture and custard. Repeat layers. Refrigerate, covered, until serving. Top with the whipped cream, additional cranberries and toasted almonds.
1 CUP: *430 cal., 14g fat (6g sat. fat), 152mg chol., 209mg sod., 71g carb. (55g sugars, 2g fiber), 6g pro.*

RECIPE INDEX

This index lists every recipe in the book in alphabetical order. Just search for the titles when you want to find your favorites. On page 240, you'll find an index of special bonus content—including tips, how-tos and a little bit of Christmas history!

P. 159

P. 143

P. 187

P. 194

P. 8

BONUS CONTENT